THE
AMERICAN
APOCALYPSE

TERRY JAMES

HARVEST HOUSE PUBLISHERS

EUGENE, OREGON

Cover by Left Coast Design, Portland, Oregon

THE AMERICAN APOCALYPSE
Copyright © 2009 by Terry James
Published by Harvest House Publishers
Eugene, Oregon 97402
www.harvesthousepublishers.com

Library of Congress Cataloging-in-Publication Data
James, Terry, 1942-
The American apocalypse / Terry James.
    p. cm.
Includes bibliographical references.
ISBN 978-0-7369-2505-1 (pbk.)
1. End of the world. 2. United States—Civilization—21st century. 3. United States—Forecasting. 4. Bible—Prophecies—Eschatology. I. Title.
BT877.J36 2009
236'.9—dc22

                                                                        2008020666

Printed in the United States of America

        09 10 11 12 13 14 15 16 17 / BP-SK / 11 10 9 8 7 6 5 4 3 2 1

This book is dedicated to Dr. Tim LaHaye, whose encouragement, generosity, and most of all, example has been an inspiration in my life and the lives of so many others. Truly, he is one of God's foremost spiritual champions in these last times.

Acknowledgments

★ ★ ★ ★ ★

My love and gratitude to those of my family who helped in so many ways while I wrote this book—Margaret, Terry Jr., Nathan, Jeanie, Dana, and especially to Angie, whose editorial acumen is second to none.

Thanks also to Todd Strandberg, my partner in raptureready .com—whom I also consider in my family—for his encouragement and research input while working on this book.

My special gratitude for writing the foreword to this volume goes to Jack Kinsella. His years of devotion to presenting God's Word with absolute integrity, and in dynamic fashion, have shone brightly as an example for us all.

Most of all, I am thankful to the Lord Jesus Christ, who makes it possible for us to be together in God's family for all of eternity.

Contents

★★★★★

Foreword 9

Setting the Stage 13

Section I: Prophecy Takes Shape

1 The Explosion 27

2 The Discipline-Blessing-Discipline Roller Coaster 43

3 The Israel-America Miracle 63

4 Soaring Superprowess 85

Section II: End-times Illness

5 Societal Symptoms 105

6 Geopolitical Palsy 127

7 Economic Epilepsy 141

8 Religious Fever 157

9 Probing the Prognosis 173

Section III: Future Headlines?

10 International Community Demands Role in Iraq 189

11 Globalists Seek Economic Control 209

12 Peace Puzzle Coming Together 225

13 Religious Leaders Propose World Unity 243

14 World Stunned as Millions Vanish! 255

15 United States Pursues Place Within
   Changed International Order 269

Are You Prepared? 287

Notes 289

FOREWORD

★ ★ ★ ★

I 've followed and been a fan of Terry James's work on behalf of the Lord for almost a decade, and so was honored when he asked me to consider writing the foreword to his latest book, *The American Apocalypse.*

Like Terry's previous books, *The American Apocalypse* is well-researched and carefully documented, and it tells a tale of a nation suffering from a form of spiritual madness it can neither identify nor treat.

Terry also tells the tale of another nation, the Jewish State of Israel, whose fate is inextricably intertwined with ours, and the role both play in the unfolding drama of history as foretold by the Hebrew prophets.

While Terry's book bears the somewhat gloomy-sounding title of *The American Apocalypse,* it is not a gloomy foretelling of impending doomsday; rather, it points to the beacon of hope that current events portend.

One looks to the future, irrespective of one's philosophy, and what looks back is the picture of the future as reflected in popular television and movies. And, to quote the great Yogi Berra, "The future just ain't what it used to be."

The TV series *Star Trek* was wildly popular in its earlier incarnations, when it was set in unknowable centuries from now. As the franchise developed, it produced a series of prequels that traced the *Star Trek* legend, in reverse, back toward the present.

Set four centuries in the future, humanity is peaceful and caring, wars have been abolished, and the earth is clean and beautiful and as pristine as it was on the day of creation. *Star Trek* became a cult classic. Anything connected to the *Star Trek* franchise was instant gold.

The final show in the franchise was set in the twenty-first century. It failed miserably. It lost its element of believability. It is too hard to see how we got from where we are obviously headed to the utopia of the twenty-fourth century. Imagination can only carry hope so far.

The secular futurist outlook is, in many ways, more, er, *apocalyptic* than the outlook presented by John's apocalypse in the Bible. The "Mad Max" future of popular culture is one of hopelessness and despair for the survivors of the inevitable carnage to come.

This future outlook permeates popular culture because it is believable, and it is believable because it is probable. Bible prophecy presents what is overall a very similar outline, but with one important difference.

To the rest of the world, the headlines offer the promise of chaos and confusion and certain carnage to come. The Bible offers assurances that that picture is really evidence of hope. It is proof positive that what so terrifies the world is evidence that history is following a predetermined script.

As the book of Isaiah recorded some 2500 years ago: "I am God, and there is none else; I am God, and there is none like me, declaring the end from the beginning, and from ancient times the things that are not yet done, saying, My counsel shall stand, and I will do all my pleasure" (Isaiah 46:9-10).

Because God foretold the events that led us to this point in history with 100 percent accuracy (as Terry's book proves beyond a reasonable doubt), that means He remains on the throne, intimately concerned with and involved in the affairs of men.

It means that the Bible is true, and so too, are its promises—including the promise of salvation to all those who trust its Author.

It is my sincere prayer that this book will be both a blessing and a lifeline of hope to its readers in these uncertain times. I pray that you will find in its pages the answer to the question repeated around the world every time a new atrocity tops the news: What's this world coming to?

I recommend this as a must-read for anyone who has ever asked that question or struggled to provide an answer when asked. In Terry's book, you *will* find the answer you seek.

And if you can grasp the full import of the message contained in the book before you, you will come to realize that you have no reason to be afraid of what is to come: "He that cometh to God must believe that he is, and that he is a rewarder of them that diligently seek him" (Hebrews 11:6).

May God richly reward you as you proceed on your quest for His truth.

—Jack Kinsella
April 12, 2008
www.omegaletter.com

SETTING THE STAGE

★ ★ ★ ★ ★

America: Is anything foretold about this nation in Bible prophecy?

That question, in one form or another, is one of the most frequently asked when I speak on topics involving Bible prophecy.

No nation in modern times stands more at stage-center than the United States. None in all of recorded history has had more influence or has more directly affected countries contemporary to its time of nationhood than America. Its contributions to moving the world from the speed a horse can run to light speed through near-instantaneous communications technologies are staggering.

There is no peer to American creative industrial genius when considered in context of civilization-enhancing contributions by all generations prior to the twentieth century. The United States of America, as a result of her genius and industry, stands alone as the most materially endowed nation-state ever.

Sounds like pompous, typically ugly American elitism, you say? Well, to borrow from, quote, and expand a bit upon the words of that renowned philosopher, one-time St. Louis pitcher Dizzy Dean, "It ain't braggin' if you can do it."

Section I of this book, "Prophecy Takes Shape," provides evidence that America's accomplishments stand far above and beyond the achievements of all other nation-players in bringing mankind to the current degree of technological progress. The most gifted history revisionists would be hard-pressed to construct even moderately believable sophistry that would offer contradictory evidence to America's role over the last 100 years in bringing mankind to the amazing technological point at which the world presently stands.

Again, Dizzy would say that it ain't braggin' because this nation has done it. The very fact of America's spectacular achievement would, one would think, secure its place within the final prophetic disposition of nations. Yet this nation is referenced by name nowhere in Bible prophecy. That no mention of the most powerful and wealthiest nation in recorded history is made in the Bible seems a profoundly strange omission.

Recognizing and acknowledging that this super nation-state is not even alluded to by name, there nonetheless remains room to ponder. Therefore we return to the question, though slightly altered: Is America in Bible prophecy, even if not specifically named? We must first address another question even more pressing: Does there exist a Supreme Judge of all things who therefore has the final say on human conduct and contributions to the furtherance of man?

The fact that we are considering the possible position of America in Bible prophecy gives the answer to this question from the standpoint of this book's perspective. Indeed, there is a God in heaven. He is, rather than existential in His dealings with planet Earth, the one and only deity, who is hands-on and who cares about His creation called man. He has definite things to say about individuals and nations when it comes to responsibility in matters involving conduct within human affairs. Regarding the individual and the nation-state, God's Word says: "Unto whomsoever much is given, of him shall be much required" (Luke 12:48).

Judgment of Nations Coming

According to Bible prophecy, a judgment of nations is coming. That judgment is given in the following prophetic scriptures:

- "When the Son of man shall come in his glory, and all the holy angels with him, then shall he sit upon the throne of his glory. And before him shall be gathered all nations: and he shall separate them one from another, as a shepherd divideth his sheep from the goats: And he shall set the sheep on his right hand, but the goats on the left. Then shall the King say unto them on his right hand, Come, ye blessed of my Father, inherit the kingdom prepared for you from the foundation of the world" (Matthew 25:31-34).

- "Then shall he say also unto them on the left hand, Depart from me, ye cursed, into everlasting fire, prepared for the devil and his angels" (Matthew 25:41).

These prophecies generate additional questions, including:

- What criteria will Christ use to judge the nations that are allowed to inherit the millennial kingdom and to judge which ones will be cast into the fires of damnation for eternity?

- Will America appear before Jesus Christ in this sheep/goat judgment?

- If so, will America be a sheep nation or a goat nation?

This book will attempt to address these and other questions as they relate particularly to the United States of America.

One thing is sure: Before any nation is judged at this great prophesied gathering, it will first have to survive the coming time of unprecedented trouble on this planet. About that time, Jesus prophesied, "For then shall be great tribulation, such as was not since the beginning of the world to this time, no, nor ever shall be" (Matthew 24:21).

God has stated specific guidelines for His future judgment of the nations. Some of the guidelines are general; they describe how He deals with nations throughout history. Others relate specifically to

His dealing with nations during the time known as the apocalypse. Interestingly, most all judgments upon nations, whether general or specific, have one element in common. This ingredient, in itself, comprises a study that has required numerous volumes to encapsulate its many aspects.

The ingredient of which I write is at the forefront of news today. Its influence on most every facet of life, when fully explored, is astonishing. The prophet Zechariah long ago foretold this all-important entity would be the catalyst for great turmoil just before Christ's return. No other nation than America is more at ground zero as a result of this one element prophesied thousands of years ago to bring all peoples on earth to the Middle East to do battle: "In that day will I make Jerusalem a burdensome stone for all people: all that burden themselves with it shall be cut in pieces, though all the people of the earth be gathered together against it" (Zechariah 12:3). "And it shall come to pass in that day, that I will seek to destroy all the nations that come against Jerusalem" (Zechariah 12:9).

Jerusalem and Israel are inseparable in God's economy. The prophet Zechariah seemed to be speaking directly to our present day with his words of forewarning. One senses, if attuned to world news in this present hour, that Jerusalem, Israel's capital city in God's economy, will from now until Christ's second advent be at center stage. Just as Zechariah prophesied, Jerusalem is in the process of becoming a "burdensome stone" (verse 3) and a "cup of trembling" (verse 2) to all other nations of the world. The burden created by the nations trying to force a tranquility that cannot come except from the Prince of Peace and His direct intervention will literally cut in pieces those humanistic endeavors to bring about Mideast peace.

Tragically, this places America at the very heart of the Zechariah prophecy. This nation presently leads the contingent of geopoliticians pressuring Israel to divide the land that belongs to the God of Abraham, Isaac, and Jacob.

God's Word foretells the strongest possible condemnation for those who do what today's international community, led by the so-called

"Quartet" (the United States, the European Union, the United Nations, and Russia), is attempting to do in the matter of Israel versus its avowed enemies: "I will also gather all nations, and will bring them down into the valley of Jehoshaphat, and will plead with them there for my people and for my heritage Israel, whom they have scattered among the nations, and parted my land" (Joel 3:2).

All nations will be brought together to be judged by the Lord God Jehovah of Israel. This, of course, is Armageddon, the last and most violent battle of the war, which will have begun sometime during the Tribulation era: "He gathered them together into a place called in the Hebrew tongue Armageddon" (Revelation 16:16).

America and Israel Linkage

America's relationship with the modern State of Israel began so differently than things are today. Those who have spiritual discernment to see the hand of God moving in the affairs of man know beyond any doubt that America was raised up in large part to bring Israel back into the Promised Land in preparation for the windup of history.

The United States has indeed been a golden cup in God's hand, used to bless the nations of the world. This nation and its history validate God's promise to Abraham: "I will bless them that bless thee, and curse him that curseth thee: and in thee shall all families of the earth be blessed" (Genesis 12:3).

The United States, it is abundantly obvious to this observer, has been under the watchful eye of the Creator of all things, the God of Abraham, Isaac, and Jacob. It is as if the Almighty put all of human history in fast-forward on some cosmic video screen with America's founding and subsequent movement forward over the ensuing centuries. His dealings with this country have been a shaping and molding process unparalleled in history.

Sometimes the fast-track molding has been painful—for example, the blood shed during the Revolutionary, Civil, and other internal wars. The agonizing correction applied during the 1930s Great Depression and dust bowl years all pushed America up against God's grinding stone of course correction. A primary reason for the painful grinding process was to prepare a people who would be strong enough and sufficiently discerning of God's direction to be midwife for Israel's rebirth as a nation in mid-twentieth century. In retrospect, we can say World Wars I and II tempered America and steeled it as the greatest power in history. The horrendous battles America fought and won made the nation capable of standing by God's chosen people, the nation of Israel, during the severe hatreds they would face while rising to their feet on May 14, 1948 and beyond.

The blessings America has received for this act of being friend and protector of Israel in modern times cannot be missed by the honest historian.

Greater Purpose for America

Next we must consider the profoundly greater purpose that one attuned to God's reasons for raising up America in these latter days should not miss. The purpose fits precisely with America acting as the nation-state protector for modern Israel. The connection is a matter that only the omniscient hand of the God of the universe could perform.

The Bible prophecy involved is the key manifestation of God's mercy that must take place before the return of Christ at the second advent: "This gospel of the kingdom shall be preached in all the world for a witness unto all nations; and then shall the end come" (Matthew 24:14).

We begin to understand the amazing master stroke by the conductor of this great symphony in which all of humanity has been involved. God chose Israel to bring into the world of lost humanity the Redeemer, the Savior, the Lamb slain from the foundation of the world: His only begotten Son, Jesus, the Christ. The Creator of all that is chose America, the most powerful nation-state ever to have been upon the planet, to have a part in keeping His promises to Abraham, Isaac, and Jacob. Through those patriarchs, all nations and all generations would be blessed.

The most astounding blessing God could give the generations of earth is redemption. This redemption is found in Christ, and in Christ alone. There is no other name by which we can be saved (see Acts 4:12).

This is the "good news"—the gospel of Jesus Christ! If we believe in Jesus Christ for redemption, we will be saved from the deadly result of sin—everlasting separation from God the Father and heaven.

The United States, despite her degeneration into gross immorality and turning in directions other than to the God who raised her up, nonetheless has to be the one nation on earth that gets the gospel message, literally, to the whole world. The supernaturally arranged ties cannot be missed unless the intention is purposely to do so. The very finger of God tied the gospel, Israel, and America together.

So, is America in prophecy? The answer, to this writer at least, is a resounding yes! By name, no, but by presence and influence, absolutely! America is predestined by God Almighty to preserve and protect God's chosen people through whom the Savior came. The Lord of heaven also chose America to serve an infinitely higher purpose. He chose this nation to get the gospel message to the whole world. God has thus demonstrated His great mercy, manifesting the truth that He keeps His promises. He demonstrates today that His prophetic Word will come to pass—and in fact, *is* in the process of coming to pass right now. We again see that truth in the previously presented prophetic passage: "This gospel of the kingdom shall be preached in all the world for a witness unto all nations; and then shall the end come" (Matthew 24:14).

Lest We Become Self-aggrandized

All this talk of the United States being a golden cup in God's mighty hand should, to those who earnestly desire to know the mind of God in the matters, bring sobering thoughts rather than thoughts of self-aggrandizement. We have only to turn to the prophetic Word of God to learn the fate of a humanistic instrumentality once used by God then turned against Him:

Babylon hath been a golden cup in the LORD's hand, that made all the earth drunken: the nations have drunken of her wine; therefore the nations are mad. Babylon is suddenly fallen and destroyed: howl for her; take balm for her pain, if so she may be healed. We would have healed Babylon, but she is not healed: forsake her, and let us go every one into his own country: for her judgment reacheth unto heaven, and is lifted up even to the skies (Jeremiah 51:7-9).

Dangerous Delusions of Grandeur

Israel and America also stand bound together in perhaps the most dangerous of all false teachings of our time. This should not surprise, because the very first forewarning in Christ's Olivet Discourse involved the deceivers who would proliferate at the end of days:

- "As he sat upon the mount of Olives, the disciples came unto him privately, saying, Tell us, when shall these things be? and what shall be the sign of thy coming, and of the end of the world? And Jesus answered and said unto them, Take heed that no man deceive you. For many shall come in my name, saying, I am Christ; and shall deceive many" (Matthew 24:3-5).

- "Many false prophets shall rise, and shall deceive many" (Matthew 24:11).

Paul the apostle gave further prophetic word on the times when false teachings would attempt to deceive: "The time will come when they will not endure sound doctrine; but after their own lusts shall they heap to themselves teachers, having itching ears; and they shall turn away their ears from the truth, and shall be turned unto fables" (2 Timothy 4:3-4).

Replacement Rantings

False teachings about which Jesus and Paul forewarned are at the heart of the delusion that infects Christianity today. The claimed replacement of God's chosen people, the Jews, with Christ's church and with certain nation-states helps make up the matrix of the infection.

Indeed, many have come on the contemporary scene preaching and teaching that today's Israel is not the Israel of God's prophetic Word. These proclaim that the Jews in the world today are not the Jews of God's promises to the patriarchs. The Jews, by race, have, they say, been replaced through God's promises to Christians. Christians are the *real* Jews that are God's chosen people, according to the misguided replacement theologians of these last days.

Some take the matter much further. They declare that the ten tribes of Israel were somehow lost to history but are now found, and the nations of Great Britain and the United States are their homes. These national entities, they say, are now Israel in God's economy of things.

A large majority of the articles and books that popped up when researching for information on the topic of the United States in prophecy were materials distributed by those who claim the Jews of the Old Testament have been replaced by the church, so far as God's prophetic promises are concerned. Also, publishers of the teachings involved in the ten lost tribes being Britain and America turned up in profusion with each search for relevant information.

The Reform church institutions—those who left Catholicism with the Martin Luther-engendered Protestant Reformation—have continued to hold to the Catholic view that the church has now inherited the promises given to the Jews by race.

God, however, has made certain promises that are unconditional. That is, they were one-sided, with the Lord God of Israel telling the physical descendants of Abraham, Isaac, and Jacob that He guaranteed they were His people forever, no matter what:

> I will establish My covenant between Me and you and
> your descendants after you throughout their generations
> for an everlasting covenant, to be God to you and to your

> descendants after you. And I will give to you and to your
> descendants after you, the land of your sojournings, all the
> land of Canaan, for an everlasting possession; and I will be
> their God (Genesis 17:7-8 NASB).

The proposition that God has broken His covenant to the literal descendants of the patriarchs Abraham, Isaac, and Jacob is an untenable one from the reading of Scripture. To those who say God's covenant with Israel concerning the nation and land is conditional, I suggest considering the Lord's declaration regarding Israel's King David and all of Jacob's literal offspring through the ages to come:

> If his sons forsake My law and do not walk in My judgments,
> if they violate My statutes and do not keep My commandments, then I will punish their transgression with the rod
> and their iniquity with stripes. But I will not break off My
> lovingkindness from him, nor deal falsely in My faithfulness.
> My covenant I will not violate, nor will I alter the utterance
> of My lips. Once I have sworn by My holiness; I will not
> lie to David. His descendants shall endure forever and his
> throne as the sun before Me. It shall be established forever
> like the moon, and the witness in the sky is faithful (Psalm
> 89:30-37 NASB).

The church (Christ's body of believers since the establishment of His church) is not the Israel of these promises. Britain and the United States have not now been given the promises God gave Abraham's descendants through Isaac, then Jacob. There are no ten lost tribes. God knew where each and every individual of each and every tribe was in the centuries past. He knows where each and every Jew is at present. He has always known. The Jew is the inheritor of God's promises forever!

Israel: Catalyst of Apocalypse

America, then, is not the new Israel. But, as already stated, America is providentially linked with Israel, and has been since Israel's

God-inspired conception and birth. America's fortunes—from here through the end of human history, as it is presently known—are intricately connected to Israel's future.

Satan's hatred for God's chosen people became excruciatingly evident on September 11, 2001, when the 19 Islamic terrorists crashed the huge commercial jet aircraft into the World Trade towers in New York City, and another into the Pentagon at Washington, D.C. This seems to me to have been the opening salvos of Lucifer's final assault on God and His chosen people.

Israel is the catalyst that will bring all on planet Earth to near extinction. But it is not Israel who has precipitated or perpetuated the building end-times conflict. Satan is leading all humanistic efforts to make Israel appear to be the illegitimate, warmongering troublemaker for the Middle East and the world, who will foment and bring to conflagration history's final war. The "spirit of the antichrist" (1 John 4:3) is at the heart of hatred for the Jew, and it is this spirit we will examine in due course.

The United States, in my view, is key to Israel's fortunes from this point until Christ's return at Armageddon, although not in precisely the way some will infer from this statement. America's influence, from its conception, is supernaturally imprinted upon the final act of history.

The American Apocalypse will, I hope, bring that truth to light in a way that can't be missed by anyone who reads it and is intellectually honest about its conjectures, postulations, and conclusions.

Section I:

PROPHECY TAKES SHAPE

★ ★ ★ ★ ★

1

THE EXPLOSION

★ ★ ★ ★ ★

The United States of America has been at the very heart of the explosion of human technological progress. America has no peer in this regard, even to this present hour. Just as God's hand of providence guided the founding fathers in bringing the country to birth in 1776, so His omnipresence inspired the American genius and industry resident in the nation to achieve things essential to the opening of the book of end-times prophecy.

The prophet Daniel's words resonate in our day: "Thou, O Daniel, shut up the words, and seal the book, even to the time of the end: many shall run to and fro, and knowledge shall be increased" (Daniel 12:4).

This foretelling by Daniel ranks as perhaps the foremost signpost encapsulating the present generation's place on God's prophetic time line, when considering the question about whether America is anywhere in Bible prophecy, even if not mentioned specifically by name.

The prophet's words tell us:

1. There is a book that has written in it the end of all things regarding the human realm.

2. That book was purposely shut in order not to reveal details about the end.

3. The book was sealed during Daniel's time, and no one would be able to break that seal.

4. The world would experience a great population explosion near the end.

5. The people of that future time would go at phenomenal speed to and from points all over the earth.

6. Man's knowledge would increase tremendously.

Many, including this writer, believe this detonation of knowledge at the very end includes knowledge about end-of-days prophecies from God's Word, as well as human knowledge that has erupted to an extent like no other time in history, in what we now call the information age. The major implication in the first part of the prophecy is that the book of understanding end-times matters would be opened at the time of the running "to and fro" and of the exponential increase in knowledge. Therein is the validation of our claims that this generation is bumping up against the very end of the age, and that the signals we are witnessing today are, indeed, signs of Jesus Christ's soon return to planet Earth.

Again, the United States of America is inarguably the matrix out of which the geometrical progression of knowledge, and the spectacular increase in ability to travel to and from anywhere on earth, has grown. The unsealing and opening of the book that the angel mentioned to Daniel might well have taken place during one specific incident about which we've all learned in our rudimentary studies of American history. The occurrence certainly seemed an explosive epiphany, with God reaching down to man in spectacular fashion. More than coincidentally, one of America's most famous founding fathers was the recipient of this brilliant stroke from the heavens.

Benjamin Franklin's Shocking Experience

Benjamin Franklin, whom we know as one of the key founding fathers of the United States, in fact appropriated through his God-inspired genius the catalyst to the greatest discovery of mankind. His use of a key opened mankind to new vistas dreamed of by only a very few inventive minds in previous history.

Franklin believed electricity could be harnessed from lightning. So he tested his theory in 1752 through use of a contrivance with which we have all become somewhat familiar by way of our history books. Details of his experiment and of those leading up to the dramatic initial test remain murky, but enough information emerged to determine that Franklin's primitive, highly dangerous experimentation seems—at least to this writer—the opening of Daniel's foretold travel and knowledge.

Franklin originally thought to test his theory using a spire atop a Philadelphia church. He concluded after a time of thinking on the matter that his experiment would be better served by using a kite and the mobility it offered, instead of a spire fixed to a building.

So Franklin tied two sticks vertically to a kite string, and ran a strand of wire up the kite string. He attached a metal key to the string and the wire. His hypothesis: The wire would draw electricity from the lightning in the thunderstorm, thus proving that lightning was unharnessed electricity. The key, he postulated, would gather and retain the charge for a time.

Franklin conducted his experiment in a field in Philadelphia, and wanted to keep it just between him and his 21-year-old son—initially, at least. Apparently he wanted to avoid the ridicule he feared would be forthcoming if friends saw him playing with a child's toy to carry out his scientific investigation.

The kite flew amidst the ominous clouds, but nothing happened. He was about to pull in the string and give up for the day when he noticed the twine beginning to exhibit strange changes. Strands stood out from its core, and this made Franklin think perhaps a stream of electricity from the lightning above, indeed, was flowing downward toward the device he held.

He slid his hand up the string until his knuckle touched the key. Some reports say the resulting shock knocked the soon-to-be founding father to the ground. The jolt, however, was—thankfully for future

Americans—mild, and he quickly recovered to excitedly proceed with experiments that led to the astonishing inventions that pleasure our lives today.

American Industriousness on Display

Of course, much groundwork was laid by others as well as Americans for the explosion of modern technological achievements, But it is American industriousness—a genius for taking groundwork laid and rocketing into the future with that foundational creativity—that makes the United States unique among the nation-states of history. Electricity and its many fantastic applications have continued to be the fuel that powers the still-surging explosion of knowledge and travel in the twenty-first century.

One is led, when considering the profound aspects of the information age, to again think on electricity and the moment Benjamin Franklin appropriated the thought to experiment with the kite and the key. The connection is thought-provoking.

The Creator of all things seems to have reached His finger directly into the affairs of man with the power within the thunderstorm. It was electricity, as man has termed it, that set in motion all that has developed since.

Electricity, experts in the science involving the human brain tell us, fires from neuron to neuron in our synapses, giving us power of reason and creativity. It is this cognitive ability, perhaps, that was supercharged that day when the lightning, though well-governed, sat the industrious Mr. Franklin on the seat of his knickers. Certainly from that point forward he laid much of the foundation for science that would fire the imagination of future men of science. And it is not far-fetched, if one is faith-based in worldview, to wonder whether this significant founding father of America didn't experience a boost in reasoning ability that would influence the birth of the most technologically advanced country in human history.

Daniel's prophecy can't be summarily ruled out as coming to pass in our day. Anyone who is willing to examine the progress of civilization in terms of technology, from a perspective that puts aside bias against supernatural intervention into the affairs of mankind, must acknowledge the similarities. Daniel 12:4 contains the precise prophetic exigencies that erupted from the relative technological darkness of the nineteenth century and are massively burgeoning in this generation. These are...

- the ever-expanding base of knowledge, and

- physical travel that can jet anyone to anywhere on earth in a matter of hours.

Additionally, we are "transported" by communications devices that move our expressed thoughts instantly around the globe.

Again, we consider the prophecy: "Thou, O Daniel, shut up the words, and seal the book, even to the time of the end: many shall run to and fro, and knowledge shall be increased" (Daniel 12:4).

Increase of Knowledge

The "increase of knowledge" the angel spoke of to Daniel, I believe, began with Johannes Gutenberg's invention of movable type printing. God's Word, the Bible, soon became more widely available as printing processes advanced. God's wisdom is true knowledge of the most beneficial sort. His Son, Jesus Christ, is the Word (John 1:1).

So we begin our look at the inventions that rapidly began spreading the Word of God, as well as other information, to a world basically in informational darkness until then. Although America wasn't a nation when the knowledge floodgates were partially opened, by the mid-nineteenth century, with Benjamin Franklin's early experiments in electricity as a foundation, Americans began to assert what can only be described as God-inspired inventiveness.

Invention Time Line[1]

- 1455—Johannes Gutenberg invents printing press with metal, movable type

- 1560—Camera obscura, a primitive image-making device, invented
- 1650—Leipzig, first daily newspaper, launched
- 1714—Englishman Henry Mill receives first patent for typewriter
- 1793—Claude Chappe invents first long-distance semaphore (visual or optical) telegraph line
- 1814—Joseph Nicéphore Niépce creates first photographic image.
- 1821—Charles Wheatstone reproduces sound in primitive sound box—the first microphone
- 1831—Joseph Henry invents first electric telegraph
- 1835—Samuel Morse invents Morse code
- 1843—Samuel Morse invents first long-distance electric telegraph line
- 1861—Alexander Bain patents first fax machine
- 1861—United States starts Pony Express mail delivery
- 1861—Coleman Sellers invents Kinematoscope, a machine that flashes a series of still photographs onto a screen
- 1867—American Sholes invents first successful and modern typewriter
- 1876—Thomas Edison patents mimeograph, an office copying machine
- 1876—Alexander Graham Bell patents electric telephone
- 1876—Melvil Dewey devises Dewey decimal classification system of organizing library books

- 1877—Thomas Edison patents phonograph, with wax cylinder as the recording medium

- 1877—Eadweard Muybridge invents high-speed photography, creating first pictures that capture motion

- 1887—Emile Berliner invents the gramophone, a system of recording that can be used over and over again

- 1888—George Eastman patents Kodak roll-film camera

- 1889—Almon Strowger patents direct-dial telephone or automatic telephone exchange

- 1894—Guglielmo Marconi improves wireless telegraphy

- 1898—First telephone answering machines introduced

- 1899—Valdemar Poulsen invents first magnetic recordings using magnetized steel tape as recording medium; this is foundational for both mass data storage on disk and tape and the music recording industry

- 1899—Loudspeakers invented

- 1902—Guglielmo Marconi transmits radio signals from Cornwall to Newfoundland, first radio signal across the Atlantic Ocean

- 1906—Lee de Forest invents electronic amplifying tube or triode, allowing all electronic signals to be amplified, improving all electronic communications—i.e., telephones and radios

- 1912—Thomas Edison demonstrates first talking motion picture

- 1914—First cross-continental telephone call made

- 1916—First radios with tuners launched, allowing listeners access to different stations

- 1923—Vladimir Kosma Zworykin invents television or iconoscope (cathode-ray tube); first television camera
- 1925—John Logie Baird transmits first experimental television signal
- 1926—Warner Brothers Studios invents way to record sound separately from film on large disks and synchronize sound and motion picture tracks upon playback—an improvement on Edison's work
- 1927—NBC starts two radio networks
- 1927—CBS founded
- 1927—First television broadcasts in England
- 1927—Warner Brothers releases *The Jazz Singer,* the first successful talking motion picture
- 1930—First television broadcasts in United States
- 1930—Movietone system of recording film sound on audio track right on film invented
- 1934—S. Joseph Begun invents first tape recorder for broadcasting; first magnetic recording
- 1938—Television broadcasts able to be taped and edited rather than aired only live
- 1939—Scheduled television broadcasts begin
- 1944—Computers such as Harvard's Mark I put into public service; the age of information science begins

The years 1944–1948 were pivotal—this span of time witnesses an explosion of change relevant to Daniel's prophecy. Things leading up to that year of the computer were not without their own fascinating aspects. World War II in 1941–1945 and the invention and use of the first atomic bombs in 1945 brought mankind to a place where the biblically prophesied Armageddon was possible. The year 1947 saw the discovery of the Dead Sea Scrolls at Qumran in February, and an interesting phenomenon taking on greater scrutiny with credible reports of flying saucer-discs, followed by a strange crash of something at Roswell, New Mexico, in July 1947, which remains a controversial mystery to this day.

But it is 1948 that is most significant. The Jewish State of Israel was reborn on midnight of May 14. In that foretold rebirth (see Isaiah chapter 66), end-times prophecy took on a whole new meaning. Now the stage was set for all prophecies leading up to the return of Christ. A world organization of earth's nation-states was born, and America was the nation—the world's only superpower—that oversaw and assured both the birth of modern Israel and of the United Nations.

The dam that seems to have held back man's progress blew apart, and technology flooded in every direction. We continue with an overview of the results of the increase of knowledge wrought by the invention of the computer, among other things:

- 1948—Long-playing vinyl record invented (played at 33 rpm)

- 1948—Transistor invented, enabling miniaturization of electronic devices

- 1949—Network television starts in United States

- 1949—45 rpm record invented

- 1951—Computers now sold commercially

- 1958—Chester Carlson invents photocopier, or Xerox machine

- 1958—Integrated circuit invented, enabling further miniaturization of electronic devices and computers

- 1963—ZIP codes invented in United States

- 1966—Xerox invents Telecopier, first successful fax machine

- 1969—ARPANET, first Internet, started

- 1971—Computer floppy disc invented

- 1971—Microprocessor invented; considered a computer on a chip

- 1972—HBO invents pay-TV service for cable

- 1976—Apple Ihome computer invents first nationwide programming via satellite, implemented by Ted Turner

- 1979—First cellular phone communication network starts in Japan

- 1980—Sony Walkman invented

- 1981—IBM PC first sold

- 1981—First laptop computers sold to public

- 1981—Computer mouse becomes regular part of computer

- 1983—*Time* magazine names computer man of the year

- 1984—Cellular phone network started in United States

- 1984—Apple Macintosh released

- 1984—IBM PC AT released

- 1985—Cellular telephones in cars become widespread

- 1994—The American government releases control of Internet and World Wide Web is born, making possible communication at fast speeds

Increase in Travel

Man's rapid growth in his ability to travel runs parallel to his increase in knowledge. The physical act of traveling from place to place is even more manifest than communications developments because we can *see* vehicular traffic. Electrons flashing our thoughts at light speed across wires by satellite and through cyberspace are not so easily observed.

Just as America has been dominant in the field of knowledge-gathering, it has stood far above all nation-states in creating travel technologies. U.S. industrial genius has produced the ability to run to and fro beyond the wildest imaginations of all but a few people a century ago. Those thinkers foresaw things to come. However, no one could have anticipated the increase in travel that has truly been prophetic in its many dimensions.

Even a cursory look at the stupendous movement from the tens of miles per hour steam engines could travel less than two centuries ago to rocket engines that roar across space at many thousands of miles per hour today should engender thoughts about Bible prophecy for Christians who are intellectually honest. Anyone who looks at Daniel 12:4 should be provoked to wonder if our day is "the time of the end" spoken of by the angel to Daniel.

Travel Time Line

- 1492—Leonardo da Vinci first to seriously theorize about flying machines, with more than 100 drawings illustrating his theories on flight

- 1620—Cornelis Drebbel invents first submarine, a human-oared submersible

- 1662—Blaise Pascal invents first public bus: horse-drawn, operates on a regular route, maintains according to a schedule, and employs fare system

- 1740—Jacques de Vaucanson demonstrates his clockwork-powered carriage

- 1783—First practical steamboat demonstrated by Marquis Claude Francois de Jouffroy d'Abbans—a paddle-wheel steamboat

- 1783—Montgolfier brothers invent first hot air balloons

- 1787—Steamboat invented
- 1789—First self-propelled road vehicle invented by Nicolas Joseph Cugnot
- 1790—Modern bicycles invented
- 1801—Richard Trevithick invents first steam-powered locomotive (designed for roads)
- 1807—Isaac de Rivas makes hydrogen gas-powered vehicle, the first with internal combustion power, but his is a very unsuccessful design
- 1807—Robert Fulton's *Clermont,* the first steamboat with regular passenger service, is launched
- 1814—George Stephenson invents first practical steam-powered railroad locomotive
- 1862—Jean Lenoir makes gasoline engine automobile
- 1867—First motorcycle invented
- 1868—George Westinghouse invents compressed air locomotive brake, enabling trains to stop with fail-safe accuracy
- 1871—First cable car invented
- 1885—Karl Benz builds world's first practical automobile powered by internal combustion engine
- 1899—Ferdinand von Zeppelin invents first successful dirigible
- 1903—Wright brothers invent and fly first engined airplane
- 1907—First helicopter introduced; however, it features an unsuccessful design
- 1908—Henry Ford improves assembly line for automobile manufacturing

- 1908—Hydrofoil boats—boats that skim water—
  co-invented by Alexander Graham Bell and Casey Baldwin

- 1926—First liquid-propelled rocket launched

- 1940—Modern helicopters invented

- 1947—First supersonic jet flies

- 1956—Hovercraft invented

- 1964—Bullet train transportation invented

- 1969—First manned mission (Apollo) to the moon
  launched

- 1970—First jumbo jet flown

- 1981—Space shuttle launched

End-times Catalyst

America's influence within its brief duration of nationhood has brought mankind physical comforts, luxuries, and relief from drudgery that no other era has provided. Although vast areas of the world still wallow in squalor, technologies produced for the most part by this nation are available to bring those victims out of their tragic conditions. It is the greed of tyrants—for the most part, dictators—that keeps the very poor of the world under oppression.

The United States has been at the forefront of reaching out to other lands and their peoples, almost to a fault. Much of the largesse that has poured from the American treasuries into these dictatorships has been scarfed up by the despots and put into their own bank accounts around the world.

Many examples can be cited. Saddam Hussein, Manuel Noriega, and Idi Amin, to name but a few whose time has passed, along with many still in power, have banked billions of dollars, many of those dollars provided by American State Department-types who would rather placate than confront tyranny. When politicians try to cajole dictators, more often than not the cost ultimately is far more expensive in lives and money when military force becomes necessary to face down the bullies of the world.

So while American technological advances have made life better in the Western world, these advances have been slow to reach the masses living elsewhere on the planet.

Whereas the Daniel 12:4 prediction about the exponential increase in knowledge and travel at the time of the end relates more to the Western world, there is another prophecy—from the lips of Jesus Himself—that has the entire world in view: "Then shall be great tribulation, such as was not since the beginning of the world to this time, no, nor ever shall be. And except those days should be shortened, there should no flesh be saved: but for the elect's sake those days shall be shortened" (Matthew 24:21-22).

Christ's prophecy speaks to the time leading up to Armageddon and the very moment of His return to earth. He foretells that this is a time when all of humankind, indeed flesh of every sort, will be about to become extinct.

What could be so horrific as to cause the denouement of all flesh?

There is coming a time when all the world's armies will be gathered in the valley of Jehoshaphat (Joel 3:2). God Himself will gather them to the place called Armageddon (Revelation 16:16). It doesn't take a stretch of reasoning to think of something of a technological nature that could end all flesh upon planet Earth. It is technology that had its genesis at Alamagordo, New Mexico, with the first explosion of the atomic bomb. Not much time was wasted in demonstrating just how destructive that technology was to human flesh!

Still photographs and motion pictures recorded shadows in the form of human bodies on the sidewalks and streets of Hiroshima and Nagasaki, Japan, following the dropping of the atomic bombs near the end of World War II. The people had been literally vaporized, indicating horror not unlike the result of a future judgment as described by the prophet Zechariah: "This shall be the plague wherewith the Lord will smite all the people that have fought against Jerusalem; their flesh shall consume away while they stand upon their feet, and their eyes shall consume away in their holes, and their tongue shall consume away in their mouth" (Zechariah 14:12).

The explosion of knowledge mentioned in Daniel 12:4 brought the technology that can make man's life on earth a blessed existence. And that knowledge, combined with great advances in travel, has produced the ability to deliver destructive power from the air, the likes of which no other generation could even fathom. Make no mistake: America is at the very heart of the end-of-days book being opened. And open it is!

2

THE DISCIPLINE-BLESSING-DISCIPLINE ROLLER COASTER

★ ★ ★ ★ ★

There is a story that has always stuck in my mind, clutching at my patriotic spirit. It is about George Washington, who was kneeled upon the ground in an early morning mist among trees that allowed sunlight to filter and stream through them and strike the general's bowed head.

A British soldier moving from an advance post back to his regiment came upon the scene. He recognized Washington as leader of the rebel forces that continued to bedevil the English army. Washington didn't notice the soldier, so engrossed was he in beseeching the Almighty aloud.

The trooper raised his rifle and took aim at Washington. He then lowered it when he heard the general's words. They were spoken fervently, with passionate pleading for God's righteous will to be done and a request for forgiveness of anything that he might have done in putting himself above God, honor, and duty to the American cause. The British soldier lowered the rifle barrel and moved silently away, leaving the American commander to his meeting with the Lord.

When the soldier reached his regiment, his comrades noticed the grim look on his face. They asked what tragedy had befallen him in the woods. He replied that their cause was lost. God was on the side of their foes. Providence was the vanguard of the American cause.

We know that the story of George Washington chopping down the cherry tree is likely myth, as is the tale of his throwing a silver dollar across the widest point of the Potomac River. But one has to entertain the thought that this account of Washington and the British soldier is steeped in fact. God certainly saw the American forces through to victory; history reveals no other explanation for the ragtag American forces defeating the British against all odds.

Reality versus Revisionism

Our children are taught a much different story about America's founding today. Public education tends to paint a picture of the group of men who founded this country as wanting no mixing of Christian religious beliefs in the process of bringing America to birth.

Public education in the United States has endured a dumbing-down process that is...well...dumbfounding! Values clarification, moral relativism, situational ethics—these are the philosophical/psychological tools of inculcation that have been used to bludgeon educators and students alike into a profoundly changed view of America's founding principles. The apropos term here is *revisionism*.

The "progressive" mind-set of many politicians, primarily through judicial fiat, has skewed reality on most every issue. Christianity's true influence on the founding of America is perhaps the most obvious victim of this travesty. Facts surrounding our nation's beginning have been turned upside-down by the revisionists. The nation continues to be under corrective divine discipline, in my view, because the revisionists have run rampant in propagandizing the American people. The lies they have printed as facts reflect the mind of the one whose humanistic religion they follow: "Ye are of your father the devil, and the lusts of your father ye will do. He was a murderer from the beginning, and abode not in the truth, because there is no truth in him. When he speaketh a lie, he speaketh of his own: for he is a liar, and the father of it" (John 8:44).

From Truth to Lies

America's founding was set upon spiritual concrete. Today the nation sits in spiritual quicksand. We need to understand what has happened to change the moorings and why that change has taken place.

I like to quote America's most renowned founding fathers when addressing the nation's foundational principles. Here are a couple of my favorites quotes, which I believe tell the story of America's structure being set in spiritual concrete:

- President George Washington said in his 1796 farewell address, "Reason and experience both forbid us that national morality can prevail in exclusion of religious principle."

- John Adams, America's second president, said, "The United States Constitution was made only for a moral and religious people. It is wholly inadequate for the government of any other."

We have only to look at what is inscribed upon the edifice that houses the U.S. Supreme Court and what is etched in the surfaces of walls that frame other government buildings to identify the "religion" to which Washington and Adams referred as the basis for America's "morality." The Ten Commandments so influenced the founding fathers of America that they saw His directions for godly living as inseparable from their own governance.

Providential guidance under the Almighty's hand shaped the founding years and continued to do so until the humanistic religion called evolution began its eroding subterfuge. When God became more and more marginalized while the humanists were allowed their man-centered way within the national political process, the guiding hand of God became the harsh grip of corrective discipline.

Even within that painful correction, we can see heaven channeling the United States into its manifest destiny. We will look at that supernatural process momentarily. For now, let us examine how the rebellion against that providence developed in America's earlier years.

Turning to Fables

The father of lies pulled from his bag of deception his favorite trick in dealing with America. The apostle Paul's letter to Timothy describes a time when this luciferian sleight-of-hand will be done with the very Word of God: "The time will come when they will not endure sound doctrine; but after their own lusts shall they heap to themselves teachers, having itching ears; and they shall turn away their ears from the truth, and shall be turned unto fables" (2 Timothy 4:3-4).

Satan has done all he can to turn even the most well-grounded evangelical churches of the United States away from sound Bible doctrine. He wasn't long in using the same mind-twisting perversion on the political leaders, educators, and even the clergy of this nation when it comes to the arena of principled government. The seduction came in the form of pseudoscience. Actually, it was a religious system melded with so-called science.

The pseudoscience that has come, in effect, to pervade and influence just about everything in American life is evolution. It is a mixture of religion and "science," because to believe its premise calls for more faith than is required by any religious belief system one can name. Evolution says everything that is came to be quite by chance, from nothingness. Things, so the specious postulation goes, are progressing toward bigger and better.

This flies in the face of reason. The very law of entropy—the second law of thermodynamics—necessarily projects, even admitted by evolutionary scientists, that things of this world are deteriorating. Falling apart. Corroding.

We have only to consider the biblical worldview versus the evolutional worldview to see the luciferian influence. God says in His Word that He created all things perfectly. He created one man and one woman, the progenitors of all of mankind. Adam and Eve disobeyed. And since that fall of man in the Garden of Eden, all things have been deteriorating. The history of mankind and the physical world within which man interacts is degenerating. We get old and die, or die from disease before reaching average longevity. Our automobiles end up corroding and rusting in junkyards. Our bridges eventually collapse. The same happens with our houses, our clothing, with everything around us. Ours is a world that is passing away, says the Bible.

Evolution teaches just the opposite. Everything began in chaos. Man was not created, but climbed out of primordial slime (about whose origin no scientist can explain), moved through many stages of development to become primate, part ape, part man, then fully man. (No scientist can prove the linkage from one stage to another.) Now, so the preachers of evolution say, man will continue to progress to the highest possible state, as long as people take care of the environment and have good intentions toward all of mankind under the leadership of the humanists-elite.

Yet we look at our news headlines and see that man is not getting better, but worse. Our headlines—when the reports are accurate and not twisted to fit a political agenda—tell us that man is more dastardly than ever. This conforms to God's prediction through the apostle Paul: "Evil men and seducers shall wax worse and worse, deceiving, and being deceived" (2 Timothy 3:13).

The evolutionary worldview is one of the primary influences bringing about the fulfillment of this prophecy. That luciferian religion turns the minds of lost people farther from God every day. Thus, the worsening of the things of this world proves God's worldview to be the correct worldview, and evolution to be the false.

It is more than interesting that the man held up as the icon for the religion of evolution was educated within a Christian seminary. Charles Darwin entered seminary when his father determined that his son didn't have the resolve necessary to pursue secular academic goals within higher education. In some key cases there has been a connection between people who have made a nefarious mark upon humanistic developments throughout history and their relationship, at some point in their lives, to being interested in Christian theological training. Some who come to mind are Charles Darwin, Karl Marx, Joseph Stalin, and Adolf Hitler. These and a considerable number of others seemed to have just enough interest in Christianity to make them dangerous to mankind.

Evolution has replaced Christianity as having chief influence on this nation, so blessed by Providence from its inception. The influence of its Christian roots fades with each revisionism-based mandate issued by the government. That humanistic religion has turned America from truth to fables.

The Rewriters at Work

Revisionists of American history continue to be hard at work. Their efforts began early in America's first century of existence as a nation, but we will look for the most part at the process as it developed and is moving today through our national life.

Revisionism is the retelling of the facts about the nation in order to change the perceptions of those being deceived. The only purpose one can fathom is that this is done to subvert American society and culture. One who is honest in appraising such rewriting, upon careful observation of the revisionists at work over the decades, must conclude that the revisionism is done to prepare the minds of citizenry to accept reason for change in public policy.

The prime example to look at is the movement to install a Darwinistic view of the origin of man into the public thinking. This hasn't been easy for the revisionists to do. The Scopes "monkey trial" in 1925 seemed, at first glance, a failure for the evolutionist proponents, but from it came a full-blown, governmentally approved teaching of evolution as the "scientific" approach to origins in public schools. From the acceptance and approval of this faith-based system (it is a religion, make no mistake) came the constant lie that man is not created by God, but is from a chance happening that has somehow eventuated in all that we are and all that we perceive around us.

The bottom line, from the revisionist/evolutional view: Man owes allegiance or obedience to no higher being. Thus man can, without worrying about offending a god, determine whether a human fetus will be brought to birth. There is no higher moral authority than man himself, so the evolutional model presents.

The founding fathers were crucial to the birth of the nation. This, everyone knows. That cannot be written out of the American psyche. So the founding fathers' actual part in the formation of America must be revised so the citizenry will accept that they too saw no deity as influencing their man-centered thoughts and ideals in creating the United States.

This revisionist approach has been applied at every level of the social issues that are at the center of the American political process. And for the most part, Americans are left out of that political process, in terms of being able to vote them up or down. And Americans' elected representatives are also left out of many of the critical decisions that affect the country. For example, the decision of *Roe v. Wade* in 1973 was rendered by the Supreme Court without Americans having any say in its becoming a government-stamped law. Nearly 50 million babies have been aborted since. And I, for one, believe God considers abortion to be murder in the womb.

Revisionism by Omission

Subterfuge in the revisionists' playbook is not always as blatant as in the case of creating an entire religion (evolution) to undermine the nation. More subtle, but just as effective, has been the revisionism done by leaving out key thoughts that appear in some of America's foundational documents. These omissions have been perpetrated upon America's children for many decades through public school textbooks.

Following are a couple of examples of revisionism by omission:[2]

The Mayflower Compact (1620)

The textbook says:

> We whose names are under-written...do by these presents
> solemnly and mutually in the presence of God, and one of

another, covenant and combine our selves together into a civil body politick.

The full declaration reads:

> We whose names are under-written having undertaken for the glory of God, and advancement of the Christian faith and honor of our king and country, a voyage to plant the first colonie in the Northern parts of Virginia do by these presents solemnly and mutually in the presence of God, and one of another, covenant and combine ourselves together into a civil body politick.

Patrick Henry (1775)

Another familiar declaration, by one of the nation's most famous patriots, has been dissected for whatever revisionist reasons. Certainly the omission of this patriot's giving God preeminence is detrimental to understanding American's Christian roots.

The textbook says:

> Is life so dear or peace so sweet as to be purchased at the price of chains and slavery?…I know not what course others may take, but as for me, give me liberty or give me death.

Patrick Henry said:

> Is life so dear or peace so sweet as to be purchased at the price of chains and slavery? Forbid it, Almighty God! I know not what course others may take, but as for me, give me liberty or give me death.

Parents, Guardians of Truth

God has charged parents with safeguarding children against the many dangers that lurk, seeking to deceive and seduce them. Chuck Missler, in my view, gives accurate analysis and wise counsel in the matter of safeguarding America's children against the lies of the revisionists. His words, framed within the context of the question about America's place in Bible prophecy, are thought-provoking indeed:

> We debate the conspicuous absence of the United States in the final biblical scenario, and we somehow conclude that maybe America's decay is just a predestined prelude to the return of our Saviour. And so we become passive.
>
> But if our Lord did return today, what would we have left to give Him from the wreckage of our rich spiritual heritage and the incredible blessings that He has bestowed on this country?...
>
> Liberal engineers of social change have made the claim that, given just one generation, they can radically alter a society. And they have proven their point...
>
> Perhaps we need to consider that God doesn't hold us as accountable for governments and policies and social orders as much as He does for the spiritual inheritance that we give to our own children. Perhaps, in His providential plan, it would be enough if only we would master the task of safeguarding God's truth from father to child, one generation at a time...
>
> However close our relationship with God, no matter how strong our own convictions, we need to understand this principle of teaching the next generation.
>
> Otherwise our faith dies with us, and our children are left to fashion a world of their own choosing.[3]

Missler pinpoints the causes and effects of deserting godly principles:

> The fallout from the takeover of secular humanism in America has been staggering, and nowhere is it more evident than in the lives of our youth. When we examine the course of the

last couple of decades in this country, we see a chronicle of what happens to a nation that turns its back on God...

There is no lack of historical evidence that this country was founded on Christian principles. Document after document confirms an original commitment to God and to His laws.

Patrick Henry stated, "It cannot be emphasized too strongly or too often that this great nation was founded not by religionists but by Christians, not on religions but on the gospel of Jesus Christ."

If we assume that 200 years ago the majority of people in America were followers of God, then what happened in the intervening years to bring us to where we are today? The answer may be that we lost something crucial. We lost the foundation, the reference point, of our Christian faith. And without the foundation of God's authoritative Word, we no longer had anything substantial to pass on to the next generation. So we substituted relativity for truth, and "values clarification" for God's moral absolutes.[4]

Revisionism Must Be Exposed

It would be remiss to fail to point out to parents and educators of America's children the warning signs to look for in textbooks. In his article "Revisionism: How to Identify It in Your Children's Textbooks," David Barton offers the following advice:

When examining a text, always remember that your children do not know as much about history as you do and consequently have no basis for identifying bias. Therefore, examine each text as if you knew nothing at all about history except what is presented in that text; on that basis, will you be pleased with the tone toward America inculcated in your child through that text? If not, then urge your school to get a better text or be diligent to supplement for your children what is missing or wrongly presented in the text. It is not melodramatic to state that America's future rests on what is taught to our children, for as Abraham Lincoln wisely observed: "The philosophy of the school room in one generation will be the philosophy of government in the next."

Famous American educator Noah Webster therefore rightly admonished:

"The education of youth should be watched with the most scrupulous attention…[It] lays the foundations on which both law and gospel rest for success."[5]

Revisionists' Erosion Moves Nation in Wrong Direction

America, placed by the hand of providence within a foundation of Christian principles, began pulling away from its moorings. The farther people moved from that moral center geographically as well as philosophically, the more the nation strained in opposition to the traces in which God had harnessed America, thus to guide it toward its destiny. That national destiny would be reached; God would see to that. But not without the disciplining hand of heaven.

The nation's history has been one of a roller-coaster-like ride of ups and downs, of blessings and discipline. Let us look at the dichotomy involved in rebellion and obedience, the powerful dynamics that have throughout its history made a societal and cultural impact upon this nation's movement toward its end-times destination.

Morals Go South as Americans Go West

Horace Greeley's exhortation to "Go west, young man. Go west!" wasn't necessary in order to open the floodgates of migration from East to West in the early 1800s.

Towns in the American West sprang forth in profusion during the nineteenth century. Entrepreneurs, including the ne'er-do-well sorts, built lucrative (if less than morality-based) businesses alongside wagon trails, outside army forts, at river crossings, at railheads, and in mining areas.

The quickest monetary gain came from the vices that followed the rail workers, soldiers, miners, and cowboys. The first structures built, then, for the most part, were made for the entertainment of these men. And it was indeed a man's world, catering to every carnal pursuit imaginable. Recreation for the almost totally male population inevitably meant the "triple-W" vices of wine, women, and wagering.

Saloons, brothels, and gambling halls seemed to sprout from the sagebrush-strewn ground overnight. One authority writing on the era of expansion says the following:

> [The earliest] structure might be only a lantern-lit, dirt-floored tent, the bar simply a board stretched between two whiskey barrels, the prostitution facility just a cot in a wagon bed for the use of a single female strumpet, and the gambling outfit only a rickety table, a few chairs and a greasy, dog-eared deck of cards. As the towns grew and prospered, these primitive facilities were replaced by one-story wooden buildings with false fronts to make them appear even larger. And if the community developed into a city, saloons were housed in imposing brick buildings with ornate bars, huge back-bar mirrors and brilliant chandeliers. Some brothels became elegantly furnished parlor houses with attractive "boarders" managed by madams whose names were famous throughout the West.[6]

Comstock Lode Erupts

The fabled Comstock Lode silver strike hit in the 1860s and Virginia City, Nevada blossomed. Soon it flourished as had San Francisco. An agent of the U.S. Geological Survey studying recreational opportunities in Virginia found that the town of 18,000 had a gambling house for every 150 inhabitants.

Railroad and the Rowdies

The completion of the Transcontinental Railroad during the late 1860s was one of the great achievements in America's history.

The Union Pacific ran through the Great Plains and joined with the Central Pacific at Promontory Utah Territory on May 10, 1869. A number of towns came into existence as a result of the railroad's progress westward, and these towns attracted large numbers of the lower members of society, including cheating gamblers and other forms of riffraff who lived nefarious lifestyles. These towns came to be called "Hell on wheels," and as the railroads advanced further west, most of these towns disappeared. The occupants would load up their worldly goods and move along to the next location along the route. A few such towns survived, however, and are thriving communities today— including Julesburg, Colorado; North Platte, Nevada; and Cheyenne, Wyoming.[7]

Cowboys and Cattle Towns

The great cattle drives of the 1870s brought the creation of cattle towns and debauchery as decadent as the earlier movement westward. Abilene, Newton, Wichita, Ellsworth, and Dodge City welcomed the cowboys after their back-breaking longhorn trail drives up from Texas.

Some of the famous gunfighters, many of whom followed the gambling circuits associated with the cattle drives, made their reputations both as guns for hire in the cattle business and as lawmen. James Butler ("Wild Bill") Hickok, Wyatt Earp, Bat Masterson, and others added to the lore and lusty reputations of the trail towns and later the established cities.

Reformers Reach for Return to Reason

Finally, enough of America's citizenry became fed up with the wanton lifestyles of many in their midst. Their anger over the unbridled drinking, carousing, and otherwise godless activity created openings for crusading reformers, who were up to the task of taking matters into their own hands. The historian reports:

> The great age of Western gambling ended with the closing of
> the frontier and the rise of antisaloon and woman suffrage

reform movements that swept across the nation in the first decades of the 20th century. These led inevitably to constitutional amendments prohibiting the manufacture and sale of alcoholic beverages and establishing the enfranchisement of women. State after state passed legislation outlawing casino gambling.[8]

Gilded Age and Robber Barons

The era termed "the Gilded Age," from the 1870s to 1900, was the time of the polarization of wealth in the United States. The so-called "captains of industry" were, to the have-nots of much of the country, the "robber barons."

These businessmen built their fortunes on the backs of large numbers of workers who were at their mercy concerning wage and labor matters. The disparity and animosities brought labor unions and the thuggery attendant to those determined to rule the labor class with an iron fist, although claiming great respect for the rights of the common, working man.

Gangland types in particular prospered from the deals made in all the wrong places, usually to the detriment of the working class that was caught in the middle of the money powers and union leadership. Despite the societal and cultural schism created by the volatile disagreements between employers and laborers, America produced the most powerful industrial base to exist on earth:

> The entrepreneurs of the Second Industrial Revolution created industrial towns and cities in the Northeast with new factories, and contributed to the creation of an ethnically diverse industrial working class which produced the wealth owned by the rising super-rich industrialists and financiers such as Cornelius Vanderbilt, John D. Rockefeller, Andrew Carnegie, Henry Flagler, and J.P. Morgan...

> The wealth of the period is highlighted by the American upper class's opulent self-indulgence, but also the rise of the American philanthropy (Andrew Carnegie called it the

"Gospel of Wealth") that endowed thousands of colleges, hospitals, museums, academies, schools, opera houses, public libraries, symphony orchestras, and charities.[9]

The sumptuous lifestyles of the wealthy, known as "the leisure class," didn't go without notice by those who struggled just to get by. The green pastures looked better on the other side of the economic divide, and certain elements within the American have-nots were, despite restrictive laws that would cramp their style, determined to create their own version of how to enjoy life.

Prohibition Proceeds

Drunkenness and the debauchery and depravity that spun from alcoholic consumption were out. Sobriety and a return to what the middle class considered morality were in. Prohibition descended upon the liquor industry like an Oklahoma thunderstorm. Liquor-related politicians were targeted, as well as the distillers who corrupted them with lobbyist bribes and cajoling activities that affected and infected the fabric of American society through officials in local, state, and national governments.

World War I began, and shortly after America joined the fight, in 1918, Congress passed the Eighteenth Amendment to the Constitution. The law prohibited the manufacture, transportation, and sale of alcoholic beverages.

President Herbert Hoover called the effort to abolish liquor in the United States. "a noble experiment." But soon the thirst of many Americans for the altered states of mind alcohol produced generated rebellion against the authorities they saw as preventing the good times.

Before long, such terms as *bootlegger, bathtub gin,* and *speakeasy* became household words. Gangs of thugs became more powerful as they trafficked in illegal alcohol.

Flapper Frenzy

Young women of the era who loved the loosening of moral restraints joined the craze the age of bootleg liquor produced. The flappers jitterbugged, did the Charleston, smoked cigarettes, drank the illegitimate booze, and wore the glittering, body-exposing attire of the lascivious lifestyle they chose for themselves.

In yet another way, America was pulling away from the godly moorings upon which the founding fathers had secured the nation. The following excerpts from a historical perspective summarize the flapper influence:

> Writers and artists in the United States such as F. Scott Fitzgerald, John Held Jr., and Anita Loos popularized the flapper look and lifestyle through their works, and flappers came to be seen as attractive, reckless and independent...

> Flappers went to jazz clubs at night where they danced provocatively, smoked cigarettes through long holders, sniffed cocaine (which was legal at the time) and dated. They rode bicycles and drove cars. They drank alcohol openly, a defiant act in the American period of Prohibition. Petting became more common than in the Victorian era. Petting Parties where petting was the main attraction became popular...

> Despite its popularity, the flapper lifestyle and look could not survive the Wall Street Crash and the following Great Depression. The high-spirited attitude and hedonism simply could not find a place amid the economic hardships of the 1930s. More specifically, this decade brought out a conservative reaction and a religious revival which set out to eradicate the liberal lifestyles and fashions of the 1920s.[10]

Gangland versus Government

The Roaring Twenties brought gangsterism into full bloom in America. Gambling, prostitution, and mass murders—these and every other crime imaginable pervaded the nation when Al Capone and his nefarious colleagues ruled as the crime kings of the time of Prohibition.

The public either looked the other way during the gangland

activities, or participated by frequenting the speakeasies and buying the illegal alcohol. The results of this acquiescence sent American culture onto a course toward a deadly destination that would take the hand of God to set right.

During the Jazz Age, as it was also known, society demanded that the freewheeling partying be soaked with all of the feel-good things the senses of fallen men and women most desired. The gangsters were more than pleased to provide everything needed to fulfill the human lust for fleshly pleasures. Capone's organization controlled the flow of much of the forbidden alcohol. The Purple Gang, centered in Detroit, was in charge of much of the booze that flowed from Canada, delivered over frozen waterways during the winter and by boat during warmer times of the year.

Al Capone resented the Purple Gang, which was run by hoodlums purported to be even more ruthless than Scarface, as Capone was nicknamed. Capone's organization and the Purple Gang had an uneasy working relationship, but one that was mutually remunerative, so they co-existed to saturate America in illegal beer and liquor.

With the customers clamoring for as much of the commodity as the gangsters could supply, many policemen were hamstrung in their efforts to curb illegal alcohol production and distribution. Many didn't even try. They joined in the many rackets.

> Illegal liquor was the second biggest business in Detroit at $215 million a year in 1929, just behind automobiles. During Prohibition, the trade in alcohol employed about 50,000 people in the Detroit area, according to *The Detroit Free Press*. There were as many as 25,000 blind pigs operating in the Detroit area, and authorities were not only helpless to stop it, many were part of the problem.[11]

Great Depression Discipline

The Roaring Twenties ended with a whimper. But it was an agonizing whimper, when on Black Thursday, October 24, 1929, 16 million shares of stock were sold in panic by investors. The stock market crash came when stockholders who had lost faith in the American economy rushed to divest themselves of what they perceived as worthless stock.

They were right. The Great Depression developed. The ramifications were global and profound, eventuating in the most destructive conflict in world history: World War II. Worldwide depression helped bring Adolf Hitler to power in Germany. Hitler waged war on God's chosen people, the Jews, murdering as many as six million in Europe.

Nearly 25 percent of America's total work force, 12,830,000 people, were unemployed at the height of the Depression in 1933. The rest of the world suffered as much, and some countries even more.

Income for workers fell almost 43 percent from 1929 to 1933—that is, for workers lucky enough to keep their jobs in the worst economic calamity ever in U.S. history. The drastic fall in prices caused many farmers to lose their homes and land. Many went hungry. Families, in many cases, split up because there wasn't enough to eat. Many teenage children resorted to riding the rail lines to seek whatever work they could find. Many migrated and lived in shantytowns constructed of cardboard lean-tos, old abandoned cars, scraps of tin and wood, or anything else that could be used for makeshift shelters. These compounds were called "Hoovervilles" because of public anger directed at President Herbert Hoover, who was in large part blamed for the dire economic circumstances in which people found themselves.

A case can be made—if speculative—that the Great Depression was the Lord's corrective hand of discipline due to America's pulling out of the traces meant to guide the United States to the destiny He planned from its conception. Certainly, this is my view and that of many others who look at American history through the lens of a biblical worldview.

In the course of all that happened during this era, Christianity was shoved to the margins of national life. People wanted little or nothing to do with the moral compass provided by the Creator of all things.

When God's creation, called humanity, refuses to acknowledge Him, nature itself eventually cries out. This is what the book of Revelation starkly presents in chapters 6 through 19. In the apocalypse, the Tribulation era, 21 specific judgments—most all of them involving nature being utilized to punish rebellious mankind—affirm the words of Jesus as stated in Luke 19:40: "I tell you that, if these should hold their peace, the stones would immediately cry out."

The pious Jewish religionists were upset and angry at the people, who shouted hosannas of praise while Jesus rode the donkey into Jerusalem. He was coming to offer himself as Israel's long-awaited Messiah. The Jewish religious leaders wanted Jesus to make the people stop praising Him. They considered their praise blasphemy. Jesus was, in effect, falsely claiming to be God's anointed one, so far as the leaders were concerned. That's when Jesus warned that if He silenced the people's praise, creation itself would cry out and convulse in a mighty way.

This seems akin to what happened following the Roaring Twenties. The people of America, for the most part, had pushed God aside. They had grasped to themselves the raucous good times of the hedonistic age. God was denied to the extent that the stones (nature itself) cried out.

I'm convinced that the Dust Bowl was a case of the very stones crying out because God was not honored. Still, it was not apocalyptic in its severity. It was corrective, in my view. We get a brief look at the terrible conditions of that era through the following account:

> The year 1934 was an important year in terms of the Dust Bowl. The drought of 1934 would be one of the worst of the decade. Also, 1934 was a year of many record high temperatures. The extreme heat caused numerous deaths on the Great Plains…
>
> Dust storms during the time period could last for several days. The large amount of topsoil which was blown around could turn day into night, and leave behind something that

looked like a brown snowfall. One particularly bad dust storm occurred on April 14, 1935, a day which came to be known as "Black Sunday." A huge dust storm engulfed the town of Boise City, OK. Many people were caught off guard because the bright, sunny day was quickly turned into night by the worst dust storm of the year…[12]

Writer John Steinbeck captured this era in his novel *The Grapes of Wrath*. And it was indeed an era when the crops of corrective judgment, whose seeds of refusing to follow the God-designed course for America had been planted more than a decade earlier, came to fruition.

Again, the tremendous Dust Bowl of the 1930s, I'm convinced, was a corrective measure while God prepared the American people for the second world war—a conflict God didn't cause, but certainly used to temper and harden this nation to make it ready to meet its destiny.

That destiny was primarily to bring modern Israel to birth on May 14, 1948, and included spreading the gospel to the world through advancing communications technologies. The United States was blessed economically from that point onward, making it the wealthiest and most technologically advanced nation that has ever existed.

3

THE ISRAEL-AMERICA MIRACLE

★ ★ ★ ★

The United States of America and modern Israel have been joined at the hip, as they say, since the first rumblings of Israel again becoming a nation following the Jews being scattered to the whole world after A.D. 135. The Jewish state has returned, and in a supernatural fashion. To begin comprehending the scope of the miraculous return and America's part in the nation being back in its ancient land, we need to understand the prophetic implications.

Many who look at world conditions and examine the issues and events of our time believe they are witnessing Bible prophecy being fulfilled. Things seem aligned geopolitically, socioeconomically, religiously, and in most any other category of end-times signals one might care to examine.

It is relatively easy to make the case that Bible prophecy is being fulfilled today. Jesus' Olivet Discourse (Matthew 24–25) seems to outline almost without exception each of the many things leaping from today's news headlines.

In this discourse, Jesus gave end-times prophecies in answer to His disciples' questioning:

> As he sat upon the mount of Olives, the disciples came unto him privately, saying, Tell us, when shall these things be? and what shall be the sign of thy coming, and of the end of the world? And Jesus answered and said unto them, Take

heed that no man deceive you. For many shall come in my name, saying, I am Christ; and shall deceive many. And ye shall hear of wars and rumours of wars: see that ye be not troubled: for all these things must come to pass, but the end is not yet. For nation shall rise against nation, and kingdom against kingdom: and there shall be famines, and pestilences, and earthquakes, in divers places. All these are the beginning of sorrows (Matthew 24:3-8).

Fulfilled Prophecies?

Jesus answered some of His closest disciples' questions about signs of the end of the world and the ushering in of His kingdom. The Lord foretold the signals that would immediately precede His kingdom coming into its full authority and power:

1. People will come in His name, claiming they are Christ, but they will be deceivers.

2. There will be unusually widespread wars.

3. There will be rumors of even greater wars.

4. Nations will rise in conflict against other nations.

5. Kingdoms will be in conflict with kingdoms.

6. There will be famines.

7. There will be diseases and other natural disorders.

8. Earthquakes will occur in many places.

Jesus called these times the "beginning of sorrows." The language used is likening these prophetic signals to birth pangs—to labor like that of a pregnant woman who is about to deliver her baby.

A Closer Examination

1. FALSE PROPHETS, FALSE TEACHERS

Jesus foretold that many people would come saying, "I am Christ."

This tells us two things. First, it means that people will come declaring they speak in Christ's name. They will say Christ is Lord. Second, people will come on the scene claiming to be Christ, or to have the "Christ spirit." These will be deceivers.

Certainly many today claim they come in the name of Jesus Christ, but they deny that He is the only way to redemption, as stated in John 14:6. The New Age movement and some religions that don't fit the biblical prescription for true Christianity—for example, Scientology—are prominent in the news, with celebrities like Tom Cruise and John Travolta leading the way. Such movements of groups don't hold forth Jesus Christ as the only way to salvation. Rather, they preach man-centered ways to redemption.

Other false prophets and teachers say that they themselves are the Christ. One such well-known guru who made this claim in recent decades is Lord Maitreya. His John-the-Baptist-type false prophet, Benjamin Creme, pointed to him as the Christ.

2. Widespread Wars

Jesus prophesied that at the time just before He returns, war will be rampant upon the earth. His words indicate unprecedented bloodshed.

World Wars I and II were the most horrific ever, with the latter concluding only after hundreds of thousands of Japanese civilians were killed by atomic bombs dropped by American planes on Hiroshima and Nagasaki. Adolf Hitler's rage against the Jews ended with as many as six million of God's chosen people murdered in the Holocaust.

The twentieth century saw violence through war on a scale unmatched in any other era in human history.

3. Rumors of War

Following World War II, fear of the possibility of a nuclear war became part of the psyche of America and the world. It is now possible for intercontinental ballistic missiles (ICBMs) to carry thermonuclear payloads that could kill massive populations of people in a matter of minutes. And the fact terrorists might possess weapons of mass destruction places us under a cloud of great uncertainty at this hour.

4. Nations Rise Against Nations

This is one of the more profound indicators of Bible prophecy juxtaposed against the realities of our times. The word used for "nation" in Jesus' Olivet Discourse is from the Greek word *ethnos*. This translates to *ethnic* in English. Jesus was saying here that ethnic group rising against ethnic group will mark the time just before He returns to planet Earth.

No matter which way we turn to observe what is happening in the socioeconomic and geopolitical arenas in today's world, the central aspect of conflict between peoples involves race. Jesus predicted that the races of mankind will be in great conflict as the time of His return nears.

We think on the ethnic elements of recent wars and know the profound truth of Jesus' words of prophecy. The Serbs/Croatians, Turks/Armenians, Arabs/Jews, and many other ethnic disputes ring the globe. In America, rival youth gangs have their senseless violence steeped in ethnic differences. America, land of the free, increasingly suffers from ethnic rages that rob people of liberty and even of life through drive-by shootings and bloody battles—just for the sake of racial pride.

Armageddon will have racial hatreds at its core. The Oriental world will invade the Occidental when the 200-million force from east of the Euphrates invades the Middle East (Revelation 9:13-16).

5. Kingdom Rises Against Kingdom

This has been a human history-long problem for mankind. Nationalism steeped in lust for what other nations possess. Dictator-spawned hatreds and greeds. These and other fallen humanistic evils make this prophecy one that was in process even as Jesus gave it.

The Lord, of course, was foretelling a greater conflict between kingdoms than those in which even the Romans had engaged in order to build the world-dominating empire they enjoyed during Christ's time.

6. FAMINES

There have been many great famines since Jesus foretold this horror as marking the very end of the age. Two world wars caused massive starvation and suffering, but dictatorships of more recent vintage, combined with the natural harshness of arid lands like Ethiopia and the Sudan, have caused starvation that can only be described as apocalyptic. Jesus indicates a time of famine that makes even those just described seem relatively mild by comparison.

7. PESTILENCE

Planet Earth has seen humanity-staggering pestilence. The bubonic plague that caused the Black Death during the Middle Ages and the outbreaks of cholera and other diseases that have killed millions are pestilences we've all heard about but haven't experienced so much in this generation. AIDS is the plague we think about today. This always-fatal disease threatens to wipe out entire nations in Africa. Yet the Lord foretold a time when the thing called "pestilence" will become much worse.

8. EARTHQUAKES

Much controversy rumbles throughout the prophecy-watch community today about this indicator. Earthquakes are on the increase and are being reported from most every point on the globe. It seems the whole planet is quaking to one degree or another. Some say the greater profusion of quakes is due to better detection and reportage in these more technologically advanced times. Others believe the planet is convulsing in testimony to Christ's soon return.

The magnitude of the temblors experienced just in the twentieth and twenty-first centuries have indeed been impressive. The 9.2 Alaska quake in 1964 and the 9-plus shaking in the Indian Ocean in 2004 that spawned the tsunami that killed more than a quarter of a million people makes this the most pronounced era of reported earthquakes, to be sure.

The Sure Indicator

An increasing number of Bible prophecy students are declaring that the signals explored above signify that the prophecies given by Jesus are occurring today. Prophecy *is* being fulfilled in our time, they declare.

Although the issues and events inundating our daily lives look quite similar to the prophecies Jesus foretold in His discourse, I don't believe the things we are seeing now are the exact things about which the Lord spoke. This opinion is based upon a number of factors that would involve an extensive body of scriptural explanation. Space limitations require that I must say only that rather than seeing actual Tribulation or apocalyptic things happening right now, this generation is in the midst of witnessing the *stage being set* for the things Jesus foretold will prevail during the last seven years of human history (the time known as Daniel's seventieth week, the Tribulation, as outlined in Revelation chapters 6 through 19).

The Great Storm of Apocalypse

The best way to describe where we are as an end-of-days generation is to think of ourselves as looking out across a great plain. We can see all the way across the flat distance to the horizon.

Boiling on that vast horizon are ominous, black clouds. The closer the storm gets, the more we can see the wicked, jagged flickers of lightning. We sense the audible distant rumbles and soon our ears are assaulted by thunderous crashes of violence rushing our way.

The many prophetic signals Jesus foretold are similar. We are not yet in the midst of that great apocalyptic tempest, but we certainly recognize that it will soon overtake our still relatively tranquil surroundings.

The world stage is setting up for the era about which Jesus said, "For then shall be great tribulation, such as was not since the beginning of the world to this time, no, nor ever shall be" (Matthew 24:21).

The Exception?

There is an exception to every rule, so the saying goes. Even God's Word sometimes has exceptions to the rules contained therein. But never in the case of unalterable truth, such as the following: "Neither is there salvation in any other: for there is none other name under heaven given among men, whereby we must be saved" (Acts 4:12).

The exception to the rule in the case of end-times prophecies not being fulfilled during the current dispensation (church age) might well be Israel once again being a nation.

Modern Israel's rebirth—in my mind, at least—can be likened to Jesus being the only way to salvation. Israel being back in the land of promise, with its language, Hebrew, once again the national language, is the dramatic manifestation of God's unalterable truth. Israel will be His nation forever. Here is God's very word on this truth through His Old Testament prophets:

1. God's first promise to Abraham about a nation:

> The LORD appeared unto Abram, and said, Unto thy seed will I give this land (Genesis 12:7).

> I will establish my covenant between me and thee and thy seed after thee in their generations for an everlasting covenant, to be a God unto thee, and to thy seed after thee. And I will give unto thee, and to thy seed after thee, the land wherein thou art a stranger, all the land of Canaan, for an everlasting possession; and I will be their God (Genesis 17:7-8).

2. To those who say God's covenant with Israel concerning the nation/land is conditional:

> If his children forsake my law, and walk not in my judgments; if they break my statutes, and keep not my commandments; then will I visit their transgression with the rod, and their iniquity with stripes. Nevertheless my lovingkindness will I not utterly take from him, nor suffer my faithfulness to

fail. My covenant will I not break, nor alter the thing that is gone out of my lips. Once have I sworn by my holiness that I will not lie unto David. His seed shall endure for ever, and his throne as the sun before me. It shall be established for ever as the moon, and as a faithful witness in heaven. Selah (Psalm 89:30-37).

Thus saith the LORD, which giveth the sun for a light by day, and the ordinances of the moon and of the stars for a light by night, which divideth the sea when the waves thereof roar; the LORD of hosts is his name: If those ordinances depart from before me, saith the LORD, then the seed of Israel also shall cease from being a nation before me for ever (Jeremiah 31:35-36).

Now the LORD had said unto Abram, Get thee out of thy country, and from thy kindred, and from thy father's house, unto a land that I will shew thee: and I will make of thee a great nation, and I will bless thee, and make thy name great; and thou shalt be a blessing: and I will bless them that bless thee, and curse him that curseth thee: and in thee shall all families of the earth be blessed (Genesis 12:1-3).

3. Abraham's idea for Ishmael, versus God's plan:

Abraham said unto God, O that Ishmael might live before thee! And God said, Sarah thy wife shall bear thee a son indeed; and thou shalt call his name Isaac: and I will establish my covenant with him for an everlasting covenant, and with his seed after him (Genesis 17:18-19).

Give thee the blessing of Abraham, to thee, and to thy seed with thee; that thou mayest inherit the land wherein thou art a stranger, which God gave unto Abraham (Genesis 28:4).

4. God reveals His plan for the land/nation to Jacob:

Behold, the LORD stood above it, and said, I am the LORD God of Abraham thy father, and the God of Isaac: the land whereon thou liest, to thee will I give it, and to thy seed; and thy seed shall be as the dust of the earth, and thou shalt spread abroad to the west, and to the east, and to the north, and to the south: and in thee and in thy seed shall all the families of the earth be blessed. And, behold, I am with thee, and will keep thee in all places whither thou goest, and will bring thee again into this land; for I will not leave thee, until I have done that which I have spoken to thee of (Genesis 28:13-15).

5. God's words to Moses:

Behold, I have set the land before you: go in and possess the land which the LORD sware unto your fathers, Abraham, Isaac, and Jacob, to give unto them and to their seed after them (Deuteronomy 1:8).

6. God's words to Joshua:

Moses my servant is dead; now therefore arise, go over this Jordan, thou, and all this people, unto the land which I do give to them, even to the children of Israel. Every place that the sole of your foot shall tread upon, that have I given unto you, as I said unto Moses. From the wilderness and this Lebanon even unto the great river, the river Euphrates, all the land of the Hittites, and unto the great sea toward the going down of the sun, shall be your coast...Be strong and of a good courage: for unto this people shalt thou divide for an inheritance the land, which I sware unto their fathers to give them (Joshua 1:2-4,6).

7. God's promise to return Israel to the land:

Yet for all that, when they be in the land of their enemies, I will not cast them away, neither will I abhor them, to destroy them utterly, and to break my covenant with them: for I am the LORD their God. But I will for their sakes remember the covenant of their ancestors, whom I brought forth out of the land of Egypt in the sight of the heathen, that I might be their God: I am the LORD (Leviticus 26:44-45).

> I will bring again the captivity of my people of Israel, and they shall build the waste cities, and inhabit them; and they shall plant vineyards, and drink the wine thereof; they shall also make gardens, and eat the fruit of them. And I will plant them upon their land, and they shall no more be pulled up out of their land which I have given them, saith the LORD thy God (Amos 9:14-15).

The Israel-America Miracle

The reestablishment of Israel in the land God promised His chosen people affirms that God's promises never fail. This is the one element pervading the entirety of end-times matters that can verify fulfillment of prophecy in our day for those who make that case. Israel's amazing relationship with America, likewise, gives the United States considerable credence as a nation of prophetic destiny.

Scripture is replete with profound assurances given by God to Israel that the land promised to them was *theirs*. Remember, this is a people who were scattered throughout the world and persecuted—without a country—for almost two millennia! "The LORD thy God will turn thy captivity, and have compassion upon thee, and will return and will gather thee from all the nations, whither the LORD thy God hath scattered thee...And the LORD thy God will bring thee into the land which thy fathers possessed, and thou shalt possess it" (Deuteronomy 30:3,5).

A Stunning Fulfillment?

Isaiah the prophet was given a view down the corridor of time to see God's people scattered, violently mistreated, and then brought back together as one. Ezekiel the prophet foresaw a similar thing in the valley of dry bones prophecy recorded in Ezekiel 37. Isaiah's prophecy is remarkably more dramatic than other prophecies—even than Ezekiel's vision—because of the stunning precision with which his prophecy was given and with which it came to pass. I wrote about Isaiah's marvelous prophecy some time ago.

[Israel is the one sign] Jesus gives that seems most directly to signal the beginning of the end. We have been living a part of that most dramatic sign since 1948, when the nation of Israel was born in a single day—May 14.

Of that time of Israel's rebirth, Jesus—speaking in parabolic language to His disciples—said, "Now learn a parable of the fig tree; When his branch is yet tender, and putteth forth leaves, ye know that summer is nigh: So likewise ye, when ye shall see all these things, know that it is near, even at the doors. Verily I say unto you, This generation shall not pass, till all these things be fulfilled" (Matthew 24:32-34).

Jesus, in speaking to His disciples in the Olivet Discourse, looked down through the eras of future man; He spoke to future disciples—to the generation that would be alive at the time of His second advent.

The nation Israel, in the symbolic language sometimes utilized in God's Word, is likened at times to a fig tree in that God intended the children of Israel to be fruitful, a blessing to all the world. Such references to Israel as a fig tree are found in Judges 9:10-11, Joel 1:7-12, Habakkuk 3:16-17, and in many other passages.

Jesus clearly used the fig tree parable to tell the last generation of believers that the reestablishment of the nation Israel would be a key sign of His nearing second advent as well as a sign of the end of the world system. All other signs given by Jesus would accompany this major sign as the end of the age approached.

Since Jesus had told of the destruction of Jerusalem—and implied the dispersion of the Jewish people—just prior to giving the parable of the fig tree, He spoke most pointedly of the time when Israel would be regathered and begin to "shoot forth" its leaves. The golden summer of His millennial reign would be near when this came to pass. His coming again would be imminent.

First, however, the black winter clouds of apocalypse would have to storm upon a world gathering to commit collective suicide.

Possessing the Land

The prophet Ezekiel spoke of the Diaspora and rebirth of God's chosen nation—the same nation that made the world tremble nervously in anticipation of its reaction to Saddam Hussein's Scud missile attacks during the Persian Gulf War.

> And I scattered them among the heathen, and they were dispersed through the countries: according to their way and according to their doings I judged them...For I will take you from among the heathen, and gather you out of all countries, and will bring you into your own land (Ezekiel 36:19,24).

God's promises to this beleaguered, precariously perched nation, the nation most prominent in the process of pursuing world peace, are numerous throughout the Scriptures.

Consider the profound assurances given through Moses: "That then the LORD thy God will turn thy captivity, and have compassion upon thee, and will return and will gather thee from all the nations, whither the LORD thy God hath scattered thee...And the LORD thy God will bring thee into the land which thy fathers possessed, and thou shalt possess it..." (Deuteronomy 30:3,5). And "Shall the earth be made to bring forth in one day? or shall a nation be born at once? for as soon as Zion travailed, she brought forth her children. Shall I bring to the birth, and not cause to bring forth? saith the LORD" (Isaiah 66:8-9).

The exodus of Jews from the Soviet Union, since the supposed benevolent institution of *glasnost* and *perestroika,* has been staggering. The dissolution of much of Eastern Europe's communist superstructure has freed many more to migrate to Israel. They stream from Ethiopia and from around the globe to the Land of Promise. We are witnesses to God's promises to Israel in ways unthinkable a few years ago. God is indeed making manifest, through the Jews, His great prophetic truth in this generation!

Dry Bones, Live!

Put yourself in the prophet Ezekiel's place for a moment. While you do so, think of the things you know about the Jews in the day in which we now live.

Think for a moment on the blowing sands of the Palestinian region and of the empty, desolate places, void of human life for the most part.

Now, remember the stark black and white images of starving, dying people you've seen on documentary footage of the death camps called Auschwitz, Buchenwald, Dachau, Mauthasen, Sachsenhausen, Treblinka. Remember the trenches, the bulldozers, the skeletal forms beneath loose, pasty-white skin. See again the corpses, intermingling and meshing together—rolling over each other as the bulldozers did their work of pushing the bodies into the ditch-like, common graves.

Recall the scenes of the allied commander, Dwight D. Eisenhower, as he and his staff walked among the pathetic, sticklike, human figures following the liberation of the concentration camps. See again the German people, robust, well-fed, even though bone-weary of war. Picture them in your mind's eye as they held handkerchiefs to their noses, some of them weeping, others retching, and some trying to leave the lines in which they were forced to walk while viewing the rotting bodies of the dead Jews.

Remember all this as you put yourself, for one moment, in the place of God's prophet, Ezekiel:

The hand of the LORD was upon me, and carried me out in the spirit of the LORD, and set me down in the midst of the valley which was full of bones, and caused me to pass by them round about: and, behold, there were very many in the open valley; and, lo, they were very dry. And he said unto me, Son of man, can these bones live? And I answered, O Lord God, thou knowest. Again he said unto me, Prophesy upon these bones, and say unto them, O ye dry bones, hear the word of the Lord. Thus saith the Lord God unto these bones; Behold, I will cause breath to enter into you, and ye shall live: and I will lay sinews upon you, and will bring up flesh upon you, and cover you with skin, and put breath in you, and ye shall live; and ye shall know that I am the Lord. So I prophesied as I was commanded: and as I prophesied, there was a noise, and behold a shaking, and the bones came together, bone to his bone. And when I beheld, lo, the sinews and the flesh came up upon them, and the skin covered them above: but there was no breath in them. Then said he unto me, Prophesy unto the wind, prophesy, son of man, and say to the wind, Thus saith the Lord God; Come from the four winds, O breath, and breathe upon these slain, that they may live. So I prophesied as he commanded me, and the breath came into them, and they lived, and stood up upon their feet, an exceeding great army. Then he said unto me, Son of man, these bones are the whole house of Israel: behold, they say, Our bones are dried, and our hope is lost: we are cut off for our parts. Therefore prophesy and say unto them, Thus saith the Lord God; Behold, O my people, I will open your graves, and cause you to come up out of your graves, and bring you into the land of Israel (Ezekiel 37:1-12).

The Nazis would have built their Reich atop ground filled with the dry bones of God's people of destiny. Adolf Hitler, Heinrich Himmler, Joseph Goebbels, Hermann Goering,

Reinhard Heydrich, Martin Bormann, and the other elitist, Aryan monsters of the Third Reich fired the engines of satanic, ideological hatred with the skeletal remains of more than six million of the house of Israel. The final solution, once and for all, would have rid the world of the despised Jew. Instead, Hitler's ashes lie scattered in the bloody soil of German shame. The bones of all the other Nazi diabolists are strewn in ignominy—who knows where. Yet, the Jew remains, thrives, and prospers the world in every facet of life from the arts to industry, medicine, science, and beyond.

"Never Again!"

God began His chosen nation's restoration to Palestine nearly a century before the Nazi beast began its genocidal work. Migration, though a trickle at first, began about 1838. The revival of national Jewish life in that land started in earnest in 1878.

Then came the event that distinguishes it as perhaps the most important signal that apocalypse is near, that Armageddon approaches. Jerusalem was reclaimed for the Jew in precisely the manner the prophet Isaiah had foretold more than twenty-seven hundred years earlier: "As birds flying, so will the LORD of hosts defend Jerusalem; defending also he will deliver it; and passing over he will preserve it" (Isaiah 31:5).

In 1917, General Edmund Allenby, commander of occupied Palestine for the British Empire, was ordered to take Jerusalem for the Jews. He found the city in possession of the Turks. To take the city by force meant risking initiation of hostilities that might so inflame the region as to cause a massive conflict to result. Bloodshed could have raised the indignation of the whole world.

Allenby, seeking advice from his government, was told to use his own judgment. He again contacted his superiors, who told him to pray, offering no further counsel in the matter.

Allenby then ordered the commander of a fleet of airplanes to fly over Jerusalem. This action so terrified the Turks that they surrendered the city without a shot being fired.

Isaiah's prophecy was thus fulfilled: "As birds flying," God "delivered" Jerusalem; the city was "defended" while aircraft "passed over."

As a result of this action, the Balfour Declaration was signed on November 2, 1917, recognizing Palestine as the rightful homeland for the Jew. The regathering began to take on new dimensions. So, too, did the ugliness of anti-Semitism.

Hatred for the Jew seemed driven by dynamics that transcended reason, reaching fever pitch in Germany on the evenings of November 9 and 10, 1938. During these "Crystal Nights," as they have become known, Jewish homes and businesses were ravaged and destroyed, and many Jewish people were brutally assaulted.

Nazi inner-circle members haughtily termed it the "Week of Broken Glass." Hitler's plan, taken from the pages of his prison-dictated writings, *Mein Kampf,* had taken root. The persecution had become full blown.

From the valley of dry bones—the crematorium/gas chamber hells of Nazi Europe—arose a God-breathed spirit that screamed then and screams still: "Never again!" The crucible of holocaust tempered a people for the rebirth prophesied almost three millennia earlier.

Modern Israel was born on May 14, 1948. The Jews have miraculously prospered. From a people near extinction in 1945, they are today the focal nation of the world. Surely, Israel is the premiere sign that God's prophetic clock approaches the midnight hour...

The Center of the Storm

What is the true source of the world's rage against Israel? "And there appeared a great wonder in heaven, a woman...And she being with child cried, travailing in birth, and pained to be delivered. And there appeared another wonder in heaven; and behold a great red dragon...and the dragon stood before the woman which was ready to be delivered, for to devour her child as soon as it was born. And she brought forth a man child, who was to rule all nations...and her child was caught up unto God, and to his throne" (Revelation 12:1-5).

Here is found the nucleus of the geopolitical storm presently gathering in the Middle East. More than a mortal storm, it is a cosmic, universal maelstrom of eternal consequence.

Lucifer, that fallen angel—Satan, that serpent called the devil—stirs the black, brewing tempest that will soon unleash his fury into man's final war.

His hatred for the people through whom God chose to give fallen man His supreme love gift, His only begotten Son, Jesus Christ, in order that people can be reconciled to the Creator, grows more intense and more manifest by the hour.

The Jew, the nation Israel, is the centerpiece of the Mideast turmoil. Why? Because the Jew, Israel, is at the center of that struggle over which man and his intellect have philosophized since antiquity but have never comprehended. The struggle is between good and evil. Many governments have tried to deal with the trouble in this region. Some seemed for a time to succeed in their efforts. But, the ancient conflict goes on, and more and more often, inflames to the point of eruption.

The wars are legendary by their very nature. Modern Israel, though surrounded on three fronts by forces thirty times greater and backed against the Mediterranean Sea, has not only survived major assaults in 1956, 1967, and 1973—in fact, it was born in the midst of battle in 1948—but, it has miraculously and completely routed the enemies each time while gaining additional territory. Now Israel faces a subtle aggression, but one much more virulent and dangerous.

Diplomatic cries for peace and safety through a negotiated solution to the problem of a homeland for the Palestinian refugees are becoming demands. The "Palestinian problem," the diplomats say almost without exception, "is the key to war and peace."[13]

Israel, America's Saving Grace

This brings us to America's second-most important reason for existence—second only to this nation's destiny in broadcasting the gospel of Jesus Christ to the whole world. This secondary use of the phenomenally powerful American nation is among the most profound indicators we can find that America, indeed, is in Bible prophecy. God has used America as a midwife in Israel's modern birth into the land promised to Abraham, Isaac, and Jacob those thousands of years ago.

President Harry S Truman—who said he had read the Bible through a number of times—insisted despite many voices of opposition that the embryo country still in the womb of the Holy Land, Israel, come to birth on May 14, 1948. America stood by Israel's struggle to get to its feet and its battles against its attacking, hatred-filled enemy neighbors.

A careful look at the times leading up to Truman's presidency after Franklin D. Roosevelt died in 1945 makes it obvious God's hand was at work in unseen ways.

Truman had, as just mentioned, read God's Word through a number of times. He told those around him that the Jews had promises from God concerning the land. He apparently believed that America must bless, not curse, Israel. Historians would say that coincidentally, perhaps even ironically (but I am convinced that the word should be *providentially*), Truman had a Jewish friend—Edward Jacobson—with whom he had co-owned a haberdashery. Jacobson convinced Truman early on of Israel's prophetic destiny.

Although Israel now has its own nuclear arsenal, it is America—in human terms—that has provided the most strength, militarily, which discourages overwhelming assaults against the Jewish state. But, looking beyond the physical earthly protection for Israel, it is the Lord of heaven who provides the ultimate hedge of protection.

God has proved in war after war throughout Israel's earlier and latter incarnations that He keeps His promises to protect the people from absolute destruction, despite their many diasporas and their tribulations as captives and outcasts. He uses human military to accomplish His promise that the Jew will always be His chosen people. Many strange reports have come out of some of those battles, reports proclaiming supernatural activity having turned the tide. And, at a spiritual warfare level in the sense of Ephesians 6:12, conflicts unseen by human eyes continue.

Christian Soldiers

Israel's nuclear capability and America's stupendous military and technological might are strong defensive ingredients for modern Israel's protection. But while surrounded by forces of overwhelming numbers whose satanic rage cannot be stemmed, a most unconventional army is Israel's greatest ally.

This ally contingent holds the joint Israeli-American defensive coalition in place and in God's prophetic plan. It is a spiritual force that is Israel's closest friend. Christians, particularly those in America, make up the spiritual army that supports Israel's right to exist as does no other group on earth.

I must qualify that statement because today there are so many divergent claims to the name of Christ, and differing views about what it means to be a Christian. The definition I use here for *Christian* is one who has been "born again" (John 3:3). This means that a person has been born into the family of God for all eternity. The only way for this to happen is for an individual to accept Christ's sacrifice on the cross at Calvary—His shed blood—to pay for the individual's sin, which separates the individual from God. Those who are born again make up this army of defenders of Israel's right to exist in its ancient homeland.

This army doesn't bear physical arms or fight literally on the bloody fields surrounding Israel. This army fights with prayer for the peace of Jerusalem and does spiritual battle for Israel while that Jewish state moves in blind unrepentance toward its ultimate great destiny—to be the head of all nations during the millennium, Christ's 1000-year reign on planet Earth.

America Plunges While the Church Arises

America, the golden cup in the Lord's hand for more than two centuries—having disseminated the gospel to the world, and having been the midwife of Israel's birth into modern times, then its protector—is not mentioned in Bible prophecy by name. However, supposedly lesser nations of history are mentioned, such as Persia (present-day Iran), Syria, and others. Russia fits into the region known in ancient times as the area that Scripture calls "Rosh." But this once-shining city on the hill called America is nowhere to be found as the very end of days unfold.

So what happens to the United States of America?

We have looked at my view—which I believe is the biblical view—that God's people, the Christians of these end times, are Israel's most fervent friends. But, again I must write a word of qualification. Not all of the born again believe Israel is God's chosen nation as given in the Old Testament. Many Christians today don't even think in terms of Israel and its prophetic destiny one way or the other. This is because in many cases they aren't taught the truth of these matters by their pastors and teachers. Also, they may not do enough study on their own to open their spiritual minds on these things so God the Holy Spirit can instruct them regarding Israel and prophecy yet future. They are ignorant of these things; many are willfully ignorant. So it is a relatively small group of Christians who observe prophetic matters as outlined in God's Word.

No matter the tragic state of the spiritually weakened church in these last days, God hasn't let slip from His mighty grasp the Israel-America miracle He began to form in history now long past. Be assured, those among the heaven-bound, end-times Christians who do understand Israel's place in God's holy eyes are key to America's ultimate destiny.

4

SOARING SUPERPROWESS

★ ★ ★ ★

Roaring engines and the liftoff of the gargantuan space shuttle rockets, with blasting flame and volcanic-like clouds boiling violently, symbolize America's rise to superpower status in the twentieth century. Neil Armstrong, the first man to walk on the lunar surface, said it all when he hopped in what appeared to be slow motion from the rung of the ladder on the lunar lander: "That's one small step for a man, one giant leap for mankind."

The feat proved beyond any doubt which nation was the true superpower. Even the most brilliant visionaries at the time when America was a fledgling could not have foreseen its phenomenal growth to the eagle nation it became when it soared to the moon and back many times. Yet the words of the founding fathers seem to reveal that they understood the nation they were birthing would eventually rise to God-ordained greatness:

- No people can be bound to acknowledge and adore the invisible hand, which conducts the affairs of men more than the people of the United States. Every step, by which they have advanced to the character of an independent nation, seems to have been distinguished by some token of providential agency (George Washington, first inaugural address, April 30, 1789).

- All eyes are opened, or opening, to the rights of man. The general spread of the light of science has already laid open to every view the palpable truth, that the mass of mankind has not been born with saddles on their backs, nor a favored few booted and spurred, ready to ride legitimately, by the grace of God (Thomas Jefferson, letter to Roger C. Weightman, June 24, 1826).

- All of us who were engaged in the struggle must have observed frequent instances of superintending providence in our favor. To that kind providence we owe this happy opportunity of consulting in peace on the means of establishing our future national felicity. And have we now forgotten that powerful friend? Or do we imagine that we no longer need his assistance? I have lived, Sir, a long time, and the longer I live, the more convincing proofs I see of this truth—that God governs in the affairs of men. And if a sparrow cannot fall to the ground without his notice, is it probable that an empire can rise without his aid? (Benjamin Franklin, to colleagues at the Constitutional Convention on June 28, 1787).

- The sacred rights of mankind are not to be rummaged for, among old parchments, or musty records. They are written, as with a sun beam, in the whole volume of human nature, by the hand of the divinity itself; and can never be erased or obscured by mortal power (Alexander Hamilton, *The Farmer Refuted,* February 23, 1775).

- It ought to be commemorated, as the day of deliverance by solemn acts of devotion to God Almighty. It ought to be solemnized with pomp and parade, with shows, games, sports, guns, bells, bonfires and illuminations from one end of this continent to the other from this time forward forever more. You will think me transported with enthusiasm but I am not. I am well aware of the toil and blood and treasure, that it will cost us to maintain this Declaration, and support and defend these States. Yet through all the gloom I can see the rays of ravishing light and glory. I can see that the end is more than worth all the means. And that posterity will triumph in that day's transaction, even altho' we should rue it, which I trust in God we shall not (John Adams, in a letter to Abigail Adams, July 3, 1776).

Eaglet Tests Wings

It is astonishing to realize that now, in the early twenty-first century, some still with us were alive when the phenomenal technological renaissance took off—literally.

The 1903 Flyer 1, the Wright brothers' first powered aircraft, made four short flights on December 17, 1903, at Kitty Hawk, North Carolina. They had made great headway with earlier glider-type craft, which took mankind beyond achievements made by the inventors of the glorified kites that allowed a few men to glide somewhat earlier. Wilbur and Orville Wright's invention, then innovations of yaw, pitch, and roll instrumentalities, made controlled flight a possibility. Adding powered flight to the technology equation caused mankind to literally launch into the future with incredible swiftness.

The invention of powered flight was not long in finding its way into the usual channels human minds too often direct their creativeness. Following their flying exploits of 1905, the Wrights contacted the United States War Department. They also contacted people individually and within governments in England, France, Germany, and Russia.

The Wrights' offers to sell a flying machine were turned down time and time again by government bureaucrats who thought the brothers were a bit mentally challenged. Others, after exploring and reviewing what the inventors had accomplished, expressed their thoughts that if two bicycle mechanics could build a successful airplane, they could do it themselves. But the brothers were persistent, and in late 1907 the

U.S. Army Signal Corps requested an aircraft. A French syndicate of businessmen agreed to purchase another early in 1908.

Both buyers wanted an airplane capable of carrying a passenger. The Wright brothers adapted their 1905 Flyer, equipping it with two seats and installing a more powerful engine.

The Wrights continued developments of powered aircraft, achieving great successes and suffering some tragedies, with accidents that took lives. They demonstrated their work before a million onlookers at one point, and were among the most famous celebrities of their day.

The American nation had tested its wings, and soon it would streak into the future at speeds undreamed of at the time of the first powered flight at Kitty Hawk.

Eagle's Prophetic Influence?

America's invention of powered flight and subsequent developments almost certainly had an impact on Israel coming back into the land of promise in the early twentieth century. It is good to revisit a strange incident that was part of that influence by bringing in a historical fact I mentioned previously. On page 78, I shared the account regarding General Edmund Allenby's action of flying a fleet of airplanes over Jerusalem. This frightened the Turkish inhabitants, who surrendered the city.

Although at this time the United States had not yet achieved superpower status, its star was rising while the sun was setting upon the British Empire. Israel was at the center of both realities. Britain would go on to deal with the Jewish people in a somewhat unscrupulous way while the Jewish leaders tried to move toward nationhood for Israel. America would, during the same era, more and more work to help bring Israel back to nationhood in its ancient homeland.

Beneath the barren soil of this region lay oil in quantities that would make many of Israel's Arab nation neighbors fabulously wealthy. That fact set up the industrializing West for future involvements beyond any that the leaders of the budding American superpower or other Western nations could fathom.

World Goes to War

In the second decade of the twentieth century, hostilities led to war, with England, France, and others against Germany. President Woodrow Wilson of the United States wanted to keep America out of the conflict. But Germany—despite pledges to the contrary—attacked a number of nonmilitary ships, killing a number of civilians as well as American military personnel. When Wilson received a formal note that the Germans would continue to attack such ships, he consulted with Congress, requesting a declaration of war on April 2, 1917.

In his request, Wilson laid out Germany's violation of its pledge to suspend unrestricted submarine warfare in the North Atlantic and the Mediterranean. He also pointed out Germany's attempts to convince Mexico to enter an alliance against the United States. On April 4, 1917, the U.S. Senate voted to declare war on Germany. The House concurred two days later. The United States declared war on Germany's allies, Austria-Hungary, on December 7, 1917.

Historians still debate why Wilson didn't declare war earlier, in 1915, following the sinking of the British passenger liners *Lusitania* and *Arabic,* which had led to the deaths of 131 U.S. citizens. Most assert that the American public, in the president's opinion, was not yet aware of the Germans' unwillingness to stop attacking civilians with submarine warfare. But one who holds a biblical worldview can reasonably conclude that God's guiding hand held back budding American power to conform with His providential plans for the nation. It shouldn't surprise anyone that God's timing coincides precisely with the return of His chosen people to the land He promised them.

Always the Israel Equation

America, from the early twentieth century forward, has been linked to Jacob's progeny as no other national entity. No look at the rise of the United States to history's all-time top superpower status can be undertaken without an in-depth examination of Israel's reestablishment in its God-granted land.

Modern Israel Under the Microscope

Let us turn now to the history of Israel's reappearance as a somewhat unified entity in the nineteenth century.

God prepared His people to return to the land He gave them. The preparation was tough love. Although Jews have been returning to the land of promise a few at a time since their last scattering, it wasn't until the 1800s that they started going home in significant numbers.

Many Jewish people were inspired by Zionist* ideas, and some Jewish settlers purchased considerable plots of land around Jerusalem for farming. Soon, new Jewish communities were springing up. Due to overcrowding of the land in and around Jerusalem, eight new Jewish neighborhoods were built just outside the walls of the city.

Jews comprised the majority of the population in the area by 1880. Large portions of land were purchased, bringing about more and more rural Jewish communities. As the Zionist movement gained backing, plans were made by more Jews to return to the land.

Two sizeable immigrations of Jews soon came from the eastern European continent. They worked hard to homestead some swampy areas, turning the swamps into farmland. By 1900, they had built new settlements on the reclaimed land. This laid the groundwork for the thriving agricultural economy to come.

As can be expected, the new Jewish population was opposed at every turn. To begin with, the land was at first hostile. Mosquitoes infested the swampy areas and it took extremely hard work to reclaim the land so crops could grow as they should. The Turkish Ottoman Empire's governing authority also did all it could to make things difficult. That government imposed restrictions on completing paperwork necessary to allow cultivation of the land and to do other things necessary to make progress.

The Jewish population in Israel reached 85,000 by the time World War I began in 1914. This compared to only 5000 Jews populating the land early in the previous century.

---

* A Zionist is one who believes God's Word foretells that Israel, God's chosen people, will be the chief nation among all nations that inhabit planet Earth during the millennial reign of Christ.

Balfour Brings Rage

God had laid the groundwork for the return to nationhood of His chosen people. *Miraculous* was and is the term used (in some cases by even nonreligious historians) when considering how Israel was reborn as a country.

The Jews had been widely and thoroughly scattered worldwide, then suddenly they were back in the land of the Bible. This took by surprise many of those who didn't think there was such a thing as a Jew left on the planet. Those surprised and amazed included many preachers and religious scholars.

The terrible, treacherous teaching that God was finished with the Jews as a race of people had grown greatly during the years when Israel was out of the land of promise. But now they were back, just as the Bible said they would one day be. God was preparing to prove the world and erroneous religious teachers wrong. The chosen people would yet be used to glorify God's holy name!

The British Empire, upon which the sun was said to never set, was moving into its twilight hours. Yet even at this time God was using Britain's government to help bring about the rebirth of Israel.

As stated earlier, there were about 85,000 Jews in the land by the beginning of World War I. The British government, needing money to fight the war, endeavored to make friends with the Rothschild banking house and other Jewish money interests. British Foreign Secretary Arthur J. Balfour issued on behalf of England the Balfour Declaration on November 17, 1917. This indicated approval of the Jewish goal of bringing about a Jewish state in Palestine.

The document read, in part, "His Majesty's government views with favor the establishment in Palestine of a national home for the Jewish people."

Arab zealots reacted angrily to the British declaration. They stepped up their violent terrorist activity whenever possible. Finally, Arab pressures caused the British to back away from their Balfour Declaration promises. But the seed of desire to establish a Jewish state was deeply planted. There hasn't been a moment of true Mideast peace since that troubled time.

Besieged Settlers

The great hatred Satan has for God's chosen began to boil within the minds of the anti-Semite Nazis and others. The increased persecutions and murders of Jews in Europe soon made those once reluctant to leave their homes and businesses flee for their very lives.

The last great wave of 165,000 immigrants entered the land of promise before Adolf Hitler and his henchmen began to shut off the flow of fleeing Jews. Tragically, the British authorities, following the large influx into Palestine, began turning back thousands of would-be Jewish immigrants. Those authorities didn't want the Arabs to become even more upset at the imbalance in numbers between Arabs and Jews in the region.

Even more tragically, other nations, including the United States, refused to let shiploads of Jews land in their ports. The Jewish people had no choice but to eventually be returned to the Nazis.

The Jews who made it safely to the land of promise found it far less than paradise on earth. Although it was a thousand times better than the horrors being endured by those under Hitler's control, life was hard.

Hate-filled Arabs attacked the Jewish settlers at every opportunity. Their anger exploded. They burned forests and fields belonging to the Jews. Jewish transportation of people and materials such as building supplies, agricultural implements, seeds, and other things were viciously attacked. The tactics were effective at delaying the settlers' firm toehold in the land. But God was with them, and their return to the land was well underway.

World War II and America's Launch to Superpower Status

America's move from pacifism to dealing with the exigencies of Adolf Hitler's megalomania was dramatic. The recognition that Britain was the only national entity standing between the United States and the Nazi dictator revved America's potential into full speed ahead.

World War II brought the nation out of the Great Depression, with full employment replacing the soup lines of poverty. The wartime economy, as a matter of fact, did what Roosevelt's New Deal couldn't: create jobs that there weren't enough workers to fill.

By 1941, rather than the eight million unemployed the previous year, there were labor shortages. Women soon joined the workforce—especially as men went to war—and "Rosie the riveter" became a part of the American lexicon. Women made up 36 percent of the workforce by 1945.

America's industrial base, because of progress in war aircraft technology, set the stage for the phenomenal explosion of knowledge in every aspect of human endeavor that would come at war's end. That quantum leap in knowledge, through computer-related technological achievements, developed in confluence with America's efforts to bring Israel back into its ancient homeland and establish it as a modern nation.

Truman Trumpets Return

"This is what the LORD says, he who appoints the sun to shine by day, who decrees the moon and stars to shine by night, who stirs up the sea so that its waves roar—the LORD Almighty is his name: 'Only if these decrees vanish from my sight,' declares the LORD, 'will the descendants of Israel ever cease to be a nation before me'" (Jeremiah 31:35-36 niv). How anyone can read those words from Scripture with a heart desiring understanding, then think that God is finished with the Jews and the nation of Israel, is far beyond my amazement.

Add to that scripture what the historical record in recent times has dramatically displayed for the whole world to see about Israel and the Jews, and it seems insanity to think God is done with His chosen people. He says through His holy Word that He will not give up on the seed of Abraham, Isaac, and Jacob.

Can it be that America, a nation of such prodigious technological achievement, bringing mankind from the darkness of relative ignorance to exponential enlightenment in mere decades, is not a miracle of divine design? Can it be just coincidence that the most powerful nation on earth at the time of Israel's rebirth threw its might behind

the right of the tiny nation to come forth? Can it be mere coincidence that the president of the United States just happened to have
as a personal friend a Jewish man with whom he at one time ran a
clothing business (a business that failed miserably, but a friendship
that succeeded to such an extent that it, in my view, helped bring
prophecy to pass)?

Harry S Truman, thirty-third president of the United States, didn't
talk publicly to the pregovernment leaders of Israel just before it won
its statehood. And he refused to agree with the very insistent advice
against supporting an Israeli state given by his secretary of state.

Instead, historians report that Truman's decision was based upon
his many conversations with his former business partner. Those conversations, along with Truman's apparent personal religious beliefs about
Israel, reportedly helped him make up his mind to throw America's
great influence behind Israel's rebirth.

America Supports Struggling State

Truman was up to his ears in diplomatic and military problems
when modern Israel was about to be born. The Soviet Union (USSR)
threatened all of Europe. It had already begun tightening its strangle-
hold on Eastern Europe and threatened West Berlin with starvation.
The USSR's blockade of West Berlin made world peace questionable.
Soviet dictator Josef Stalin took advantage of Western Europe's war-
fatigued economy to flex his military muscles.

President Truman was worried with the task of asking the U.S.
Congress to reinstate the military draft. Britain's Winston Churchill
was warning of the menace of war from Stalin's forces. The fighting
and turmoil in the Middle East was not at the top of the list for the
president's attention. The people about to declare Israel's independence, thus its nationhood, didn't have Truman's ear.

But a historian and researcher recently found that there was bitter
debate within the Truman administration about the founding of the
Jewish state. George C. Marshall, the powerful U.S. Secretary of State,
and those within the U.S. State Department were absolutely against

America's support for establishment of the Jewish state. Marshall and the State Department bureaucrats, whom Truman called with both irritation and amusement "the striped pants set," were so angry about Truman's possible support of Israel that Marshall threatened to quit the administration. Not only that; he told Truman he would vote Republican rather than Democratic in the next presidential election. Marshall and the others argued that the oil-rich Arab countries would react by cutting off relations with the United States. That would mean the flow of oil from the Middle East would stop or be severely slowed.

Marshall, a former top general in the U.S. Army, argued that the Arabs would join with the Soviets against America, using the refusal to sell oil as a powerful weapon. He also argued that 44,000 Jews facing more than three million angry Arabs while holding no strategic military positions in the land couldn't survive.

But despite opposition by the State Department and Secretary of Defense James Forrestal, President Truman recognized Israel as a nation. He gave America's official recognition only 11 minutes after Israeli prime minister-to-be, Ben Gurion, gave the address declaring Israel's independence from the former British territory of Palestine.

According to the research, Truman kept quiet about the fact that he had made up his mind to support the establishment of the Israeli state two months before the May 14, 1948, birth of the nation. The president, in telling why he came to that decision, said, "Historical claims, and claims of humanity, both pointed in the same direction."

The decision was made, the research shows, during a meeting with future Israeli president Chaim Weizmann. And the meeting was arranged by none other than Eddie Jacobson, Truman's former business partner.

The researcher said Truman told Weizmann that he favored the partition of Palestine in order for Israel to create a state, and that Jacobson's longstanding friendship with Truman was the key to the successful meeting. Truman had previously refused to meet with American Jewish leaders to discuss the issue of a future Israeli state.

The recognition of Israel passed the U.S. Congress with ease. George C. Marshall never made his angry opposition public and stayed with the Truman administration, later becoming the U.S. Secretary of Defense.

According to the researcher, Truman reacted to the founding of the nation of Israel and his part in it by saying it was "one of the proudest moments of my life."[14]

Bedeviled Birth

Arab countries surrounding the tiny newborn state declared war the moment they learned of the nation's announced independence. Yet Israel soundly defeated the Arab military forces in a number of successive battles. Despite that fact, the oil-rich Arab nations cut off neither diplomatic relationships with nor petroleum flow to the United States. As the clouds of war began to thin out, the modern nation of Israel stood like the dry bones in the prophet Ezekiel's vision in Ezekiel 37. Still, Israel's freedom was not secured.

The nations of the Arab league were blood-oath vowed to push the infant state into the Mediterranean Sea. Egypt, Syria, Jordan, Lebanon, Iraq, and Saudi Arabia positioned military forces for an all-out assault. The courageous, battle-hardened Israeli people, though outnumbered six nations to one and by millions of troops, took up arms and fought back valiantly.

Even seasoned reporters of the scene were dumbfounded by what happened next. The Israeli forces counterattacked on all fronts. Not only did Israel defend its territory, but it won half again as much territory through victory after victory!

Many strange battlefield incidents have been reported and retold in relation to the time of Israel's rebirth. Some call these incidents coincidence, and others call them miraculous.

Refereeing the Ruckus

Things quickly got much worse for Israel's enemies. Within less than a month, the Arab forces were in full retreat on all fronts. Israel was gobbling up more and more of the land from those who had attacked them. Of course, it was really Israel's land. God had said so thousands of years before.

The United Nations got into the act, calling on Israel to cease pursuing its backpedaling, sometimes fleeing enemies. Things had gotten totally out of hand, and there was uncertainty about the security of the oil fields in the region. The internationalist powers that be managed to bring about a sort of calm. Finally, the United Nations brokered a truce, sparing the Arab league further loss of territories and greater humiliation.

The United States and United Nations

In 1945, the United States was instrumental in setting up the United Nations, an international organization purportedly set up to establish peace and security throughout the world. At first the organization's membership was made up of only the victorious Allied countries that defeated the Axis powers of Germany, Japan, Italy, and others. Today the United Nations claims more than 150 member nations.

The United Nations is successor to the League of Nations, an ineffective organization ostensibly dedicated to the same goals and objectives as the United Nations. The League of Nations, supported by American president Woodrow Wilson, failed primarily because it never could win the support of Congress.

America was the only nation with the wherewithal to fund the founding of and support the United Nations. And today, the United States continues to be the chief contributor to its funding, accounting for at least a fourth of United Nations monetary resources on an annual basis.

It is a strange bedfellow situation in which America finds itself as chief supporter of an organization whose constituent nations consistently choose, through voting on various issues, to go against anything that is pro-Israel. Israel is deliberately marginalized at every point— especially in matters that involve the Palestinians and their clamor for a homeland in proposals that always demand Israel give up its land—land Israel has won in hard-fought battles against aggressors who have attacked them.

The United Nations seems, these days, to cater to the dictators of the world, particularly to those in the Middle East. Most every one of these Islamic leaders is blood-vowed to eradicate Israel.

Again, the situation that continues to develop looks more and more like the prophecy given by the Old Testament prophet Zechariah:

> The burden of the word of the LORD for Israel, saith the LORD, which stretcheth forth the heavens, and layeth the foundation of the earth, and formeth the spirit of man within him. Behold, I will make Jerusalem a cup of trembling unto all the people round about, when they shall be in the siege both against Judah and against Jerusalem.

> And in that day will I make Jerusalem a burdensome stone for all people: all that burden themselves with it shall be cut in pieces, though all the people of the earth be gathered together against it (Zechariah 12:1-3).

One must wonder whether America, with its support for such an anti-Semite world organization that could be considered somewhat analogous to Nimrod's Babel (Genesis 11), might be the recipient of the Genesis 12:3 cursings, considering the problems that continue to plague the nation in the midst of its phenomenal successes.

World War II Liberates United States' Potential

World War II took Americans out of the poverty of the Depression years. However, the war also made it all but impossible to purchase anything other than nonrestricted goods. And the restricted goods (materials and items that could be used only in the war effort) were few and far between—most often not things for which there was a pent-up need or desire.

Rubber for tires, petroleum, many foodstuffs, material for clothing—all were legally unavailable. Not even the black market could produce much in the way of things that were off-limits. To the credit of the American citizenry, the reason black market items were in small supply and demand was because of patriotism. In this regard, Americans of the era were indeed "the greatest generation," as former NBC news anchor Tom Brokaw's book title put it.

America ended the war far better off economically than any other nation on earth. The burgeoning defense industry drew workers to the coastal areas and the nation expanded beyond anyone's wildest dreams.

Every conceivable product for relieving toil at home and on the job developed from the genius viscerally a part of U.S. industry. Washing machines, air conditioners, television sets, and myriads of other devices great and small made life easier for a vastly expanding leisure class.

Professional athletes returning from the war brought sports into the American culture in a big way, and the entertainment industry joined other industries in saturating society with products quickly grabbed up by consumers anxious to raise families as far as possible from memories of the Great Depression.

The late 1940s and the 1950s saw a major trend toward a return to church attendance, and evangelism—led by Billy Graham—seemed to show movement of the nation toward a return to its Christian roots.

The industrial-military complex, as American power to produce goods and services was now beginning to be called, expanded at a rate that created economic prosperity beyond which the government was sometimes prepared to control. Labor unions and the businesses for which they provided workforces often came into conflict, and the wage-price cycles spiraled the country to the edge of inflationary pressures that threatened recession. At the same time, the leisure time brought about by the fewer hours worked for higher and higher wages began to have deleterious effects.

The late 1950s saw social unrest begin to rise. The integration crisis in 1957 began a movement that would produce increased cultural changes in the 1960s. The changes in America's prejudices within some areas had to be dealt with, but the divisions some of the civil rights dynamics engendered caused additional problems as detrimental to racial and national harmony as did the bigotry the government sought to end.

While America's military might and industrial strength grew beyond those of any nation's in the annals of history, the internal turmoil grew even faster.

Suppressed Superprowess

America's status as the only possessor of atomic bombs didn't last long. Soon after the close of World War II, the Soviet Union joined the elite club, and the world moved under the ominous clouds of the era to become known as the Cold War.

The race to develop weapons of more awesome power and in greater quantities was underway. America tested a number of hydrogen bombs at the Bikini Islands in the Pacific. Stalin's regime worked just as diligently to stockpile its arsenal with horrific weapons of unimaginable power. But the most troubling was yet to come.

The means to deliver these weapons of mass destruction was where the Cold War really heated up. This would ignite an effort that would produce truly earth-changing technologies.

The term that developed out of this contest to get top-billing in military capability, at one point, was a political weapon used by the Democratic party to frighten American citizens into voting them into the presidency. That Eisenhower had allowed a "missile gap" to develop that favored the USSR became the fearful condemnation of the Republican party following the Soviet's becoming the first to put a satellite into orbit around earth. Sputnik, though simple by today's standards, was perceived as an incredible leap forward. The missile gap now made it possible for the USSR to put a nuclear warhead (rather than a tiny ball that was nothing more than a glorified transmitter) on the tip of a rocket that could reach the North American continent in a matter of minutes. Yet the missile gap, it was learned decades later, never existed. Americans were probably further advanced than the Soviets in most every aspect of military technology. But propaganda won the day, politically, for the Democrats—at least it was a major factor in John F. Kennedy's election in 1960.

War or Peace, Technology Reigns

Technological progress made during the late 1940s and early 1950s moved forward at a pace slower than military planners wanted. With the Soviet advances in catching up with the H-bomb and delivery capability, and with the success of Sputnik, American scientists, industrialists, military, and government leaders put efforts into high gear. The intercontinental ballistic missile (ICBM) was the answer to those involved in the American effort, and great quantities of money were channeled toward the development of such weapons.

Much publicity about civilian use of the rocket and associated technologies by the ones in charge of producing the missile defense system prepared the American public for the even greater amounts of tax dollars that would be required to engage in the "space race," as it came to be called. Although Yuri Gagarin, a Soviet cosmonaut, was the first man to ride into space, the U.S. economic power base and innovative genius quickly overwhelmed the civilian efforts of the Soviets. The bellicose nature of the Soviet bear was made more dangerous by America's spectacular demonstrations of superiority in space-age technologies. The Soviets concentrated on military applications, losing numbers of cosmonauts in the process—something the American public never would accept in the case of the U.S. space program.

Some Soviet experts believe it was as much America's ability to afford the expenditures to achieve stupendous space feats as it was the USSR's overreach in expanding its hegemony that caused the dissolution of the Soviet Union in 1989. It was the Ronald Reagan era threat to produce the Space Defense Initiative (Star Wars Defense, as it became known) that seems to have been most instrumental in bringing the Soviet Union to its fall from superpower status.

On the other hand, America's status soared to new heights while the nation exploded with breakthroughs in computer science and in many other technological industries. The information age, with knowledge increasing exponentially (often doubling within less than two years), represents a breakthrough worthy of being considered fulfillment of Daniel's prophecy that "to the time of the end: many shall run to and fro, and knowledge shall be increased" (Daniel 12:4).

Section II

END-TIMES ILLNESS

★★★★★

5

SOCIETAL SYMPTOMS

★ ★ ★ ★ ★

Every great culture has gone through the following cycle in one
form or another:

- The formation/founding based upon ideals

- A rise to a highly productive society that uniquely contrib-
utes to civilization

- An acquisition of power, wealth, and ever-increasing taxation, in confluence with leisure, marked by a fixation with
entertainment

- A decline into immorality and debauchery that leads to
overthrow or dissolution

It is saddening to have to say that the United States of America has
not escaped this pattern. Rather, it fits precisely the bell-curve model
for decline and fall, according to the cycle just outlined.

Onset of Illness

The first signs of America's symptomatic fever came with the
economic recession that raised America's temperature during the mid-
1950s. Wage and labor tensions and conflicts brought union actions
and more aggressive lobbying within the halls of Congress, and this

spawned a civil rights movement that got underway in earnest during the Little Rock Central High crisis in the fall of 1957.

Civil unrest spread from the nation's southland, where African Americans demanded—rightfully so—that there be equal rights. Other causes—not so noble, in my view—hitched themselves to the integration movement and soon brought challenges to the U.S. Constitution. These incessant assaults began an avalanche of humanistic demands that eventuated in America's present state of declining national health.

Clever legal minds of liberal ilk, equally yoked ideologically with national news and entertainment media propagandists, were able to desensitize the executive and legislative branches to morality, finally convincing them to let the judiciary handle certain socially sensitive issues. The "New Frontier" of the John F. Kennedy administration, most within its ranks holding to a worldview of moral relativism that saw the Constitution as an organic document that changes with the times rather than one rooted in absolutes, presented the ideal incubation chamber for the humanistic ideological bacterium that would begin a moral landslide. It was a downward-spiraling malady from which America has never recovered. Some believe it is a systemic malignancy in the terminal sense.

Robert H. Bork, former acting U.S. Attorney General, wrote in his book *Slouching Towards Gomorrah* that "American culture is complex and resilient. But it is also not to be denied that there are aspects of almost every branch of our culture that are worse than ever before and that the rot is spreading."[15]

Death of Innocence

The rot festering within American national life is manifest nowhere more prominently than in the killing of babies within their mothers' wombs. The landmark case decided by the U.S. Supreme Court was *Roe v. Wade* on January 22, 1973.

> According to the *Roe* decision, most laws against abortion in
> the United States violated a constitutional right to privacy

under the Due Process Clause of the Fourteenth Amendment. The decision overturned all state and federal laws
outlawing or restricting abortion that were inconsistent with
its holdings...

The *Roe v. Wade* decision prompted national debate that continues to this day. Debated subjects include whether and to
what extent abortion should be illegal, who should decide
whether or not abortion is illegal, what methods the Supreme
Court should use in constitutional adjudication, and what
the role should be of religious and moral views in the political
sphere. *Roe v. Wade* reshaped national politics, dividing much
of the nation into pro-Roe (mostly prochoice) and anti-Roe
(mostly prolife) camps, and inspiring grassroots activism on
both sides.[16]

Decisions regarding the deaths of millions of innocents following
this judicial dictate now rest in the hands of the few who say the right
to choose whether to end the life of human beings can be decided by
other human beings. Ironically, the same mind-set that gave the nation
the right to choose to snuff out babies in the womb generally comes
down adamantly against the death penalty for murderers. God's Word
again proves to be true: "Woe unto them that call evil good, and good
evil; that put darkness for light, and light for darkness; that put bitter
for sweet, and sweet for bitter!" (Isaiah 5:20).

Upside-down thinking is among the final of the symptoms of societal ills leading to the downfall of individuals and of nations. Delusion
and deception easily beset thinking that has cast God out. This is
what happened in 1963 when the U.S. Supreme Court decided—
without any voting input from the American electorate—that God
was not necessary in public schools. The lie that the founding fathers
wanted no relationship of religion to government—particularly no
relationship of Christianity to government-run schools—meant prayer
and Bible reading were out. Evolution, on an increasing scale, was in
as the replacement doctrine, with humanism the religious system of
choice.

As outlined above, the result of this reeducation to godlessness in public life eventuated in *Roe v. Wade* in 1973 and the subsequent legal killing of 50 million children in the womb. It isn't unfair, based upon the national political experience, to state that most who believe God has no place in public venues (government schools, courthouses, etc.) also hold to the firm conviction that society has no right to take the life of a convicted murderer. And they demonstrably prove time and again that they believe society must at all costs protect the environment and the habitat for the smallest of creatures, such as the snail darter or the unhatched eaglet, but not baby humans.

While it is wise and good to protect wildlife and our environment, it is contradictory to deny such protection to babies in human wombs. It is the reprobate mind that succumbs to such upside-down thinking, and Scripture makes it clear that God condemns willful perversion of His order of creation and governance: "Even as they did not like to retain God in their knowledge, God gave them over to a reprobate mind, to do those things which are not convenient" (Romans 1:28).

Camelot to Perilous Times

Excitement that approached giddiness bubbled from the news anchors and reporters upon the inauguration of John F. Kennedy on January 20, 1961. The new administration was soon dubbed *Camelot,* and the young Kennedy couple and their small daughter, with another child on the way, were followed by news journalists like paparazzi chasing after Hollywood-type celebrities. But a few short years later, the charismatic aura would turn to black clouds of mourning. The blazing lights of Camelot were snuffed with rifle bullets in Dealey Plaza in Dallas on November 22, 1963.

The Onset of Decline

Although saying so will likely be viewed by many as cynicism at best and as blasphemy against the American dream at worst, the chickens seem to have come home to roost, as the well-worn adage goes. The seeds of supplanting the God of heaven with humanistic authority began to reap the whirlwind of a bitter harvest. America was changed that day on sunny Elm Street in Dallas. The nation lost whatever innocence was left in the milliseconds when Kennedy was shot and he slumped over dead, drenching his wife with his blood. The sickness that gripped the American core being aged us instantly, and the progression of the disease continues to do its debilitating work.

Decline is evident in most every realm of the national life. Although America continues to lead the world as the lone superpower, it bleeds from self-inflicted wounds to, among other things, its economic core.

Consider the significant foreign ownership of American companies today. Such ownership extends to our banking institutions as well. More and more American jobs are being outsourced to overseas workers. The concepts of sovereignty and nationalism are on their way to extinction, thanks to those who work toward bringing together global trading blocs—such as the North American Union (NAU)—blocs that look eerily like a foreboding prophecy yet future: "The ten horns which thou sawest are ten kings, which have received no kingdom as yet; but receive power as kings one hour with the beast. These have one mind, and shall give their power and strength unto the beast" (Revelation 13:12-13).

While the beast regime of this prophecy continues to lurk in the shadows of the prophetic horizon, the foundational infrastructure for its eventual institution has been under construction in America as in no other national entity.

Fall of the Family

The removal of God's influence from America's public school classrooms by forbidding prayer and Bible reading continues to have ramifications. The American family is the chief victim of the societal/cultural disease stemming from the official rejection of the Almighty.

The following, from the Spring 2001 issue of *Legislating Morality*, speaks to the troubling matters involved:

> James Davison Hunter, professor of sociology and religious studies at the University of Virginia and director of the Institute for Advanced Studies in Culture, points out that although "American culture has always been in flux," since about the middle of the 20th century there has been growing confusion over such basic issues as the meaning of family, "family values," how to raise children, the meaning of life, and the rules for living an honorable life. "Where a consensus remains in our moral culture," he states, "it does so only in terms of the shallowest of platitudes."
>
> Hunter contends that "the changes that have occurred are not just cultural. They have been accompanied by profound changes in the social environment in which children grow up. The increases in family instability, the absence of the father from children's lives, the number of hours children are left alone and unsupervised by adults, and the role of television and other electronic media of popular culture have all been well documented."[17]

Recent statistics paint a portrait of an America not so beautiful in terms of family togetherness.

- The current ratio of marriages to divorces is about two to one.

- Marital status for females aged 15 to 44 years old, from 1950 to 2005, shows that the population of unmarried women will soon surpass the number of married women. This indicates a growing rejection of the divine institution of marriage.

- The number of unmarried couple households is increasing steadily.

- The number of children living with only one parent has

increased from 9 percent in 1960 to 30 percent in 2005. Of those, 83 percent live in fatherless homes.

- In 2004, one out of five babies were aborted, and 20 percent of those killed were in the wombs of married women.[18]

Numbers such as these continue to worsen, and the national debt is soaring while the very fabric of American society and culture is unraveling. It's not just that no one has the ability to stop the national fabric from coming apart; the truly frightening thing is that so few seem to even want to fix the problem.

The government—under the leadership of the moral relativists—wants only to throw billions of taxpayer dollars at the problem. They have done so since the initiation of President Lyndon B. Johnson's "Great Society" war on poverty in the mid-1960s. More than several trillion dollars later, the national fabric is unraveling faster than ever. The big social spenders' proclivity for ever-expanding expenditures has not been reined in. There is no fire in the belly to buck the believers in situational ethics and no moral absolutes. The social engineers bypass the voters to ramrod down the throats of the American electorate the luciferian ideological worldview that takes us farther and farther from the God who put in America's founding fathers' thoughts the desire to bring to birth planet Earth's most blessed country in history.

Despite the fact the United States still stands head and shoulders above every other nation on earth economically and in most every other category, the tatters are showing. The dollar is now declining in a significantly problematic way against other major currencies. We are in perilous times morally and financially, and our culture exhibits the symptoms of this increasingly with each passing day.

End-times Symptoms

Paul the apostle's prophetic symptoms of the end of the age assault our senses these days. He outlines the characteristics of end-of-days mankind within his "perilous times" foretellings to Timothy:

> This know also, that in the last days perilous times shall come. For men shall be lovers of their own selves, covetous, boasters, proud, blasphemers, disobedient to parents, unthankful, unholy, without natural affection, trucebreakers, false accusers, incontinent, fierce, despisers of those that are good, traitors, heady, highminded, lovers of pleasures more than lovers of God; having a form of godliness, but denying the power thereof: from such turn away. For of this sort are they which creep into houses, and lead captive silly women laden with sins, led away with divers lusts, ever learning, and never able to come to the knowledge of the truth (2 Timothy 3:1-7).

In consideration of America's place in prophecy yet future, and thinking on its current decline, it is good to examine Paul's predictions against the things going on around us today.

The symptoms described below are excerpted from one of my earlier books. I have not had to do much revising, other than to pare them down for space limitations. These troubling characteristics are even more pronounced today than they were when I first wrote of them.

Symptom #1: Lovers of Self

Today we are told by sociologists and psychologists that at the root of practically every personality problem is lack of self-esteem. Criminals, deprived of equality in society as children, thus grew up feeling left at the bottom of the heap and becoming angry at the system that rejected them. They rationalized that it is street justice to compensate for what society had done to hurt them, and therefore society is fair game.

Psychologists say people should be taught to acquire higher self-esteem; then they will become useful, productive citizens. Self-esteem is another expression for self-love, and God's Word says that this inward-turned philosophy is the *problem,* not the cure. When people think first and foremost of themselves, others whose lives they affect inevitably suffer from their self-indulgence.

One of the most blatant forms of self-love and one of the greatest detrimental effects of egocentricity is found in the problem of teenage sex and the havoc it wreaks upon individuals, families, and society at large. Young people are shown by example that it is a natural thing to indulge in sexual activity apart from the bonds of marital commitment. The body is to be enjoyed, they are told by example. They see in movies, TV sitcoms, and their adulterous parents the "If it feels good, do it" philosophy.

Teens are now told by public school systems that sex is a natural act to be enjoyed, just as eating is to be enjoyed. After all, we are but a higher form of animal life, according to public education's adoptive religion, the theory of evolution. The only thing to be concerned about, according to a growing number of educators across America, seems to be that teens engage in so-called "safe sex."

A young man whose glands are inflamed with lust after having been issued a condom by a school-based clinician pressures a girl to give in to his egocentric drive for satisfaction and impregnate her. He feels no obligation other than, perhaps, to advise aborting the baby. The girl is harmed physically, socially, psychologically, and spiritually. A baby dies. This tragic reality is played out thousands upon thousands of times each year.

The social engineers tell us the secret to ultimately producing a healthy cultural environment is high self-esteem. A sense of self-worth will make man live up to his own great expectations.

Rather than love self, however, God's Word tells us to love others, to esteem others more than ourselves, to humble ourselves before God. This generation is obviously doing none of these.

Symptom #2: Coveters

Keeping up with the Joneses is more than a joke in America today; it is symptomatic of a society gone mad with compulsion to acquire not merely as much as one's neighbor, but much more than one's neighbor. Marketers have for years told us that we deserve the best and have urged us to go for the gusto. We continue to have our senses assaulted by advertising slogans that appeal to our human pride, to our love of self.

This materialistic drive has individually, nationally, and globally tumbled man into an economic abyss from which he will not be extricated, apart from the unprecedented (and ultimately diabolical) geopolitical and socioeconomic rearrangement prophesied in Revelation 13. The spirit of covetousness is thriving in every facet of life, from young children who desire to outdress their peers to their parents who overextend to make an impression. From there it moves to governments whose members complain of massive, unmanageable deficits yet vote themselves huge salary increases and other perks while demanding that the taxpayer tighten his belt and shell out more for congressmen's pork-barrel projects. The greed monster grows!

Coups, revolts, rebellions, and wars have at their sin-blackened centers Paul's end-time term for greed. Our generation is unparalleled in its covetousness.

Symptoms #3 and #4: Boasters, Proud

Following closely on the heels of covetousness—actually, an outgrowth of it—are the dual vanities within the heart of end-time man. These people are boasters; they are extremely proud. And God detests pride. Jesus said, "Blessed are the meek [humble] for they shall inherit the earth [the millennial earth]" (Matthew 5:5).

The father of those whose characters exhibit the antithesis of humility is Satan. Lucifer was the greatest boaster of them all: "I will exalt my throne above the stars of God," he said in his supremely prideful arrogance (Isaiah 14:13). He seduced Eve in the Garden of Eden with the same prideful boast and promise: "You will be as God," he told her. When Adam yielded, all humankind became genetic heirs to the great pride that first welled in Lucifer's heart.

Boasting and pride surface early in life—we can see it even in our very young children. We can remember our own childhood experiences. We made claims, each having to be bigger, better, farther, or faster than the boast that went before.

Politicians are living, breathing proof of boastfulness and pride while they vie for a chance to "serve" us. How quickly the boasts turn empty and ring hollow when they become inaccessible and self-willed after election time. They become little lords; we become revenue producers for the wastefulness of bureaucracy. The rhetoric of the campaign stump—whether on the courthouse lawn, door to door, or in media propaganda—is a strange alchemy of prideful boasting and humble exhortation.

Yet we who are victimized time after time have no room to complain; it is the American political process in action. It is the process we have allowed to stray far from the noble designs of the founding fathers, a process we perpetuate through our acquiescence. This is not cynicism; it is fact.

Symptom #5: Blasphemy

God's name has been all but officially removed from public education in America. This in itself is a blasphemous thing. But His name is, at the same time, in practically every theater in America. Jesus Christ is unmentionable in public forums because His holy name represents a narrow-minded viewpoint and would offend. Religion, if it is to be mentioned, must represent either an eclectic view, or an ecumenical inclusiveness.

In many films above the rating of G, the name of Jesus Christ is repeated frequently. It seems as if screenwriters are required to use His holy name blasphemously at least a minimum number of times per script. Almost always, the names of God or Jesus are used either to express frustration, exasperation, or anger, or to portray the fanaticism of one religious zealot or another (usually a character who is dangerously insane).

Is it any wonder that today's generation of young people is blasphemous and rejects discipline and self-control when adults have spent decades producing an anti-God language? It is perhaps ludicrous to even ask: Are we living in a time of blasphemous deportment such as described by the apostle Paul?

Symptom #6: Disobedience to Parents

As in the case of blasphemy, we should not be shocked at the rebelliousness of our young when they have watched their parents consume themselves with self-love to a point where the children suffer incalculable damage. There has been for years now a degeneration of respect for anything and everything that smacks of order and discipline.

Children watch adults fly in the face of authority in every aspect of life. In every level of sports, adults curse and even physically attack referees, umpires, and judges. Policemen are almost always unjust, unfair, "stupid cops" when tickets are handed out.

Likewise, when the children then refuse to follow the laws that govern society, the parents blame "the system" for being unjust and geared only to placate the wealthy and the elite. The parents refuse to accept responsibility, and the children follow suit. Each generation thus exceeds the bounds of restraint to an extent greater than the previous generation.

God's Word says there will come a time in human history when children by and large will betray parents. This has already come to pass in a significant way in at least one instance. Those in charge of the Hitler youth movement, dissatisfied with the perceived weakness of German parents, removed the children and trained them in Nazi ways for the purpose of "properly" educating them. The children became tools of the state for spying out those who resisted the regime. When parents refuse to accept responsibility, the government—ostensibly to preserve the order of things and promote the general welfare—will.

During the soon-to-come Tribulation, the Antichrist and his associates will no doubt use the same tactics as Hitler. It will be relatively easy to institute such a youth-training system because uncaring or too-busy parents will have paved the way by handing the most horrendous dictatorship in history a generation of children ripe for the picking.

We can look around us today and see the terrible consequences of rebellion taking their toll on the current generation of young people.

Symptoms #7 and # 8: Unthankful, Unholy

President Abraham Lincoln officially proclaimed Thanksgiving Day a national holiday in 1863. Thanksgiving, which is observed for the purpose of giving thanks for the blessings we enjoy in the land in which we now live, was first celebrated in the autumn of 1621, when William Bradford, governor of Plymouth Colony, called for a day of thanksgiving and prayer after the harvest. Other New England colonies gradually adopted the practice.

These godly people, regardless of what revisionist writers claim, left England first and foremost for the privilege to worship the one, true God without restraints imposed by those in positions of power. They knew to whom they were indebted for all the blessings they received. Thankfulness and holiness were inseparable in the minds and hearts of our forefathers. They were thankful to the one and only God of heaven because they sought to be holy and righteous in His omniscient eyes.

How far we have come as a nation and as a world from that first Thanksgiving in 1621! People are proud of the things they accumulate, accomplish, attain; they are grateful in some instances, to other people and to institutions. For the most part, however, they use the word *thankful* interchangeably with the words *happy* and *pleased,* not in the sense of thankfulness to God.

To be truly thankful to God one must be holy—that is, a believer that God is the provider of all good things. But we live among a generation of unthankful, unholy people. They don't know the God of the Bible, nor do they seek to know Him. The only way to know the Father is to know the Son, Jesus Christ, who said, as recorded in John 14:6, "I am the way, the truth, and the life: no man cometh unto the Father, but by me."

The world today views the biblical truth that Jesus Christ is the only way to God as a narrow or close-minded concept that cannot and will not be tolerated by an enlightened people of the twentieth and twenty-first centuries.

Symptom #9: Without Natural Affection

We all read with disbelieving eyes accounts of family members killing each other, of babies being sold or discarded by their mothers, and of fathers engaging in incestuous relationships with daughters from childhood until the daughter either kills her despicable father or reports him to family and authorities.

Accounts involving what can only be described as abhorrent behavior that is "without natural affection" abound in every nation in the world.

Abortion—Perhaps no issue in American society today so fulfills Paul's prophetic end-time characteristic "without natural affection" as that of abortion. In the great majority of cases in which unborn babies are deliberately exterminated, those doing the killing and those consenting to the extermination consider the matter to be no more than medical procedures to solve medical problems.

In most cases, those involved in the abortion process seem to feel no guilt or experience any sorrow over the taking of an unborn child's life. The multiple thousands of victims each year cannot give their views in protest of their impending deaths, so they are considered by the abortionists as nothing more than fetal tissue, refuse to be thrown away.

The proposition has even been raised that in some cases the dead fetuses can be used in the treatment of maladies such as Parkinson's disease. In that procedure, the brain cells of a fetus are transplanted into the brain of a Parkinson's disease victim. There may come a day when genetic engineers will raise fetuses for the specific purpose of maintaining a bank of tissue for use in treating humanity's medical problems.

This casual attitude toward human life—considering the unborn as nonentities, as nuisances to be eliminated, or as tissue to be utilized—is also precisely the mind-set that God's Word says will pervade the generation alive in the era immediately preceding the apocalypse, or the return of Jesus Christ to earth.

Paul the apostle says that the last generation before Christ's return will be marked by the trait "without natural affection" or without love for the most basic kind of relationship, such as the mother for her baby still in the womb. People of that generation will, God's Word says, prefer convenience to responsibility.

Hundreds of thousands of abortions, the vast majority of them nothing less than contraception after the fact, have marked the last several decades as the era of greatest infanticide in recorded history.

Homosexuality—"Without natural affection" also means unnatural affection. Homosexuality is rampant; sexual deviation and perversion of every sort are looked upon now as private matters between consenting adults. Such perverse activity is more and more becoming abominations between adults and children, and even between people and animals.

That there are no moral absolutes in the twisted rationale of humanist critical thinking and values clarification means that anything goes.

Symptom #10: Trucebreakers

In geopolitical terms, communism of the former Soviet and Chinese kind as well as every other variety present in microcosm typifies the last-days characteristics termed by the apostle Paul as "trucebreakers." The number of incidents of communists lying and going back on their word is legendary, though the liberal-minded of the West just don't seem to get it. Perestroika, glasnost, and the USSR under a new name have altered nothing.

But there is an epidemic of trucebreaking in arenas other than geopolitics. It is estimated by some sociologists that as many as one out of two marriages in the United States—that is, people now being married, not necessarily including marriages from past decades—ends in divorce. The most basic truce, treaty, or pact is that made between man and woman to be husband and wife. God ordained marriage to be monogamous and to last a lifetime.

Hollywood has represented the contemporary marriage as a contract to be broken at any time or one to be ignored whenever expediency demands a one-night stand or weekend getaway with someone other than one's husband or wife. Young people now have what seems almost a legitimate excuse to avoid marriage or to at least have an experimental live-in relationship before marriage. "Why have marriage" they can ask, "when the commitment of the marriage vow is treated so lightly in practice?"

Truly, we live in a time when trucebreaking is a way of life for a growing number of people.

Symptom #11: False Accusers

If one wishes to look to a single area within American life in which false accusations run unchecked, it is the political process. False accusations and false accusers are generally accepted as normal in today's society as a whole, but in politics, as is said of love and war, all is fair.

False accusation is nothing more or less than lying in order to seek and to gain advantage for one's self, to the denigration of the one being accused.

"The heart is deceitful above all things, and desperately wicked," says Jeremiah 17:9. Politicians today look into television cameras and deny wrongdoing even after having the proof of their guilt documented for all to see. One U.S. president recently had his law license suspended for lying to a grand jury. Party affiliation makes no difference. Scandals on all sides and at all levels are epidemic.

False accusers are rampant in politics. The very fact that so many public officials are caught red-handed in one ignoble act or another makes the other honest, hardworking public servants vulnerable to innuendo and outright lies, no matter the purity of their record.

Much of the American public can be held responsible for the real and growing evil of false accusation and false accusers. Tabloids thrive on such garbage because their readers have insatiable appetites for it. We indeed live in an era of false accusers.

Symptom #12: Incontinent

Webster's Dictionary, Third Edition defines *incontinent* as "marked by lacking control, unrestrained evil appetites; inability, disinclination to resist impulse [as in alcoholism]."

Every major civilization in recorded history has ultimately come to a time when the symptoms wrapped up in the term *incontinent* overwhelmed society. Perhaps Edward Gibbons's *Decline and Fall of the Roman Empire* is the most complete account of such deterioration. The apostle Paul tells us that the last generation of human history will also come to be predominantly incontinent, not only in conduct but in its very character.

A lack of self-discipline and self-control is a growing monster straining at the tethers of law, order, and common sense. These restraints are themselves perpetually under the abrasive, corrosive attacks of luciferic agencies that seek to replace all traces of godly influence with humanism.

So, even the human governing entities of our nation and world are confused by the author of confusion, Satan. How can we expect our young people to be less confused or more disciplined than the adults to whom they are supposed to look for leadership and example?

Alcoholism and American Youth—The following findings are quite telling about the state of this incontinent culture:

- Every day in the United States, over 5000 kids under age 16 have their first full drink of alcohol.[19]

- More youth in the United States drink alcohol than smoke tobacco or marijuana, making it the most-used drug by young people.[20]

- The average age at which young people ages 12 to 17 begin to drink is 13 years old.[21]

- In a national study, 15.9 percent of eighth graders reported having at least one drink in the previous 30 days, and 12.6 percent had been drunk at least once in the previous year.[22]

- Between 1993 and 2001, 18- to 20-year-old drinkers showed the largest increase (56 percent) in binge-drinking episodes (five or more drinks consumed on at least one occasion in the previous 30 days). This group of underage drinkers also had the second-highest rate of binge drinking, outstripped only by young adults ages 21 to 25.[23]

- Twelve- to 14-year-old binge drinkers consume 91 percent of the alcohol drunk by their age group.[24]

- Approximately 10.8 million persons aged 12 to 20 reported drinking alcohol in the previous month. Nearly 7.2 million were binge drinkers, and 2.4 million were heavy drinkers.[25]

- Ninety-four percent of the alcohol drunk by all 15- to 17-year-olds and 96 percent of the alcohol drunk by all 18- to 20-year-olds is consumed when the drinker is having five or more drinks at a time.[26]

- Almost half (48 percent) of all alcohol use reported by college students is attributable to those who are underage.[27]

- Underage drinking is estimated to account for between 12 to and 20 percent of the U.S. alcohol market. Even the lower estimate, 12 percent, represents 3.6 billion drinks each year.[28]

Sexual Addiction—Sexual self-discipline—rather, the lack thereof—is easily observable and able to be documented for anyone caring to open his eyes to the facts. We have already addressed this tragedy to some extent. We have seen that lack of control in sexuality has resulted in a significant proportion of young people emulating adult lascivious and miscreant behavior; teenage pregnancies and raging diseases continue to follow in the wake of the tidal wave of immorality.

God's Word declares prophetic truth in the 1 Timothy account characterizing end-time man. We live in a time of unbridled sexual behavior.

Symptoms #13 and #14: Fierce, Despisers of Those That Are Good

People of the end time will be fierce, despisers of those who are good. We expect to read and hear of beastly, murderous individuals such as the recently executed Iraqi dictator Saddam Hussein, who reportedly once had one of his bodyguards killed and cut to pieces, then had the body parts delivered to the front door of the man's widow. But no longer are unbelievably cruel acts done solely by strange, megalomaniacal individuals in faraway places. Such atrocities are now fodder for local news writers. What's more, society is increasingly paralyzed in dealing with perpetrators of these horrible crimes.

The well-publicized rape of the Central Park jogger is a case well in point in considering the fierceness of modern man. Four young men raped, sodomized, and bludgeoned almost to death a young woman in New York's Central Park. They were on a rampage supposedly akin to a sport they concocted, which they termed *wilding*.

One of the attackers said in court that another of the men involved had expressed delight during the attack over the force and volume of blood spurting from the woman's cut body. Mass and serial murders are only at the tip of the mountainous heap of murder cases—solved and unsolved—piling up within society today. Law enforcement agencies are in the position of having to develop expertise in investigating specific types of what were once aberrant crimes but now have become almost standard police work.

There is a pernicious movement today among despisers of those who are good. In Luke 18:19, Jesus Christ says, "None is good, save one, that is, God." Those who despise good despise God Himself, and despise Jesus Christ, who is God. All people who are redeemed through acceptance of and belief in the fact that Jesus is the one and only way to salvation are good only because they are in Christ Jesus. Only Jesus can change the inner evil of the fierce and the despisers of those who are good. Only Christ can replace that heart of hatred with wonderful inner peace.

Symptoms #15, #16, #17, and #18: Traitors, Heady, High-Minded,
Lovers of Pleasures More Than Lovers of God

Reports of military personnel selling secrets or bartering intelligence for sexual favors have become more prevalent in recent years. In some cases, we have learned of espionage involving sabotage for the sake of personal gain. Recently, an FBI agent and later a CIA agent were caught in incidents of traitorous activities. These incidents were only the most publicized of the many more going on throughout the world.

On the level of industrial and corporate subterfuge, the symptoms point to a plague of betrayal. Fortunes are made and lost weekly by those who step on or are stepped on while on the ladder leading to success or failure.

This self-uplifting while ascending on the misfortune of others is symptomatic of headiness, or high-mindedness. Satan is the highest-minded of all. He has the audacity to believe he can lift himself above the one, true, eternal God. Those who reject the truth of Jesus Christ are, through omission, heirs to the fallen one's great high-mindedness.

All who seek through their great intellect, their desire, or their superiority in the realm of power-brokerage to put themselves upon the pinnacle of godlikeness in the world they have chosen to conquer are inheritors of Satan's pridefulness. They are exhilarated by the cut-throat struggle to vanquish all obstacles, all foes.

The high-minded intellectuals of academia, of the sciences, or of the liberal clergy seek more than ever to erase all mention of God the Almighty, even at the temporary expedient of tolerating many religions and allowing those religions their many various ways to godhood.

With the intellectual exercise of plotting the planet's physical and social salvation, they are sacrificing their eternal souls on the altar of evolutionary theory. Man seeks to create his own utopia totally apart from God's moral restraints. Man will go to any lengths that his own intellectual capabilities will permit to satisfy his lustful, ephemeral desires. He seeks, like Satan promised and Eve desired, knowledge, power, and wealth because these things bring temporal pleasures.

Second Peter issues a terrifying indictment and judgment on the heady, high-minded, God-despising pleasure seekers of the last days' generation:

> The Lord knoweth how…to reserve the unjust unto the day of judgment to be punished: but chiefly them that walk after the flesh in the lust of uncleanness, and despise government. Presumptuous are they, self-willed, they are not afraid to speak evil of dignities. But these, as natural brute beasts, made to be taken and destroyed, speak evil of the things that they understand not; and shall utterly perish in their own corruption (2 Peter 2:9-10,12).

We live in days such as those delineated in 2 Timothy 3:1-5. The evidence is astoundingly abundant to anyone not wishing to be a foolish, deceived, brute beast but rather desiring to be wise unto salvation.

God's Word tells that the last generation will be like the generation that perished in the flood of Noah's day. Of that people God says,

> When they knew God, they glorified him not as God, neither were thankful; but became vain in their imaginations, and their foolish heart was darkened. Professing themselves to be wise, they became fools, And changed the glory of the uncorruptible God into an image made like to corruptible man, and to birds, and fourfooted beasts, and creeping things (Romans 1:21-23).

What is this, if not a description of modern intellectual man and his attempts to rationalize away all vestiges of the true God? It perfectly describes the writings of Charles Darwin and those who have totally fallen for the evolution lie. These, like the antediluvians, "changed the truth of God into a lie, and worshipped and served the creature more than the Creator" (Romans 1:25). These foolish "intellects" join forces with those whom they would once have termed superstitious idiots, the occultists, and New Age adherents to deify Mother Earth for the sake of ecological purity.

The most powerful nation ever to exist displays symptoms of a terminally sin-sick society. What does this mean in terms of Bible prophecy and America's future? We continue the search for the answer.

6

GEOPOLITICAL PALSY

★ ★ ★ ★

America, although young in terms of years of being a nation, shows signs of aging in disturbing ways. Her shakiness is usually imperceptible, but sometimes uncontrollable. Lately, the quivering has become persistently more pronounced, like progressive disease that sometimes afflicts the human body. She is not alone. The entire world is observably experiencing palsy of the same sort.

This great superpower exerts such dynamic force upon the world of nation-states that this likely accounts for the trembling within other countries. It is perhaps reverberations caused by being intricately linked to U.S. technologies, particularly those involving global economics, that makes the others quake.

When the World Trade Center towers fell in New York City, Wall Street spasmed mightily, and every economic market on earth convulsed. A nervousness developed from that 9/11/01 terrorist attack, causing all international financial eyes to warily watch America's reaction to fluctuations in world markets. For example, they watch to see what the ramifications are in America to the sharp rises in oil prices. Because the entire world is tightly intertwined by instant electronics and satellite, economic quakes or even just burps are instantaneously sensed and reacted to by all money market centers on the planet.

America is, for now, at the nerve center of the world financial system. I say for now because Bible prophecy foretells that Babylon will one day be at the heart of all world financial dealings. More about that in due course.

Distress and Perplexities

Jesus prophesied that the time just before His second coming will consist of unprecedented troubles. The convulsions during that time, He foretold, will be worse than any ever experienced by any generation: "There shall be signs in the sun, and in the moon, and in the stars; and upon the earth distress of nations, with perplexity; the sea and the waves roaring" (Luke 21:25).

The question to consider here is this: Do tremors that are evident in many areas of America's national life today equate to things Jesus foresaw as reported in the Luke 21:25 account? Let's give the United States a brief, three-point check-up.

Economics

There is a constant diatribe from mainstream media today. The talk is persistently of economic downturn. The news sources, it is blatantly obvious, like to present bad news. This is what sells, they believe. With nearly 90 percent of today's news journalists reportedly registered Democrats, and of an admitted progressive (read *liberal*) collective mind-set, it doesn't surprise that there is a reportorial bias in presenting bad economic news. This news slant, as much as any less-than-optimistic statistics that might appear, creates the economic jitters the nation is more and more undergoing.

The nation has experienced high employment and, in the majority of cases, ever-expanding profits. Yet more recently there has been an increase in the number of reports about layoffs, plant closings, and quarterly losses.

Talk is of the decline of the dollar against other world currencies, and trade imbalances and indebtedness running counter to the United States' best interest. Yet at the same time, the United States is owed great debt and the economy continues to expand at a quite healthy rate that is the envy of the world. America continues to be the pillar to which other nations want to tether for fiscal stability.

Still, there are the nerve-jangling jitters, the palsy that just won't go away. If we see an implosion of national economic health, it will have been in large part due to jitters created by the media's drumbeat for ideological change in Washington, D.C.

At the same time, there are legitimate reasons for concern. The recent mortgage crisis and personal credit indebtedness, with greed and avarice at every level of American society, prove that the love of money is the root of the evil that is quickly eroding American culture.

Society/Culture

We see genuine cause for the nervous shakes in looking at the deterioration of American culture. The great wealth the nation enjoys has, in some areas, become more a curse than a blessing.

Bread and circuses are the things Edward Gibbons pointed to as central to the decline and fall of the Roman Empire—or any empire, for that matter. Certainly, Americans are increasingly fat from milk and honey, with generous helpings of every other imaginable food. Entertainment-wise, we worship celebrity, and our young emulate the showbiz icons. Society degenerates while the young (and not so young) drug up and follow the "If it feels good, do it" crowd, which has changed a bit but nonetheless clings to the drugs, sex, and rock-n-roll of the 1960s hippy counterculture.

As we have noted earlier, the very "liberated" minds of that counterculture have so infected American jurisprudence that the judiciary has gotten away with kicking God out of the classroom. The new god that has replaced Him is perhaps Bacchus, the god of mirth, wine, and song. The result is a society that is producing more youth gangs and more teenage unwed mothers, and a government that has become a nanny state and a welfare dependence center for growing numbers of people who have no desire to become productive citizens. What's more, many these days are not citizens, but illegals who pour across the borders in large numbers each night.

Government

Taxation to feed the insatiable wants of bureaucracy is another thing that brings empires down. The Roman Empire was one of many to so overload the people with tax burden that the revolts throughout the widespread reaches of Roman influence tattered and unraveled. The same happened with the British Empire, and with Israel those millennia ago when Solomon's successor, his son Rehoboam, refused to listen to his father's wise counselors (1 Kings 12:3-11), and rather took advice of the taxation-minded men of his age. We remember the declaration, "Taxation without representation is tyranny!" We have representation, but it too often represents the lobby groups and pork-barrel interests, not the taxpayers.

The plan of recent vintage to give tax rebates to people who haven't paid taxes—as an economic stimulus—punctuates the degree to which American legislators have strayed from sound principles of governance. The palsy that grips the national health is exacerbated by such...well, in this case, I like the term *voodoo economics*.

Point is, in summing up the above, American society suffers with growing distress over the reprobate thinking rampant within citizenry, business, and government. Although this generation isn't yet in the age known as the Tribulation, the distress plaguing America and the world shows that we must be near the end of the age.

End-times Quaking

If we are near the end of the age, just before the beginning of the apocalypse, and America seems to be at the epicenter of the "distress of nations, with perplexity" (Luke 21:25), what role is the United States destined to play from here to Christ's second advent? Possible conclusions on this most frequently asked question perhaps lay ahead in our dissection of end-time matters.

Here's how one well-studied prophecy scholar frames Christ's forecast that there will be "distress of nations, with perplexity":

It is difficult to imagine a more appropriate description of the world today than the one presented in Psalm 2. David prophesies that the rulers of the earth will "take counsel together." All we have to do is look around us and see that there are more international organizations in the world today than at any other time in history. There are regional and global alliances, trade agreements, economic treaties, and on and on it goes. Yet the international community in our generation continues to be plagued by ethnic conflict, anarchy and colossal power struggles.

Unseen powers are at work behind the scenes that no one seems to understand. World leaders themselves are pawns in a global board game—a game in which their moves are orchestrated by people and organizations motivated by lust for power, position and monetary gain. There is no room for the Lord in the world's halls of power. The international scene, then, is evolving just as the prophets said it would. The Lord is allowing the nations to back themselves into a corner where the problems of the world seem overwhelming. This is the Lord's way of "squeezing" an out-of-control world and holding it tightly in place while He administers a sobering dosage of His wrath and judgment.[29]

Daily headlines are witness to the world leaders' determination to throw off God's bonds of restraint. Whether they ban together in the United Nations or determine individually to do things unilaterally that seem right in their own eyes, the leaders exhibit the same willful intention to build a world under their governance as did Nimrod at Babel. God is never in the picture.

Even when a leader does include God in his words, everyone knows they are but eloquent expressions of speechwriters, meant to make their bosses look good for posterity. The following excerpt from President John F. Kennedy's January 20, 1961, inaugural speech comes to mind: "...asking his help, and his blessings, but knowing that here on earth, God's work must truly be our own."

Israel: The Seismic Center

No matter which direction world angst causes the newshounds to turn, the geopolitical seismic activity surrounding Israel always draws attention back to the Middle East. This is the number one reason pre-Trib prophecy watchers can say with assuredness that we are bumping up against the end of the age. One top observer, before his death in 2006, was my friend Zola Levitt:

> For most citizens of the world, September 11, 2001 marked the beginning of the "war on terrorism." The murder of over 3,000 men, women and children in New York, Washington, D.C. and Pennsylvania by Islamic radicals created in us all a new fear—the fear of the terrorist. But for the state of Israel, the war on terrorism did not begin in 2001; it started decades before at the birth of the Jewish state.
>
> Whether attacked by Arab nations or Arab suicide bombers, Israel has defended itself like no other nation on earth in a seemingly unending struggle that continues to threaten its very existence.
>
> How has Israel survived until now? Will the Palestinian Authority succeed in its mission to destroy the Jewish people? Do the Arab nations genuinely want peace with Israel once and for all? Has the United States turned its back on the chosen people? What is the role of the church today in relation to Israel? And how does Bible prophecy detail the current state of the Jewish nation as well as its eventual restoration?[30]

These are quite discerning points and questions. Truth about the geopolitical palsy that so profoundly affects America and the rest of the world resides within these thoughts.

Terror Foretold

This is a generation that quakes within from distress and perplexity. The singular catalyst that galvanizes the fear that grips people—particularly within Western societies—is the global terrorism against which we must be guarded every second of every day.

Because this is an impossible task, fear sits within the Western psyche—particularly within the leadership—that weapons of mass destruction, in the possession of terrorists, might at any moment change life forever in their comfortable existences, or end life all together. At the same time, there is a strange façade of calm, as if the problem doesn't exist. Most realize, however, that the next 9/11 could lurk just around the corner of our daily lives.

America is still at ground zero—the bull's eye of the terrorists' satanic rage. Israel, again, is the reason for that rage. Zola put his finger on the problem with precise questions, which we will examine. However, we look at a prophecy that—in my view—speaks right to the heart of the terrorism causing so much anxiety in our day: "As it was in the days of Noe, so shall it be also in the days of the Son of man. They did eat, they drank, they married wives, they were given in marriage, until the day that Noe entered into the ark, and the flood came, and destroyed them all" (Luke 17:26-27).

Jesus, who was not only a prophet, but who is God Himself, foretold the time unfolding through our daily headlines, especially ones involving the War on Terror.

The Lord said that the days just before He returns to earth will be like they were in the time of Noah, just before the worldwide flood ended all human life except that of Noah and seven family members. Let's turn back to Genesis chapter 6 to see why God destroyed that generation, and to see what societies and cultures were like in those times. We are told, "GOD saw that the wickedness of man was great in the earth, and that every imagination of the thoughts of his heart was only evil continually" (Genesis 6:5).

God's treatment plan for the global problems was profound:

> The earth also was corrupt before God, and the earth was filled with violence. And God looked upon the earth, and, behold, it was corrupt; for all flesh had corrupted his way upon the earth. And God said unto Noah, The end of all

flesh is come before me; for the earth is filled with violence through them; and, behold, I will destroy them with the earth (Genesis 6:11-13).

Primary to consider here, in thinking on what was so bad that the Lord determined the entire world must be flooded—washed clean of human corruption—is that violence filled the whole earth. Jesus said it would be like that when His time of return to again cleanse the planet of corruption arrives.

We must ask, then: Do we see anything akin to worldwide violence?

The answer is yes. There are murders everywhere, in every culture and society. But this fallen sphere has always been filled with such deadly violence. That's nothing new that would lead one to observe worldwide violence of an unusual sort.

Then came 9/11 and the fanatic Islamic terrorists who are determined to kill every person on the planet who refuses to bow the knee to Allah. Israel is the center of the rage; America stands in the middle of the bull's eye because America stands with Israel and the chosen nation's right to exist in the land God gave the Jews.

The War on Terror plainly shows that our day is like Noah's in at least that regard. Terrorism is violence taken to the maximum degree. It includes the encouraging of the murder of even women and children. As a matter of fact, the Islamic fanatics will strap bombs on young children and mentally disabled people and send them to do Allah's will against the infidels—that is, those who won't bow the knee to Allah.

Zola's Questions

So we revisit Zola Levitt's questions as posed in the excerpt above. Their substance frames the most pronounced reasons for the geopolitical palsy that plagues this generation.

- How has Israel survived until now?
- Will the Palestinian Authority succeed in its mission to destroy the Jewish people?

- Do the Arab nations genuinely want peace with Israel once and for all?
- Has the United States turned its back on the chosen people?
- What is the role of the church today in relation to Israel?
- And how does Bible prophecy detail the current state of the Jewish nation as well as its eventual restoration?[31]

Just as "the Jewish question" was at the heart of Adolf Hitler's Nazi Holocaust and rage against the world in starting World War II, so the Jewish question is at the heart of the likes of Iranian President Mahmoud Ahmadinejad's rage against Israel. His words encapsulate fanatic Islam's hatred for God's chosen people:

> "They have invented a myth that Jews were massacred and place this above God, religions and the prophets," Ahmadinejad said in a speech to thousands of people in the Iranian city of Zahedan, according to a report on Wednesday from Islamic Republic of Iran Broadcasting.
>
> Referring to comments by Ayatollah Ruhollah Khomeini, the leader of the Islamic revolution, Admadinejad said, "As the imam said, Israel must be wiped off the map."
>
> In response to Ahmadinejad's remarks on Wednesday, Mark Regev, a spokesman for the Israeli Foreign Ministry, said that, "Unfortunately, this is not the first time we've seen such extreme statements from senior Iranian leaders."
>
> He added that, "We see today that there is a growing understanding in the international community that the extremist regime in Tehran is not just Israel's problem, but rather an issue that the entire international community must grapple with."...
>
> The White House said the comments underlined the need for the international community to work together to "keep Iran from developing nuclear weapons."[32]

Several years after Ahmadinejad's declaration, the international community remains on its quest to prevent Iran from producing an atomic weapon. Trying to keep Israel from preemptively striking Iran's nuclear laboratories remains one of the most troubling perplexities of the time. Just as the prophet Zechariah foretold, Israel, surrounded by enemies who want it to be "wiped off the map," has become a "burdensome stone" and a "cup of trembling" to the world community of nations (Zechariah 12:2-3).

Israel and the rest of the world's relationship to God's chosen people stand on God's prophetic time line as the most powerful issue causing the geopolitical palsy that is the prime subject of this chapter. We can perhaps get a good overview of that issue by looking at Zola's list one item at a time:

How has Israel survived until now?

God, when dealing with mankind, most often uses earthly situations and human beings to influence things of this realm. This was true throughout Israel's history. For example, God allowed the Babylonians and the Egyptians to take Israel captive in order to correctively punish them. He used the United States to bring Israel out of its most recent diaspora in 1948. In my view, He raised America specifically for the purpose of being the human protector of His chosen people.

But make no mistake: It is God Almighty who has seen to Israel's survival. Jeremiah 31:35-36 gives this promise:

> This is what the LORD says, "He who appoints the sun to shine by day, who decrees the moon and stars to shine by night, who stirs up the sea so that its waves roar—the LORD Almighty is his name; only if these decrees vanish from my sight," declares the LORD, "will the descendants of Israel ever cease to be a nation before me" (NIV).

America is the most militarily powerful entity ever to exist. But all of her thermonuclear force combined is as nothing in the sight of the God of Abraham, Isaac, and Jacob.

WILL THE PALESTINIAN AUTHORITY SUCCEED IN ITS MISSION TO DESTROY THE JEWISH PEOPLE?

This might seem to some an unfair question. Certainly the news pundits by and large will find it an unfair question.

"The Palestinian people want only a homeland" is the line we are consistently fed. We're told the Palestinians have no desire to do anything but to live in peace in their own nation, where they have equal opportunity.

In this regard, the American and world journalists who feed us the daily news—which has become over the years not news, but one-sided propaganda—are right about one thing. The average "Palestinian" is a poor Arab who indeed just wants to live in peace and have a better life. The fact is, however (a fact we are not told), that most "Palestinians" have many more of their needs met by the Israeli government than by the Palestinian Authority. (Here I put the designation "Palestinian" in quotation marks because it is a word made up to give the Arabs of the area a nomenclature so that those who hold sway over them among the Arab tyrants can claim a right to the lands they occupy in the heart of the land God gave Israel in perpetuity. But, that's another topic for which there isn't space here.)

The question Zola posed here is not unfair. Remember Yasser Arafat, the late Palestinian Authority leader who, when offered 98 percent of all the things he demanded during the Oslo negotiations, got up and stomped out of the proceedings because he didn't get all he wanted? His true goal as the terrorist he was is the same as the goal of the Palestinian Authority leadership today: total eradication of all vestiges of the Jewish state from the region, just like Iranian president Mahmoud Ahmadinejad told us to our faces.

Fact is, had Arafat accepted the deal he was offered, he would have been assassinated, no doubt, like Egyptian president Anwar el-Sadat for making peace with Israeli prime minister Menachem Begin in 1978.

The Islamic terrorist leadership wants Israel destroyed. But, to answer the question Zola posed—no. Israel will be a people forever!

Do the Arab nations genuinely want peace with Israel once and for all?

Perhaps at one time the answer would have been yes, the people of the Arab nations want genuine peace with Israel. However, one has only to remember the reactions of millions in the streets of all Arab nations following the attacks on September 11, 2001, when there was dancing and firing of automatic weapons into the air to celebrate the destruction of the World Trade Center.

There has been inculcation of such magnitude that the very young now have as their earliest memory that they are to hate the Jew—and America as well. The hatred is building, and in my view will culminate when the Gog-Magog attack prophesied in Ezekiel chapters 38 and 39 takes place.

Has the United States turned its back on the chosen people?

A strange dichotomy has developed in America. Like so many things taking place within the nation, there seems almost a 50-50 percentage split on this matter. Many issues seem to have developed a schism, a division that has taken on a life of its own.

We are polarized as a nation on the major social and moral issues. Abortion, prayer in school, religious expression—for example, the flap over whether to call it *Christmas* or *holiday*—the United States is a house divided. Jesus said, and it was reiterated by Abraham Lincoln, that a house divided against itself cannot stand.

If America comes down on the side against support for Israel in the strongest sense of the word *support,* we must indeed begin quaking with geopolitical palsy. America will not stand.

What is the role of the church today in relation to Israel?

The attitude of the church in relationship to Israel is the most troubling of all developments. This is where the great divide, as touched on in the previous of Zola's questions, takes on the most ominous possibilities within America's polarization. I speak of the church as being all who are born again (John 3:3). The church in this sense consists of all who have accepted Christ for salvation (Romans 10:13).

This body of Christ should be the most supportive of Israel's right to exist in the land God gave them. When I say the church should support modern Israel, I'm not talking about supporting the Jewish religious belief that rejects Jesus Christ as Messiah. I'm talking about supporting the right of the nation to exist and for the Jews to not be persecuted.

Sadly, most people of the church today are either 1) too busy being entertained—both by secular entertainment and by megachurch entertainment—to even consider the matter of national Israel and the fact Christians should support that people; or 2) members of huge church organizations whose clergy hold to the theology that the church has replaced Israel, the Jew, as God's chosen people.

More and more, I am asked questions about why Christians should support Israel. "Doesn't the church now have the promises God made to the Jews?" people ask. One person sent me an e-mail saying, "Why do Christians continue to support them, claim them to be God's chosen people, and believe in the Holocaust and the terrible persecution of the Jews? Could the Holocaust be a terrific hoax? Most experts actually believe so."

This was from a person who claims to be a Christian. He was genuinely perplexed as to why he should support the state of Israel and the Jews' right to the land God promised to the nation.

To answer Zola's question, the role of the church to Israel today is woefully underplayed. A core group of Christians firmly back Israel's right to exist. Even so, the support is the small nation's greatest strength in this time that is almost certainly bumping up against the end of the age. This support and what it means will be the focus of a later chapter. The relationship between the church and modern Israel is nothing short of staggering in its import.

How does Bible prophecy detail the current state of the Jewish nation as well as its eventual restoration?

The Bible predicts Israel's situation in the times just before Christ's second advent in frightening terms. Zechariah put his finger on almost the very place Israel will soon occupy on the end-times time line—if the nation isn't there already.

Again we look at a familiar passage:

> The burden of the word of the LORD for Israel, saith the LORD, which stretcheth forth the heavens, and layeth the foundation of the earth, and formeth the spirit of man within him. Behold, I will make Jerusalem a cup of trembling unto all the people round about, when they shall be in the siege both against Judah and against Jerusalem. And in that day will I make Jerusalem a burdensome stone for all people: all that burden themselves with it shall be cut in pieces, though all the people of the earth be gathered together against it (Zechariah 12:1-3).

This prophecy is about the time of Jacob's trouble foretold by Jeremiah the prophet:

> These are the words that the LORD spake concerning Israel and concerning Judah. For thus saith the LORD; We have heard a voice of trembling, of fear, and not of peace. Ask ye now, and see whether a man doth travail with child? wherefore do I see every man with his hands on his loins, as a woman in travail, and all faces are turned into paleness? Alas! for that day is great, so that none is like it: it is even the time of Jacob's trouble; but he shall be saved out of it (Jeremiah 30:4-7).

Jesus, Israel's Messiah, forecast the following about the end of days: "For then shall be great tribulation, such as was not since the beginning of the world to this time, no, nor ever shall be" (Matthew 24:21).

These prophecies about Israel's prophetic destiny would not have been possible if Israel had not returned to the land. But the people are back, and they are at the center of the controversy that threatens to spark Armageddon.

From a human standpoint, America is the key to Israel's future. That relationship causes the geopolitical world to quake with anxiety over things to come.

7

ECONOMIC EPILEPSY

★ ★ ★ ★ ★

Bible prophecy forecasts a time when most every person on planet Earth will be controlled through one economic system. It will be, Jesus Christ said, the worst time in history. The system that will ultimately control through buying and selling instrumentalities is found in the following passage:

> He causeth all, both small and great, rich and poor, free and bond, to receive a mark in their right hand, or in their foreheads: and that no man might buy or sell, save he that had the mark, or the name of the beast, or the number of his name. Here is wisdom. Let him that hath understanding count the number of the beast: for it is the number of a man; and his number is Six hundred threescore and six (Revelation 13:16-18).

This is the passage, of course, that gives us the ominous number 666, which Hollywood and others have made the center of things relating to the occult and devil worship. But it isn't fiction that God deals in when forewarning things to come. This will really happen. It will be the regime of the beast, the Antichrist, that will institute this evolved economic system.

Such a prophesied draconian tyranny seems far distant. Even now, however, the world suffers a sort of epilepsy—seizures caused

by instability within the community of interconnected nations—
that portends corrective action. The United States of America is at
the very center of the linkages, and when the neuron-to-neuron-like
synapses are short-circuited and America convulses, the rest of the
world shakes.

This was made clear in the aftermath of the terrorist attacks on
September 11, 2001. The falling of the twin towers of the World Trade
Center sent the markets around the globe into a tailspin.

Global Economic Implications of 9/11 Attacks

The tragic events of September 11 have affected the world
economy in a number of ways, directly and indirectly. The
direct effects became immediately visible in the short run, in
terms of losses of life and businesses operating in the World
Trade Centre. The attacks inflicted material damage and
casualities on a far greater scale than any terrorist attacks in
recent history, resulting in a sharp global economic reaction.
Between September 11 and September 25, an estimated US
$2 trillion were lost in world equity markets, 20 of the world's
major stock market indexes dropped by more than 10 percent,
and 32 national indexes dropped by at least 8 percent.[33]

Over the same period, at least 15 currencies saw their values
drop by 4 percent or more relative to the US dollar, which was
a tremendous fall over a short period. The cost of immediately
shifting business activities to other areas was colossal.

The unprecedented adverse impact of the terrorist attacks,
though very sharp, also turned out to be temporary. The
credit for that went to the US monetary policy of immediately reducing interest rates.[34]

Overall, in the short term, the terrorist attacks and the resul-
tant security precautions taken have made travel, trade, and
communications more costly. The initial disruptions in trans-
port networks threatened the functioning and efficiency of
global production chains. More significantly, business and
consumer confidence took a significant blow.

The contagion effect of the slowdown in US economy inter-rupted global trade patterns due to increased insurance and freight costs, lengthened shipping times and extended cus-toms delays. As far as sectoral implications were concerned, air travel, tourism and financial sectors, especially the insur-ance and banking sectors, were the immediate targets. The estimate of the total immediate claims in insurance and rein-surance sectors ranged from $20 to $80 billion.[35]

The impact of declined travel and tourism activity and finan-cial sectors was felt in economies mainly dependent on these industries. This has particular relevance to the East Asian economies such as Singapore and Thailand that are directly linked to the US economy in terms of exports. Similarly, European and Caribbean economies, where tourism con-tributed a significant amount to national incomes, were also affected. Tourism makes up 5% of the GDP in some of the European countries but for countries like Costa Rica and Dominican Republic and Mauritius it accounts for 6.6%, 9.6% and 13% of the GDP, respectively.[36]

The disruption in trade patterns severely strained the ability of countries with high debt-to-export ratios, such as Argen-tina and Brazil, to finance their debts. In addition, the direct involvement of some countries in the War on Terror resulted in their bearing the direct cost impact on their respective economies.[37]

It is difficult to accept that America, the center of the financial universe today, is not even mentioned in Bible prophecy as a player in end-times economic matters. No doubt the dynamics involving buying and selling goods worldwide will be the epicenter of the final judgments as God pours out His great wrath upon the humanistic system called Babylon. This is what God's Word forecasts for that system:

Standing afar off for the fear of her torment, saying, Alas, alas, that great city Babylon, that mighty city! for in one hour is thy judgment come. And the merchants of the earth shall weep and mourn over her; for no man buyeth their merchandise any more: The merchandise of gold, and silver, and precious stones, and of pearls, and fine linen, and purple, and silk, and scarlet, and all thyine wood, and all manner vessels of ivory, and all manner vessels of most precious wood, and of brass, and iron, and marble, and cinnamon, and odours, and ointments, and frankincense, and wine, and oil, and fine flour, and wheat, and beasts, and sheep, and horses, and chariots, and slaves, and souls of men.

And the fruits that thy soul lusted after are departed from thee, and all things which were dainty and goodly are departed from thee, and thou shalt find them no more at all.

The merchants of these things, which were made rich by her, shall stand afar off for the fear of her torment, weeping and wailing, and saying, Alas, alas, that great city, that was clothed in fine linen, and purple, and scarlet, and decked with gold, and precious stones, and pearls!

For in one hour so great riches is come to nought. And every shipmaster, and all the company in ships, and sailors, and as many as trade by sea, stood afar off, and cried when they saw the smoke of her burning, saying, What city is like unto this great city!

And they cast dust on their heads, and cried, weeping and wailing, saying, Alas, alas, that great city, wherein were made rich all that had ships in the sea by reason of her costliness! for in one hour is she made desolate (Revelation 18:10-19).

Many who study Bible prophecy find America in this description. However, in total context of the Babylonian hybrid entity addressed, this description seems merely to reflect the hellish system that will have developed by the time God's greatest wrath falls upon rebellious mankind. This doesn't seem to describe a specific nation or city, although of course it could be.

America, if she is the subject of John's vision here in Revelation 18, has metamorphosed to the point she represents the amalgam of the beastly materialistic entity the economy of the time has become. This system has burgeoned into a world of haves and have-nots on a scale never before to have existed. It is a tyrannical economic monster, with all the wealth in the hands of a very few elite. All others are fodder for providing its gaudy opulence things of totally self-indulgent pleasures.

Economic Epilepsy Foreshadowing Babylon

Definitive economic realities and trends are lining up with Bible predictions of the way things will be at the end of the age. One specific, powerful dynamic is driving all of mankind toward the end-of-days abyss Jesus called the Great Tribulation. John the revelator gave, through inspiration directly from Jesus Christ, prophecy about the state of the economy during history's most terrible time:

> When he had opened the third seal, I heard the third beast say, Come and see. And I beheld, and lo a black horse; and he that sat on him had a pair of balances in his hand. And I heard a voice in the midst of the four beasts say, A measure of wheat for a penny, and three measures of barley for a penny; and see thou hurt not the oil and the wine (Revelation 6:5-6).

The foreboding call for the rider on the black horse to gallop forth tells of a coming time of worldwide famine—of death from starvation—for millions. There will be, at the same time, great riches. The wine will flow sumptuously, and there will be plenty of medicinal and other of life's soothing emoluments for living luxuriantly. However, the prophecy indicates a catastrophic division of the haves from the have-nots. The rich will get richer and want for nothing while the rest of the world goes deeper into earth history's blackest hour of depression.

Earth's Economic Future

If this generation is within the general time frame of the era just before Christ's second coming, then we who believe in the Bible as God's inerrant Word are assured we can see the signals of the season leading up to the end. Jesus said in Mark 13:37, "What I say to one, I say unto all, watch." He said further: "When all of these things begin to come to pass, then look up, and lift up your heads; for your redemption draweth nigh" (Luke 21:28).

So, with the Lord of creation—the infallible prognosticator of what will happen from here to eternity—let us examine His end-time word on earth's economic future. Keep in mind that the whole Word of God is Jesus speaking to us. Scripture states, "In the beginning was the Word, and the Word was with God, and the Word was God. The same was in the beginning with God" (John 1:1-2).

It is Jesus, who is God, who gave all prophetic truth about what will happen in the end of days to the prophets of His holy Word. Prophecy comes from Jesus, no matter what Bible writer or what book we look at while we think upon things involving the end-time economy.

With this fact in our thinking, let's consider the thought expressed when we began. One specific, powerful dynamic is driving all of mankind toward the end-of-days abyss Jesus called the Great Tribulation. It is becoming more and more evident what that component of the end-time economic puzzle is: oil.

Petroleum the Catalyst

Petroleum is tugging, driving, causing all of mankind to rush toward the Middle East for the final showdown with Jesus Christ Himself.

The economic epilepsy that is the manifestation of petroleum pressures are many, and affect most every facet of life in America and around the world. Therefore, rather than looking only at oil as an energy-producing resource, I want to break down all of the peripheral issues associated with petroleum—that is, we will look at that specific catalyst for bringing the armies of Earth to do battle in the Valley of Jezreel in its many component parts of the influence oil is exerting, particularly as it involves economic pressures upon the nation-states of the world.

The prophet Ezekiel gives us, in a capsule, the end-time economic factor that is the nucleus of the movement toward Armageddon:

> Thus saith the Lord GOD; It shall also come to pass, that at the same time shall things come into thy mind, and thou shalt think an evil thought: and thou shalt say, I will go up to the land of unwalled villages; I will go to them that are at rest, that dwell safely, all of them dwelling without walls, and having neither bars nor gates, to take a spoil, and to take a prey; to turn thine hand upon the desolate places that are now inhabited, and upon the people that are gathered out of the nations, which have gotten cattle and goods, that dwell in the midst of the land (Ezekiel 38:10-12).

This is a prophecy of the Gog-Magog war scheduled for times just ahead. Some believe it might take place before the rapture, some believe it might coincide with the rapture, and still others believe the Gog-Magog assault into the Middle East toward Israel could take place within the time of Daniel's seventieth week, or the Tribulation.

It isn't particularly relevant to be concerned with the timing of that catastrophic attack here. But it is most relevant to consider what might cause the leader of this great force to have his "evil thought" and determine to bring that tremendous coalition of Israel-hating armies from the north.

It is becoming increasingly clear what that factor will likely be: oil. Oil is the one commodity on earth that could reach the degree of importance that could constitute the great "spoil" mentioned a number of times in the Gog-Magog passage. It cannot be mere coincidence that the Middle East region is where the planet was most lush, the place where the Garden of Eden was placed. If oil is, as most scientists believe, primarily decayed vegetation and animal matter that has decomposed, then this is the area where we might expect the greatest deposits of the substance we call oil. It must be more than mere coincidence, too, that this is the general region in which all of the petroleum-hungry nations of the world would have an intense interest. How much of a stretch is it then to believe that the forces of Gog-Magog would one day consider this region a chief target for invasion? And carrying this logic to its biblically prophetic conclusion, is it any wonder that Armageddon, involving most every nation on earth, will take place in this very region to do battle for the great spoil—the liquid black gold—beneath the sand of the Middle East?

Ezekiel prophesied that God would "put hooks" in Gog's jaws (Ezekiel 38:4) and bring him into the region for the Magog force's destruction. God said He will gather all armies of the world to the place called Armageddon. Seems to me the gathering process is well under way as we consider matters involved in the end-time economy.

Petroleum Makes the World Go 'Round

The world's drive to progress in technologies makes it inevitable that the need to find energy sources will more and more take center stage to power the efforts to fuel industry. This was prophesied by Daniel the prophet: "Many shall run to and fro, and knowledge shall be increased" (Daniel 12:4).

Such great explosion of travel requires massive amounts of energy, and knowledge has increased to keep pace. The drain on crude oil resources and upon refineries has increased almost as exponentially, as has the knowledge needed to produce the modern marvels of transportation in which we run to and fro. The one painfully obvious area in which we have not made stupendous achievement is in creating viable alternate sources of energy to replace that available through fossil fuels.

New, thirsty customers plus diminishing supply equals trouble of the apocalyptic kind. We will look at the newest customers lining up at the diminishing petroleum pools. But first, let us think a bit upon how oil has an impact on life just in America.

America continues to be the world's greatest drain on oil resources around the world. We produced most of our own energy needs during the mid-twentieth century. The vast, easy-to-access oil reserves in Texas and Oklahoma gave the nation a cheap supply of energy to run the machinery of our burgeoning demands.

The depletion of those fields and the subsequent search for new oil suppliers moved the United States and the world into geopolitical channels that few foresaw. America and the world, ever since being struck by the epiphany that indeed oil is a finite resource, have been powerfully drawn to the Middle East.

Israel the Key

So many rearrangements have taken place since the late 1950s that it would require a set of volumes, not a single chapter, to cover the matter. The bottom line to consider is that the rearrangements have all revolved around America's relationship to Israel.

This relationship has seemed both a blessing and a curse. America's acting as midwife for the birth of modern Israel opened new venues of economic markets. Our protection of the infant state, which quickly became the most powerful in the region (with America's help), gave the United States a presence in the region with the deepest petroleum reserves. These were needed to assure the powerful engines of Western productivity would continue to run. The geopolitical and industrial realities of the times assured America a place among the chief players of the region with the clout to keep oil flowing.

The royal Saudi family held the keys to the most copious amounts of the black gold. They needed—and need to this very moment—America's powerful military protection. All we have to do is recall the 1990–1991 Operation Desert Storm conflict to realize that truth. Kuwait fell, and Saudi Arabia would likely have been next but for America's intervention.

The rearrangements have proven to be a mutual, indispensable matter for each partner. Although the two cultures are in total conflict, survival demands a continuing and quite strong relationship.

The security arrangements have brought forth, at the same time, strange bedfellow-type situations. One recently reared its troubling head when America and the Saudis announced the likelihood that the United States would be selling advanced weaponry to Saudi for its protection. While this is a fantastic economic boon for the American arms industry, it is potentially a slash in the joined-at-the-hip relationship between America and Israel.

The royal family of Saud must have America's strength to survive, even with increased military capability of their own. The Arab nations are indeed composed of many men at the top echelons of power who are tied inexorably to the beasts that direct the terrorist organizations of the Middle East. One example is Syrian dictator Bashar Al Assad, who permits every major terrorist organization of the region to headquarter in Damascus. Because of ancient hatreds and Islam, every one of the organizations is dedicated to removing Israel and her closest ally, America, from the Middle East. They hate the Saud royal family also, considering them as in league with the infidels—all who are not fully in compliance with the laws of the Koran.

Israel looks with discomfort at the American/Saudi relationship, and becomes quite nervous over the thought that the most advanced and sophisticated weaponry on the planet might be placed in the hands of Muslims.

End-time Players

End-time economic matters come even more into focus when thinking upon the newest players in the dangerous game of who controls the petroleum pools of the Middle East and the world.

The Mechanized Dragon

The price of oil continues to edge upward while a newly awakened industrial monster steps to drink from earth's black, liquid pools in order to satiate its growing thirst.

China, which is one of the oldest civilizations on Earth, has a population of 1.3 billion and rising. That's about five times the population of the United States. It has the world's second-largest economy, and according to experts, is growing economically at a rate four times faster than that of America.

China has 22 percent of the world's population, but only 7 percent of earth's land mass. Considering the nation's rate of growth and reputation for aggressive behavior, this does not bode well for a peaceful future. This is true in part because less than 10 percent of China's land is farmable. The arable land is reported to be declining at somewhere around 750 thousand acres per year due to urbanization, erosion, and other factors. China will almost certainly look more and more to the north and west for expansion. Look for this expansionist mind-set from China's leadership to be the source of rumors of war over the coming years.

The nation's growth means its energy needs are mushrooming. China is already the largest user of oil next to the United States, with its need for petroleum having risen more than 50 percent within the past decade.

Demand Portends Trouble

This speaks directly to the end-time economy that is developing. The almost unbelievable demand for oil portends a coming crisis of frightening proportions. The petroleum industry will simply be unable to keep up with the demands of the nations, whose industrial needs are even now accelerating out of control.

Added to the great demand for petroleum by China is that nation's workforce, which has tasted the milk and honey of industrial growth and will settle for nothing less. Since the collective farms and the land were returned to the people to a considerable extent in 1978, the peasants' economic condition has improved, according to some experts, by more than 1500 percent. Millions upon millions of Chinese citizens enjoy Western luxuries such as television sets, computers, and many other items. They have come from walking or riding broken-down bicycles through poverty-stricken countryside villages to driving automobiles upon superhighways in a growing number of large cities.

All of this progress continues to move forward at the expense of the Western economies, particularly that of the United States.

Estimates are that by 2030, China will be 60 percent urbanized in the most modern sense of the word. Tens of millions of Chinese are flocking to the cities. Shanghai, for example, is already eight times the size of New York City in population. The average per capita income has risen from pennies per day at best to $1,000 per year. This seems trivial to Americans and Europeans, but that growth represents astonishing industrial dynamics that have begun to deleteriously affect the Western economies. Chief among the nations affected is America, which is losing ground to China in some key areas of technological production.

One observer of the situation regarding the United States versus China in economic productivity says this:

> They [China] are today the manufacturer of choice over the U.S., Mexico, Thailand, Singapore, or what have you. They produce more engineers per year than the United States. Their research and development expenditures are outpacing the United States. Their technical industry outpaces the U.S., Europe, and Japan. They are the ones setting the global standards for office software, operating systems, mobile phones, RFID chips, Internet protocols, and other technologies.[38]

Another analyst further assesses the China factor within the evolving end-time economy:

> China is swaggering on the world stage, and has rapidly emerged as the world's second largest trader of merchandise goods. America, in one sense, has already become China's servant as it has amassed huge holdings of US currency and fixed-income securities. Bond market trends this year already appear to indicate that the US has lost its monetary sovereignty.

> America is already in a vulnerable position, its dollar having fallen to near all-time lows against the rest of the world.

And now, the economic climate for Americans themselves is getting ugly. In tough times, what will be the priority of politicians? Keeping voters happy? Lower oil prices? Or continuing to support Israel? Unfortunately, this last policy will prove to be mutually exclusive with the other objectives.

Already, the legendary spendthrift consumer has begun to change behavior noticeably. The US consumer is beginning to conserve cash and lower consumption spending. There [are] both anecdotal and theoretical indicators of this shift...

Credit card debt increased 9.2% in May 2007, a sharp increase in growth. We consider this a sign of consumer duress, particularly as mortgage refinancing has fallen...[39]

When the Apocalyptic Volcano Blows

We have considered mostly the United States and China to this point in thinking on the end-time economy and a likely forecast for the future in terms of financial indicators. This is altogether proper, because no doubt about it, China represents the greatest challenge to the Western industrialized world.

CHINA

China's enormous need for petroleum plus its exploding demands for goods of every sort are draining the economies of the rest of the world. Top economic analysts predict that within 20 years, China will have the largest economy in the world. That nation currently uses 2500 tons of coal per minute. It uses 24 million watts of electricity per minute and 240 thousand barrels of crude oil per minute. Extrapolated to its net effect, one economic observer says China is growing at such a rate of usage of natural resources that within 30 years it will require another planet Earth to meet its needs.

China's ratio of income from America to outflow of money to the United States is staggering in its implications. Fifty billion dollars annually—that's more than $150 million per day—currently flows from America to China. China has attracted more foreign investment capital in five years than Japan has in the 50 years since World War II. That nation holds, according to one economic authority, so much of America's debt instruments that if China sold those into the world market, America would be bankrupt in about 17 minutes.

The bottom line of all these troubling things about the great dragon nation is that its economy has suddenly vaulted it to a powerful position on the world stage. Oil powers its massively growing industry, just as oil fuels the industry of America and other Western countries. Economic force is driving all of these players to a showdown at some future point. God's Word calls that showdown Armageddon.

The United States

When the end-time volcano blows, rearrangements will take place at a quantum rate as America scrambles to regain fiscal equilibrium and societal/cultural balance. I'm more and more convinced that the top will explode from the volcano when the rapture of the church occurs. Many things will have to take place immediately. Conditions will demand it.

- America's tax base will be in shambles, and ways to re-order the nation's revenue production will be sought and secured.

- Martial law and draconian means might have to be employed to assure compliance by citizenry.

- Since millions of American workers who provided the heart of the tax base will have disappeared, the nation's leadership will likely seek immediate new rearrangements with Europe, which will not be so gravely affected.

- New, electronic funds-transfer devices will be created to deal with immediate needs in the financial marketplace.

- Dynamic rearrangements with Middle Eastern dictator-ships will be sought to secure continued oil flow to the West. This will be absolutely essential because of the refusal for decades by Western world leaders to forge ahead with new exploration for fossil fuel or research to find and produce alternate fuels.

- Israel will come into play in the end-time economic re-arrangements. The Arab nations, headed by Israel-hating Islamic fanatics, will make demands the West will have little choice but to accept if the oil is to continue to flow in a westerly direction.

- Ultimately, oil will become such a concern for all world players that all will consider black gold worth a third world war.

Looking Beyond the Apocalypse

Not a pleasant forecast, right? To the contrary! It's a very pleasant prospect, not for the present world at large but for those who look for the King of kings and Lord of lords to return and institute a new, supernaturally infused economy for Christ's 1000-year reign upon this reclaimed planet.

8

RELIGIOUS FEVER

★ ★ ★ ★

America has been the haven for those seeking religious freedom as has no other nation in the history of the world. This fact has had its upside and its downside. The upside is that there has been liberty to worship in exactly the way we want to worship, so long as it isn't truly harmful to anyone else. For example, snake handlers may do so, as long as their children aren't in contact with the serpents and the handlers don't inflict the danger of being bitten by reptiles upon anyone else. The downside is that the liberty we enjoy has opened the doors to religions and modes of worship that have had deleterious effects on society. Any religious belief system that is apart from God's only way to salvation through His Son, Jesus Christ, is going in the direction opposite that which God, who knows best, wants us to go.

The proof of the ill effects of rejecting Christ can be seen upon the youth of America. Burgeoning teenage gangs, teen pregnancies, youth rebelling against authority, and young people being lost to the drug culture—all are symptoms of a nation that has tried to separate itself from God.

At the same time, this downside—freedom to worship or not and to worship as one pleases—must be accepted because God Himself made human beings free moral agents. That is, we are free to accept or reject the offer of salvation through His Son.

However, the truly egregious perpetration of the let's-have-no-God-to-rule-over-us crowd comes in their insistence that God have no part in the national public school systems. As a matter of fact, these people insist that there be no mention of God, especially not of Jesus Christ, in any public forum. This despite the fact that sessions of Congress are still opened with prayer and the U.S. Supreme Court building is still inscribed with the Ten Commandments etched upon its marbled walls. Bibles are still used to administer the oaths of office throughout the land, and presidents still invoke God's name in speeches.

America the Religious

America, the most religious nation on the contemporary scene so far as diversity of belief systems is concerned, is not mentioned once in Bible prophecy by name. Doesn't this seem strange? Should we not, if we are truly in the end of days, expect the United States, with its religiosity, to warrant mention—even if by oblique reference—as part of the end-times mix?

We have on our monetary paper and coinage the motto "In God we trust." Churches are found on practically every corner in many towns throughout the country. Megalithic edifices, practically cities to themselves these days, dominate church property landscapes. The massive church compounds are made up of superrecreational facilities and merchandising centers. They are administrated by multilevel pastoral and administrative staffs large enough to handle with ease the multiple thousands who sit in the luxuriant, theater-style seat-pews.

Many theologians today teach and preach that the world is getting better and better—this same message is taught by the motivational speakers and psychological gurus of our day. Church is big business these days, with television programs that, in many cases, appear daily many times per day and in multiple markets across America and the world.

Pop-Psychology Pulpits

Most troubling in the deception concentric to the religious fever rampant today is the fact that those who claim the name of Christ join in the psychological mumbo jumbo of the motivational path to falsely perceived redemption. Many build the gargantuan churches upon the entertainment and feel-good methodologies available through multimedia extravaganzas and marketing strategies.

There are others who are Christ-centered and have produced mega-ministries based upon Bible principles. One such minister said the following:

> Many people come to church for less than ideal reasons: to be part of something exciting, big, and thriving; to be entertained or inspired; to get a spiritual uplift to help them through the week; to give the kids some religious training; to see the preacher they've heard on the radio. Is it legitimate to use these motivations to attract the unchurched to hear the gospel?

> Thinking up a strategy to get an unbeliever to church isn't difficult. All you do is find out what their hot buttons are and press them. If they like dancing elephants, you get dancing elephants. If they want to be successful in their business, you hold a business success seminar. If they're worried about their kids, you hold parenting workshops and invite the whole world.

> I realize that's true about people, but I'm not guided by that. My calling as pastor is to lift God's people before the Lord, to bring his Word to his people, and to equip them for their calling. Unbelievers, in a sense, are incidental to that primary purpose.

> I would never think, How can I structure this service to accommodate unbelievers? or, How can I appeal to unbelievers to come? because that's not our purpose—unless we are gearing a special meeting for evangelism.[40]

Better and Better?

Psychologists and motivational speakers who follow classic

psychological training for the most part hold to the evolution-based belief that man is getting better and better. The theory is that everything came from nothing—the postulation usually based upon the model of the big bang theory. Everything began in that chaos, and through the evolutionary process is now ascending toward the highest possible order.

God's Word says just the opposite. God created all things perfect, in perfect oneness with Himself. The mystery of iniquity entered the dynamic though the tranquil scene in the Garden of Eden. Lucifer entered the garden and seduced the woman, Eve. Adam chose to disobey; thus, sin entered the world. Now, all things that were once perfect degenerate, corrode, and die, just as God said would happen if man did not obey His prescription for life on planet Earth.

These faith-based systems—biblical creation and evolution—move from each other in diametrical opposition.

We must decide, then, which view is correct. Abundant evidence makes possible an intelligent examination and analysis of which belief system is true. Is the world getting better and better, like the gurus of pop psychology tell us today? Or is the world getting worse and worse, as foretold in the following prophecy given through the apostle Paul? "Evil men and seducers shall wax worse and worse, deceiving, and being deceived" (2 Timothy 3:13).

To refute those who say the world is getting better and better, we have only to suggest a review of today's headlines. There are so many reports of murders, robberies, rapes, genocidal atrocities, and every other kind of evil that we begin to wonder if there are any good things within this fallen world to report. It seems our moment-by-moment reality contradicts that which is proposed by evolutionary thinking and psychology, as far as the direction all things human are trending.

God's Word, on the other hand, puts the finger on the crux of the matter:

> There were false prophets also among the people, even as there shall be false teachers among you, who privily shall bring in

damnable heresies, even denying the Lord that bought them, and bring upon themselves swift destruction. And many shall follow their pernicious ways; by reason of whom the way of truth shall be evil spoken of.

And through covetousness shall they with feigned words make merchandise of you: whose judgment now of a long time lingereth not, and their damnation slumbereth not (2 Peter 2:1-3).

Form of Godliness

America is in a fever of religiosity despite the rampant evil. The religionists leading the way in the false gospel fit perfectly within the prophetic description Paul said would pervade at the end of the age: "This know also, that in the last days perilous times shall come. For men shall be lovers...of pleasures more than lovers of God; having a form of godliness, but denying the power thereof: from such turn away" (2 Timothy 3:1-2,4-5).

America's religious fever deludes all affected with the love of self and the self-centered pleasures that take them away from God. They want all temporal feel-good things that can be garnered from life, including the pseudo-Christian life. These people are living out a form of godliness while denying the power thereof. They cling to the preachers and teachers who tell them they are getting better and better, and are reaching toward a place where they can be all they can be. However, they either choose to believe or deliberately ignore the fact that true godliness must include the blood of Christ for redemption and a willingness to submit to Christ and be led by the Holy Spirit under prayer and Bible study.

Tragically, many within the pop psychology-led pews today fall into the following category: "The time will come when they will not endure sound doctrine; but after their own lusts shall they heap to themselves teachers, having itching ears; and they shall turn away their ears from the truth, and shall be turned unto fables" (2 Timothy 4:3-4).

The United States is perceived by some as a nation of elevated morality and compassion. And there is some reason for the perception.

Despite those who falsely accuse the United States of being a ruthless empire builder, it has rightfully been pointed out that this country is the only nation that fights wars to liberate others, then claims none of the land for ourselves, except military bases to help keep the liberated countries free. The United States vanquishes its foes, then picks them up, dusts them off, and rehabilitates them, providing everything they need in the process to stand on their own feet—for example, Germany, Japan, Iraq. Again, we claim only enough of the land of other nations, in some cases, to serves as resting places for our dead soldiers who sacrificed to free them—such as France following World War II.

That said, America is held up as a "religious" nation by many, and as a "Christian" nation by somewhat fewer. The perception is false; America is neither. A truly godly nation must, to quote Shakespeare writing the words for Marc Antony's eulogy of Julius Caesar, "be made of sterner stuff."

The Feel-Good Church

As emphasized throughout this book, reconciliation to God the Father in heaven is the only way a person becomes godly. This is achieved by turning to Christ for salvation through belief in His sacrifice on the cross. We are all lost, in need of redemption from sin. This is God's prescription for becoming godly, whether talking about the individual or the nation. Since the fall in the Garden of Eden, there has been no chance of a truly godly nation, only godly individuals.

Many who are godly have been seduced by the siren song of the feel-good church organizations. These children of God are being fleeced like the gullible flock they have become. Let's take a brief look at some of the seducers.

Prosperity Gospel Gurus

Television broadcast airways and cables gush with the programs of the prosperity gospel preachers and teachers. These speakers pick and choose from the Scriptures words to flatter their TV parishioners, assuring them that they must give to get. Particularly, the members of the flock to which these prosperity gurus minister must sow seeds of dollars into the ministries so the givers can reap as much as a hundredfold in God's remuneration for their faithfulness and trust. The idea is to send the seed to the ministry doing the prosperity gospel promotion.

The ministers usually tell tales of their own experiences in reaping blessings. They have, they say, given; now they have the personal health and wealth God promises those who adhere to the seed-faith principle. And the ministers can indeed give testimony to their own prosperity! Most have huge homes; some have entire compounds of homes, luxury cars, and other material treasures.

The people watching all of this don't seem to get that these ministries are wealthy because they almost exclusively dwell on the seed principle. Even when these teachers get into real doctrine from God's Word, it is most often used to direct everyone's attention back to the need for the one sitting in the TV pew to get a seed-faith gift in as soon as possible to become wealthy and healthy like the preacher.

The thought that comes readily to mind when watching this fleecing of the flock on television, no matter the time of night or day, is the scripture Paul gave in prophesying perilous times for the end of the age: "For of this sort are they which creep into houses, and lead captive silly women laden with sins, led away with divers lusts, ever learning, and never able to come to the knowledge of the truth" (2 Timothy 3:6-7).

Also, the apostle Peter's words of warning and prophecy ring true in our time in regard to these prosperity gospel gurus: "Through covetousness shall they with feigned words make merchandise of you: whose judgment now of a long time lingereth not, and their damnation slumbereth not" (2 Peter 2:3).

Don't confuse this condemnation of those who fleece Christ's flock as condemnation of the principles of giving found within God's Word.

The Bible gives clear direction for godly stewardship of the blessings God bestows. But the form of seed faith that makes the aforementioned false teachers and preachers extremely wealthy is not the way to correctly give to God's work.

Workers of Wonders and Miracles

The character played by Burt Lancaster in the movie *Elmer Gantry* looks mild in comparison to some of the health-and-wealth evangelists today. Television extravaganzas all over the world, with hundreds of thousands attending at the soccer stadiums of third-world countries, capture the faces of the mesmerized throngs seeking healing. They are promised wealth and joy if they will just believe in miracles. They are asked to become Christians with the not-so-subtle hint that in order to receive blessings of miracles and wonders in their lives, they must give as much as possible to the ministry presenting the show.

This is the part that must be like a dagger to the heart of God: His Son held up as a merchandising tool, with the message that He promises great miracles of a materialistic sort to those who sacrifice all to give to the cause.

Salvation, by God's grace, is free to all. He promises one miracle— indeed, the greatest miracle of all: Those who receive His Son, Jesus Christ, for salvation will live eternally in heaven with Him. Any other gospel is false. Here is what the apostle Paul says about the things going on in these religious circus rings: "Though we, or an angel from heaven, preach any other gospel unto you than that which we have preached unto you, let him be accursed. As we said before, so say I now again, If any man preach any other gospel unto you than that ye have received, let him be accursed" (Galatians 1:8-9).

Entertainment and Star Ringmasters

America can't be accused of being a nonreligious country. The religious fever is at its peak constantly via the TV entertainment programs. The producers work to replicate secular entertainment. The "Christian" stars entertain us by belting out songs that sound exactly the same as those that come from secular venues. Many such songs lack a distinctively Christian message.

While Christian entertainment is not in itself improper if in the appropriate place and time, surely the Lord cannot look favorably on Christian music and entertainment stars who lack any distinctives that set them apart from the world and point people to Jesus Christ. Much of what we see today is done more to accommodate unbelievers rather than call attention to their need for Christ.

There is coming a generation of people who will live during the most godless times of human history. John the apostle and prophet was told to put this in his account of that Tribulation era: "I heard another voice from heaven, saying, Come out of her, my people, that ye be not partakers of her sins, and that ye receive not of her plagues" (Revelation 18:4). We wonder whether this is good advice for the people of God for this present hour.

Toleration of All but One

True Christian faith is being marginalized at a stunning rate. From the attempts to remove God from the public classrooms in 1963 (a thing not truly possible because He is God) to the latest flaps over whether to allow Christmas nativity scenes in public places because they might offend other religious faiths, the hatred for Jesus Christ grows. And hatred for Christ is at the bottom of the incessant attempts to keep His holy name from the ears of every person possible. This is Satan's ploy—to make the name of Christ at best ignored and at worst hated by all who hear it. Satan does not want people to know the truth that "neither is there salvation in any other: for there is none other name under heaven given among men, whereby we must be saved" (Acts 4:12).

Jesus had this to say about the world's opinion of Him and of those who would be His fold, the family of God:

> If the world hate you, ye know that it hated me before it hated
> you. If ye were of the world, the world would love his own:

but because ye are not of the world, but I have chosen you out of the world, therefore the world hateth you. Remember the word that I said unto you, The servant is not greater than his lord. If they have persecuted me, they will also persecute you; if they have kept my saying, they will keep yours also. But all these things will they do unto you for my name's sake, because they know not him that sent me (John 15:18-21).

Will America Turn Out the Light?

Compared to Europe, America is bright with the light Christ brings to the world that invites Him to enlighten it. But there are trends toward turning out the gospel light, trends toward America knowing the same terrible shadowy twilight that has descended upon Europe.

Many Americans still look at churches as a positive part of culture. This is no longer true of Europeans, according to one report. Christianity, in particular, is at the center of the disdain for religion.

According to the report,

> Religion is more likely to be associated with oppression, irrelevance, or simply the past. France, like most of Europe, now has church attendance of less than 5 percent of the population, most of the attendees being the elderly. Less than 10 percent of France's population thinks religion has any importance. In Europe, in general, only 21 percent sees Christianity or religion as having any importance. "As an American in Europe, when you tell Europeans that you go to church on Sunday, they look at you like a museum piece—something strange," said journalist Richard Miniter.

> The report presents a bleak picture in Europe.

> Baylor sociologist Rodney Stark said, "It's easy to have a negative religious experience going to church in Europe. The one place unbelief is rampant is in the churches."

> The study "Fragmented Faith?" found that in Britain, one

out of five Anglican pastors does not believe in the bodily resurrection of Christ. And only 60 percent believe in the virgin birth—that's a lower level of belief than among churchgoers.

Vince Esterman, a pastor who has a dynamic street ministry in Paris, assesses the situation in Europe. "Europe that was the custodian of the gospel in the very early decades now is the continent that is rejecting the gospel and Christianity."[41]

The shadows of the European sunset on the gospel are now beginning to pale the American Christian landscape. Will America go the way of its ancestral roots, Europe, and turn off the light God has so graciously bestowed?

Wedge Issues: Homosexuality, Abortion, Replacement Theology

America's religiosity continues to be the bane of its culture. The world system—humanism—works tirelessly under the "enlightened" and "politically correct" social architects and engineers.

Homosexuality

Homosexuality is held up as an issue by which America can show its truly enlightened status before the world. Although statistics show that the overwhelming majority of Americans still do not consider homosexuality a way of life that should be equated to heterosexuality as a lifestyle, progay advocates continue to do everything they can at every opportunity to make the majority bend to the homosexual agenda. They are aided and abetted by the media, especially the entertainment media, in their debauched, perverted desecration of the gift of sexuality God built into the human race.

Churches today are divided over the matter of whether homosexuality is a legitimate form of human interaction—of intimate relationship that is accepted, even condoned, by God. It is a wedge issue destined to increase the religious fever in the nation and the world. Jesus predicted as much in the following prophecy:

Likewise also as it was in the days of Lot; they did eat, they drank, they bought, they sold, they planted, they builded; but the same day that Lot went out of Sodom it rained fire and brimstone from heaven, and destroyed them all. Even thus shall it be in the day when the Son of man is revealed (Luke 17:28-30).

Abortion

Abortion is a prime wedge issue that cuts to the heart of God, the giver of life. Both homosexuality and abortion are death-dealing issues from the mind of Satan. He hates God's creation called man. He has developed—with the willing accomplices among mankind—these twin issues of doing away with human beings. Homosexuality cannot reproduce by itself, and abortion does away with new life as it is just getting started.

Christians in America and the world are divided over whether homosexuality and abortion are wrong. God's Word is very clear on which side He comes down regarding both issues.

Replacement Theology

No other biblical geopolitical issue within the vast body of those who claim to be within Christianity is more relevant than the divide that is replacement theology. The controversy gets to the heart of the religious fever that afflicts America and the world today.

Replacement theology is the belief that the church—the body of Christ—has replaced the Jew, Israel, as heirs to the promises given to the progeny of Jacob. This claim is becoming a major movement and is, I believe, destined to contribute to the overall negativity toward Israel in the last days. In this regard, much of Christendom is going the way of the humanist elite who say they know better than God when it comes to running things here on earth (see Psalm 2:2-3).

God has made promises to His chosen people that cannot be broken. We reviewed some of those promises in chapter 2 of this book, so we won't look at them again here. Suffice it to say that God's

Word places the replacement theologians in serious error in this all-important issue of His dealing with Israel (and we're talking about modern Israel as synonymous with ancient Israel).

The Reform churches that came out of Catholicism with the Reformation of Martin Luther's time have held to the Catholic line on this matter for centuries, teaching that the church has replaced Israel in God's economy. So it doesn't surprise to find reports such as the one that follows:

> The Evangelical Lutheran Church in America (ELCA), with almost 5 million members, moved toward a partial boycott of Israeli goods while conducting its 2007 Churchwide Assembly in Chicago last week.
>
> The church's top legislative authority, the Assembly, passed a resolution that called for the group to seek a two-state solution to the Israeli-Palestinian Conflict. The Assembly urged investment in the Palestinian Authority.
>
> The U.S. Lutheran body then urged "consideration of refusing to buy goods or invest in activities taking place in Israeli settlements, and a review of other economic options," said Bishop Christopher Epting, the presiding bishop's deputy for ecumenical and interfaith relations.[42]

The reason for my rant is this: The following letter is from one of many I get from around the world. Most who write to me claim to be Christians, and I might add, to be the true Jews today. They declare they have replaced the Jews who can claim genetic ties to Jacob, who became Israel.

The person who sent this follows a "ministry" that holds to the British Israel theory, or to a theory that the church has replaced modern Israel in God's promises. In the letter (excerpted here with no editing), he tells about a man who gives the following testimony:

> I have done my own research, and I have been to the concentration camp Dachau four times; once in college, and three times when I was in the military.

I had some problems with what I saw, and with what I was told. I am going to attempt to clarify myself hopefully in an outline that is understandable.

First: 1) I stood in what I was told was the gas chamber; but it was concealed as a large shower room. One question I had was very simple. Why would the Germans use a shower to conceal the gas chamber? If your going to kill the people with gas; then just do it, don't try to disguise it. There I stood in the middle of this large room looking at the shower heads; and I could smell gas; but was it coming from a vent, an outside source, or what. I couldn't tell. I thought this was somewhat strange. I even went outside the building looking for an outside source, or some kind of piping that would funnel any foreign objects into the building, but I couldn't find any. Actually, the gas smelled like the gas that came from the canisters that we used in combat training when I was in the military.

It wasn't until 12 years later when I was in the Air National Guard; and I went to Widmund Germany to support a Tactical Command fighter unit out of North Carolina, that I really started questioning what I was told earlier. I was in a combat communications unit, and in 1985 I had to go to the Air Force combat communications training school at Tinker AFB Oklahoma...

I went through training in the classroom; being trained in CPR, First Aid, Geneva Convention, and so forth, and then I went out into the field for three weeks training in combat.

This was the first time I was ever in the full MOP suite (gas mask, boots, and the entire ensemble) while in training. I was in a fox hole for six hours under the hot Oklahoma sun. One thing I was taught was that in order to have a successful gas attack; there has to be nearly perfect weather conditions.

In other words, too much wind could blow the gas that you directed at another country right back at you; and also, the rain has a way of dissolving or nullifying chemical, bacterial, and nuclear gas agents. One thing I learned was that water and steam could very well nullify any gas in the area. I started thinking, than how could the German's gas the Jews while they were taking showers? They couldn't, the water and steam would dissolve the gas to the point that the gas would be neutralized.

I realize that it is a terrible thing to come against the Jews; after all, wasn't Jesus Christ a Jew? Wasn't the Jews God's chosen people? And wasn't the Word of God given to the Jews for them to study, and use to bring the light of the Gospel to the world? The answer of course is, NO!!!

It is denials of this kind—denials that Israel is any longer in God's eternal plan—that are an especially strong indicator of where this generation stands on God's prophetic time line. It is this kind of thinking that leads to a negative attitude toward Israel that actually plays into the larger picture of the world's rejection of the Jewish people in the last days.

9

PROBING THE PROGNOSIS

★ ★ ★ ★

The United States stands at the center of the world, whether or not the other nation-states of the planet acknowledge the fact. America is the envy of the global community for the materialistic good she possesses and produces, thus giving her great wealth and great power. It seems the globalist-elitists of the world community are determined to do incrementally what they can't do any other way short of all-out nuclear war, in which there can be no winners. They want what America has. They want the wealth redistributed to create a power base of working class to support their needs to establish a worldwide humanist empire.

Does this sound like the ravings of a conspiracy nut? Maybe so. But if it's a conspiracy theory, my rave is biblically based. It is not a conspiracy of a group of world leaders from around the globe who seek to create a world-order dictatorship. I'm of the opinion that most of these people believe they have altruistic intentions. They sincerely believe, for the most part, that building a world totally controlled by the globalist-elite thinking they can provide is the way to world peace and prosperity.

However, the real maestro in this plan to create the new world order we heard the first President Bush talk so much about is none other than the greatest of all deceivers—the father of lies. His moving through the minds of men to build a world apart from God is not without precedent. We see that influence in the following:

> The whole earth was of one language, and of one speech. And it came to pass, as they journeyed from the east, that they found a plain in the land of Shinar; and they dwelt there. And they said one to another, Go to, let us make brick, and burn them throughly. And they had brick for stone, and slime had they for mortar. And they said, Go to, let us build us a city and a tower, whose top may reach unto heaven; and let us make us a name, lest we be scattered abroad upon the face of the whole earth (Genesis 11:1-4).

This account of civilization that developed following the great flood reflects the fallen mind of mankind. This mind-set has not changed over the many thousands of years since. It was an early attempt at one world order, without consideration for the Creator's input in determining the regulation of culture and society.

The Bible records how God dealt with that early rebellion:

> The LORD came down to see the city and the tower, which the children of men builded. And the LORD said, Behold, the people is one, and they have all one language; and this they begin to do: and now nothing will be restrained from them, which they have imagined to do. Go to, let us go down, and there confound their language, that they may not understand one another's speech. So the LORD scattered them abroad from thence upon the face of all the earth: and they left off to build the city. Therefore is the name of it called Babel; because the LORD did there confound the language of all the earth: and from thence did the LORD scatter them abroad upon the face of all the earth (Genesis 11:5-9).

The Creator dealt with these one-worlders by confounding their language. He erected instant verbal communication barriers between the people working on the tower of Babel and other projects in the area so that they couldn't complete the projects. God then scattered the people who had become as one culture into the whole world. Information about the dispersion is wrapped up in the name "Peleg": "Unto Eber were born two sons: the name of the one was Peleg; because in his days the earth was divided: and his brother's name was Joktan" (1 Chronicles 1:19).

God equated the common language of that day to giving the people the ability to do whatever they could imagine. Their fallen minds obviously came up with a mighty plan to shake the bonds of a God who governs (like Psalm chapter 2 predicts a future generation will attempt), and build instead a world the way they wanted it.

Today, the marvels of computer technologies have circumvented the language barriers God established. The fallen minds of men, through knowledge the angel told Daniel would increase exponentially in the end of the age (Daniel 12:4), have brought people back together as one.

The globalist-elitists are back, and determined to build one world order. Like Lucifer himself, who again leads the grandiose planning, these self-appointed masters want to put their collective throne above the throne of God. One in particular will be given the authority by the others to sit atop that luciferian throne: "The ten horns which thou sawest are ten kings, which have received no kingdom as yet; but receive power as kings one hour with the beast. These have one mind, and shall give their power and strength unto the beast" (Revelation 17:12-13).

Disease of Globalism

America is among the nation-states afflicted with the geopolitical cancer called globalism, which has recurred (never gone away, really). Bible prophecy gives definite prognoses for the various stages through which this humanistic disease will progress. Actually, globalism has metastasized, and is terminal. It will take the Great Physician—God Himself—to excise the malignancy. The Prince of Peace is the surgeon who will ultimately return to do the job. Let us begin looking at the prognosis for this sin-infected planet through the powerful microscope of Bible prophecy.

National Temperature

We begin by trying to determine the best thermometer to use to measure the fever that drives daily life in America. One such gauge is the way people look at politics and politicians.

It isn't difficult to determine that many hold politicians in low esteem, much as they do others such as lawyers in today's culture. Maybe it's a bit cynical, but nonetheless true, to say that most everyone views the politician as someone who can do something for them, while disliking the politician—sometimes quite intensely. Special interest groups abound, and each has its own needs and desires. America is fragmented in the political hodgepodge, and the percentages of the fractionalization each side occupies in the issues of the day prove the schizophrenic nature of today's America.

The self-centeredness isn't lost on the wary politicians, who themselves want to retain power and influence. If not high on the public's likability meter, they still have the power they crave. That's enough for most of them. The more they play to the people's self-centeredness, the more power they grab for themselves.

Dr. Henry Kissinger once said power is the ultimate aphrodisiac. He recently framed further thoughts on this matter with a *Wall Street Journal* reporter, who wrote,

> I began by asking [Kissinger] about the institutional atmosphere in Washington, the hothouse of American foreign policy. The capital is far more poisonous today than at any time in the recent past, I suggested—including Mr. Kissinger's heyday during the Vietnam War, when the early Cold War-era comity between the political parties and the executive and legislative branches was already degrading.

> Mr. Kissinger leaned forward to answer my questions with studied deliberation. In part, he felt that this was institutional. Congress has itself changed. The "tradition of long-serving senior politicians from both parties who were devoted to a truly national service has passed, or largely so."

The entire system, especially as it has been transformed by the communications revolution, "is now much more driven by short-term political calculations, the need to keep powerful and vocal constituencies happy, and an eye on the next election." This effect, Mr. Kissinger posited, has been enhanced by the 24-hour news cycle—"more information, and less content."[43]

The "me-first," self-indulgent proclivities of the American public are reflected in much of the nightly TV entertainment fare. The reality programs always portray the clamor for scrambling to the top of the heap, no matter what it takes, as the winner-take-all attitude needed to achieve the desires of our lusts. We scowl at the raw ambition, yet admire the achievement the attitude accomplishes.

This self-indulgence is a sin-engendered, deceptive demeanor that one future globalist-politician will use to create the earth's last and all-controlling humanistic power base. He will both exert brute force and lie, promising people anything and everything they want. God's Word says that coming superpolitician: "in his estate shall stand up a vile person, to whom they shall not give the honour of the kingdom: but he shall come in peaceably, and obtain the kingdom by flatteries" (Daniel 11:21).

One of the great scholars of eschatology in modern times wrote:

> The Antichrist appears on the scene as the conqueror of the ten-nation revival of the Roman Empire. According to Daniel 7:8, a little horn comes up among the ten horns and uproots three of them, which signifies that he has conquered three of the ten countries. From there on, although Scriptures do not explain the reasons, he is regarded as the ruler of all ten nations. In other words, he takes over as the dictator of the revived Roman empire. From this position he rises to power gradually until finally he becomes the world ruler of scriptural prophecy.[44]

Point is, the egocentric nature and activities of both the people and those who rule over them seem headed for a culmination of sinful self-indulgence that will bring upon the world scene the personality described as "the beast"—Antichrist.

Meshing with the Geopolitical Scene

After considering America's domestic schizophrenia—various interest groups demanding politicians take care of their needs and wants first—we will look briefly at how America meshes with the rest of the world geopolitically. We will particularly think on U.S.-European relationships, because a revived Roman Empire, Europe, is the entity most of us who study Bible prophecy yet future believe will be the matrix out of which will grow the beast's regime of Revelation 13: "He causeth all, both small and great, rich and poor, free and bond, to receive a mark in their right hand, or in their foreheads: and that no man might buy or sell, save he that had the mark, or the name of the beast, or the number of his name" (verses 16-17).

Certainly, looking at relationships with Europe and the rest of the world as a snapshot in time, the decade immediately following the turn of the century and millennium has marked a downward trend for love of America abroad. Too often the nation is viewed as arrogant in its dealings with the rest of the world. *Unilateralism* is the term heard most often in severe critique of the American way of executing its foreign policy.

The most recent issue in this regard is the invasion of Iraq and overthrow of Saddam Hussein as part of the War on Terror declared by the United States upon those who seek to assault America and the world. The following overview indicates the diminishing return, in terms of popularity, on American investment in military efforts to make the world safer from terrorist violence.

In 2002, strong majorities supported the U.S.-led War on Terror in the United Kingdom, France, Germany, Japan, India, and Russia. By 2006, supporters of the effort were in the minority in Britain (49 percent), France (43 percent), Germany (47 percent), and Japan (26 percent). Although a majority of Russians still supported the War on

Terror, that majority had decreased by 21 percent. Whereas 63 percent of the Spanish population supported the war in 2003, only 19 percent of the population indicated support in 2006. Nineteen percent of the Chinese population supports the War on Terror, and less than a fifth of the populations of Turkey, Egypt, and Jordan support the effort. At the time of this writing, at about 56 percent, India's support for the War on Terror has been stable.[45]

Further testimony to America's declining popularity while its involvement in matters of the Middle East grows becomes more pronounced the farther this age of humanism progresses toward the time of prophesied apocalypse.

Andrew Kohut, speaking to the U.S. House Committee on Foreign Affairs, noted that according to the Pew Center polls conducted in 2004,

> majorities or pluralities in seven of the nine countries surveyed said the U.S.-led war on terrorism was not really a sincere effort to reduce international terrorism. This was true not only in Muslim countries such as Morocco and Turkey, but in France and Germany as well. The true purpose of the war on terrorism, according to these skeptics, is American control of Middle East oil and U.S. domination of the world.[46]

AMERICAN HEGEMONY?

The United States is constantly under the criticism of other major players in the world of geopolitics. Some are well-known, such as Mikhail Gorbachev, the former Soviet premier who is now head of the geopolitical think tank Greenpeace. He said about what transpired following the American actions in initiating the War on Terror:

> The Americans then gave birth to the idea of a new empire, world leadership by a single power, and what followed?... What has followed are unilateral actions, what has followed are wars, what has followed is ignoring the U.N. Security Council, ignoring international law and ignoring the will of the people, even the American people...[47]

There is a rising tide of invective against America involving herself in other parts of the world. Most, while hurling the accusations, are not willing to do the dirty work of trying to rein in the madmen of the planet. The words of secretaries of state under the Carter and Nixon administrations were used to address the topic in a *Wall Street Journal* report:

> As Zbigniew Brzezinski, one of those critics and [Henry] Kissinger's long-time intellectual sparring partner, puts it in his recent book, what much of the world wants from the U.S. is "respect" and recognition of its "dignity" defined as the ability to manage their own affairs as they see fit.
>
> Mr. Kissinger agreed with the point that other nations will have to have scope to develop their own identities. But he pointed out that to have world order, "these identities need to be reconciled into some general consensus." An American strategy of benign neglect may, in any case, no longer be realistic in an age of increasing global integration when relatively small transnational networks or failed states can project power against democratic societies with devastating consequences.
>
> Meanwhile, most of today's international actors, "'including states, international organizations, and nongovernmental actors, are disenchanted with different aspects of the existing world order.' Unfortunately, Mr. Kissinger noted, few of these actors are willing to play a constructive long-term role, preferring merely to challenge American policies when they involve risks."[48]

TARGETED FOR HATRED

Hatred for the United States, because of the nation's involvement in matters of the Middle East in particular, was made excruciatingly manifest with the devastation of the 9/11 attacks. The militant Islamics loathe America because she stands with the even more-hated nation of modern Israel.

As stated before, it is more than coincidental that the most powerful country ever to exist, in terms of wealth and military might, stands for all practical purposes as the only true ally God's chosen nation has in these volatile times. The supernatural element of everything that surrounds America being in the right place at the right time comes into focus when considering that the United States' strength flows from its great industrial base. This foundational power-generation requires the petroleum that lies beneath the rugged terrain of Israel's neighbor antagonists. Coincidence? That word definitely is not in God's vocabulary.

The prognosis for the United States, while we probe all of the symptoms of an America and the world afflicted with the terminal disease called humanism, is that hatred looks destined to continue to build. This is because the hatred is luciferian at its very core. America—as stated earlier—is linked with the one people, the Jews, whom Bible prophecy foretells every country on earth will in the very end of days seek to conquer. All nations will be brought to account for their hatred against Israel. Again, the lust for oil seems to be the likely catalyst the Lord knew would be the magnet to bring all rebellious nations to Armageddon for their comeuppance: "I will also gather all nations, and will bring them down into the valley of Jehoshaphat, and will plead with them there for my people and for my heritage Israel, whom they have scattered among the nations, and parted my land" (Joel 3:2).

Troubling Economic Trends

Oil is the one commodity that engenders the interest and concerns, even fears, of political leaders around the world. Need for petroleum to fuel the machinery of wealth production is all-consuming to elected governments and dictatorships alike. The black, liquid gold is almost certainly the ingredient within Jesus Christ's prophecy about wars and rumors of wars that will prove key in bringing to fruition man's final rebellious stand at Armageddon.

The price per barrel of petroleum exploded as high as $140 in 2008 and shook global financial foundations, and its constant up-and-down fluctuations added to anxieties. There seem few, if any, options available to deal with the dilemma that might assuage fears within world governments—especially within Western governments, which depend heavily on oil imports.

But it is no longer just the industrialized West that dominates the market demand arena today. The following overview gives the global snapshot:

> The arguments for even higher oil prices are well known. The economies of China and India are booming and hungry for energy. Oil fields in Mexico, the United States and several other oil producers are drying up, tightening world supplies. President Hugo Chávez of Venezuela is using oil as a political weapon. Rebels in Nigeria are creating havoc in some of Africa's most productive oil fields. The war in Iraq rages on. The dollar is weakening, causing hedge funds and traders to flee to oil and other commodities as a safe haven.[49]

Prophecy students examining recent Middle East developments must consider that petroleum is possibly, even probably, the reason all nations of the world will meet in the region Armageddon.

Ezekiel foretold an attack that would storm toward that region, and within his prophecy was a fascinating word:

> After many days thou shalt be visited: in the latter years thou shalt come into the land that is brought back from the sword, and is gathered out of many people, against the mountains of Israel, which have been always waste: but it is brought forth out of the nations, and they shall dwell safely all of them. Thou shalt ascend and come like a storm, thou shalt be like a cloud to cover the land, thou, and all thy bands, and many people with thee. Thus saith the Lord GOD; It shall also come to pass, that at the same time shall things come into thy mind, and thou shalt think an evil thought: and thou shalt say, I will go up to the land of unwalled villages; I will go to them that are at rest, that dwell safely, all

of them dwelling without walls, and having neither bars nor gates, to take a spoil, and to take a prey; to turn thine hand upon the desolate places that are now inhabited, and upon the people that are gathered out of the nations, which have gotten cattle and goods, that dwell in the midst of the land (Ezekiel 38:8-12).

The key word in that passage is "spoil." The term indicates a material reason beyond the other things listed—cattle, goods, etc.—to infer that something profoundly alluring draws this great Gog-Magog force toward Israel.

Ezekiel uses the word again in announcing that the other nations protest this invasion. They seem particularly interested in this invading force wanting to take "great spoil": "Sheba, and Dedan, and the merchants of Tarshish, with all the young lions thereof, shall say unto thee, Art thou come to take a spoil? hast thou gathered thy company to take a prey? to carry away silver and gold, to take away cattle and goods, to take a great spoil?" (Ezekiel 38:13).

According to experts, petroleum deposits are dwindling at a rate that progresses geometrically. This is because of the insatiable thirsts of growing nations like China and India, which have massive populations. These countries demand their share of fossil fuels to run their burgeoning industrial bases.

Many geopolitical observers believe it is just a matter of time until the competition for this dwindling resource turns into all-out war.

Oil industry expert Matthew R. Simmons assesses the global oil outlook:

> "Sadly, the United States of America, the world's most advanced economy, has no fuel gauge of any sort to indicate when our useable spare supply of crude oil and (refined) products is nearing empty. And the stock data of the USA is the best published oil data of any country," Simmons said.

> "None of this would be alarming if 'peak oil' was decades away. But, this is a fool's dream."

Simmons [agrees] that mounting evidence points to "peak oil" having occurred more than two years ago when the Energy Information Administration reported record global crude output of 74.3 million barrels per day in May 2005.

Peak oil refers to the notion that at some point the world will reach a peak in the rate at which it can pump oil out of the ground...

With global demand projected to grow to 115 million bpd by 2020, Simmons said numerous dangers would accompany a significant depletion of world oil supplies, including social chaos brought on by widespread hoarding as well as geopolitical conflicts that could lead to war.

"Oil shortages worry me," he said. "China is extremely conscious of how flimsy oil supply is and is doing everything they can to lock up supply."[50]

Internal Trends

Looking at trends from ideological perspectives within America gives insight into the prognosis for the nation's ills while the United States and the world move toward the prophesied apocalypse. Internal factors might be the most telling of all regarding where the nation is headed, and how quickly.

Admittedly, any survey results must be viewed with a touch of skepticism. However, I find that the following survey, although from an obviously liberal source, strongly reflects the trends in America's daily life. Youth, as they say, are the future, thus it seems valid to consider current developments among our country's college-age people.

According to a survey put out by UCLA, college freshmen in 2006 are increasingly involved in politics and increasingly leaning toward the liberal viewpoints. Support for military spending is down, as well as support for the draft. More freshmen throughout the United States this year are also identifying themselves as having a more liberal view of the world, according to the survey. UCLA's Higher Education Research Institution takes the "American Freshman" survey annually. Researchers based the statistics on 263,710 freshmen at 385 of the nation's four-year schools.[51]

The survey also noted an unusual trend happening among college students. An increasing portion of students are declaring themselves in the "moderate" category, as opposed to either liberal or conservative. Interestingly, this follows the pattern among older counterparts in the general population.

Even more interestingly, this is also true of people who identify with Christianity. More and more who claim to be Christians are taking the moderate stand on doctrinal positions once considered unshakable. If I may insert a trite but true apothegm here, it is said that those who stand for nothing will fall for anything. One must wonder whether that well-worn observation might be the final word on this great nation's memorial stone.

Section III

FUTURE HEADLINES?

★★★★

10

INTERNATIONAL COMMUNITY DEMANDS ROLE IN IRAQ

★ ★ ★ ★ ★

America is central to earth's major geopolitical exigencies, as we have noted thus far. Now we begin to peer into the future a bit, trying to frame the United States within scenarios that might provide some degree of what the times just ahead portend for the nation and the world. Any speculation here will be of a benign sort that will at every point have the light of God's prophetic Word focused directly on the matters involved.

The United States of America finds itself deeply enmeshed within the region of the world that is at the heart of Bible prophecy yet future. This cannot be denied from even a cursory glance at scriptures from Jesus and the Old and New Testament prophets. This nation, in astounding reality, is at the center of the two most prophetically significant nations of the Bible. Those nations are Israel and Iraq.

Iraq, which sits at the heart of what historians have long called Mesopotamia, "the Cradle of Civilization," and which is called Babylon in the Bible, draws the collective worry of the world community. Likewise, hour by hour, warlike uneasiness in that vast region north of Israel causes students of Bible prophecy to search the headlines and research the Scriptures with anticipation. This is done with good reason. Bible prophecy refers to Babylon second only to Jerusalem and Israel in the number of mentions about cities and nations. Indeed, prophecies involving the area now called the Middle East seem poised for fulfillment today.

Israel the Key

All prophecy yet future must be considered in light of this one fact: God's chosen nation is back in the land of promise. As has been said in earlier chapters—and it cannot be overemphasized—understanding modern Israel's position in the arena of Mideastern and world affairs is critical to understanding all other geopolitical matters. That is, to know where this sometimes deadly involvement with Iraq is leading, we must carefully study that tiny though militarily powerful state called Israel.

We've already covered Israel in depth, both its ancient and modern significance in God's dealing with mankind. Babylon, being the second-most referenced nation and city, requires a closer look.

Babylon/Iraq

As we begin looking at this nation-state that has played such a large part in God's dealings with humanity, we need to understand a bit about its history. In that regard, I found this interesting time line of Babylon's forward movement into today's world.

- By 5000 BC—Agriculture moves into southern Mesopotamia, the ancient name for the territory covered by much of Iraq today. Great cities spring up along the Euphrates and Tigris rivers. Akkad in the north and Sumer in the south become dominant in the region.

- 3500–3000—The Sumerians develop the writing, counting, the wheel, and calendars.

- 2334–2279—The Akkadian Empire established by Sargon the Great.

- 1792–1750—Hammurabi, best known for developing a set of laws that bear his name, establishes Babylon as the power center of the region.

- 1400—Assyrian, Babylonian, Hurrian, and Elamite kingdoms compete to ascend and become the greatest empires.

- 722–705—Assyrian rule is strengthened by Sargon II, who constructs a palace-temple complex near Nineveh.

- 612—Chaldeans take control; Assyrian Empire collapses.

- 597—Nebuchadnezzar II captures Jerusalem. Under Nebuchadnezzar, the Hanging Gardens of Babylon, one of the seven wonders of the ancient world, are built. Nebuchadnezzar's is the last home-grown government in Mesopotamia until the twentieth century.

- 539—Babylon is captured by King Cyrus of Persia.

- 331—Babylon is overtaken by Alexander the Great, who declares it his capital. He dies there in 323 B.C.

- A.D. 226—The Persian Sassanid dynasty comes to power.

- 637—Islam comes to Iraq when the Arabs defeat the Sassanids in the battle of Qadisiya.

- 762–63—Baghdad, which becomes the center of Islamic civilization founded by Mansur.

- 1258—Baghdad attacked by Mongols.

- 1534—Suleyman the Magnificent, leading the Ottoman Turks, takes Iraq.

- 1800s—Britain begins projecting its power in the Persian Gulf to protect trade routes with India.

- 1914–18—The Ottoman Empire, in World War I, allies with Germany against Britain, France, and Russia.

- 1919—Britain is given a mandate over Iraq by the League of Nations.

- 1921—Prince Faisal is chosen king in a referendum. He

had battled alongside T.E. Lawrence against the Ottomans.

- 1932—Britain grants Iraq its independence.
- 1958—The monarchy is overthrown in a military coup by Gen. Abdel Karim Qassem.
- 1979—Saddam Hussein takes over as president.
- 1980–88—Iraq-Iran war.
- 1990—Kuwait is invaded by Saddam Hussein's Iraqi forces.
- 1991—Persian Gulf War.
- 1998—UN weapons inspectors leave Iraq.
- 2002—American president George W. Bush seeks to disarm Saddam Hussein.[52]
- 2005—Democratic elections take place in Iraq.
- 2006—Saddam Hussein dies on the gallows for crimes against his people and humanity.

Babylon's Destiny

The world watched the American-led coalition forces decimate Saddam Hussein's military in Operation Freedom. There wasn't as much angst as in Operation Desert Storm a decade earlier, when many held their breath, wondering if Armageddon had arrived. It had not, of course, and life got back to normal after each of the Mideast campaigns almost as fast as life following the anxiety-ridden time immediately after the 2001 terrorist attacks in New York City and Washington, D.C.

The presence of American military in Iraq is a politically charged issue, to be sure, but beyond that there has developed an almost ho-hum attitude so far as concerns about this eventually developing into anything akin to Armageddon.

Is there anything of prophetic significance we can make of the second war against Saddam Hussein's Iraq? Does the Bible have anything to say about end-time Iraq?

Yes, quite a bit. But Bible prophecy speaks of Iraq as being in an apparently changed form from the Iraq of today. Prophecy again calls that region Babylon, and it is in big trouble with God. Jeremiah the prophet foretold Babylon's end-time plight:

> The word that the LORD spake against Babylon and against the land of the Chaldeans by Jeremiah the prophet. Declare ye among the nations, and publish, and set up a standard; publish, and conceal not: say, Babylon is taken, Bel is confounded, Merodach is broken in pieces; her idols are confounded, her images are broken in pieces. For out of the north there cometh up a nation against her, which shall make her land desolate, and none shall dwell therein: they shall remove, they shall depart, both man and beast (Jeremiah 50:1-3).

The prophet said further:

> Therefore, behold, the days come, that I will do judgment upon the graven images of Babylon: and her whole land shall be confounded, and all her slain shall fall in the midst of her. Then the heaven and the earth, and all that is therein, shall sing for Babylon: for the spoilers shall come unto her from the north, saith the LORD (Jeremiah 51:47-48).

Babylon's Last-Days Role

It becomes obvious, if one believes Bible prophecy should be taken literally, that the area now called Iraq is mentioned prominently as having a role to play in history yet to unfold. We can be sure the prophetic scriptures haven't yet been fulfilled because the region has never been rendered completely uninhabitable as foretold by Jeremiah: "The land shall tremble and sorrow: for every purpose of the LORD shall be performed against Babylon, to make the land of Babylon a desolation without an inhabitant" (Jeremiah 51:29).

Nuclear Scenario?

Does the prophecy above indicate that nuclear devastation is scheduled for the area occupied by the nation called Iraq? Radioactivity that contaminates the land to the point it cannot be inhabited seems to fit such a scenario.

Prophecy Scholars Differ on Babylon

When it comes to the subject of Babylon in prophecy, excellent prophecy scholars hold different views. Some believe an actual city will be rebuilt on the very real estate once occupied by ancient Babylon. This, they believe, is the future great religious and commercial center that will be destroyed in one hour, as indicated in Revelation 18:9-10:

> The kings of the earth, who have committed fornication and lived deliciously with her, shall bewail her, and lament for her, when they shall see the smoke of her burning, standing afar off for the fear of her torment, saying, Alas, alas, that great city Babylon, that mighty city! for in one hour is thy judgment come.

Other prophecy scholars believe prophecies about end-time Babylon found in Revelation and Jeremiah refer to the entire world religious and economic system that will have developed by the time of the end. These prophecies, they believe, involve ancient Babylon only in that it was the matrix out of which all of the religious and commercial evils began to grow and infect mankind's activities throughout history. These prophecy students believe that the city destroyed in a single hour might be the greatest center of commerce at that time. For example, in our day, that city would be New York City, because it has the most influence over world trade, among other things.

Still others believe references to the Babylon scheduled for future destruction might refer to the United States.

Regardless of how the prophecies about end-time Babylon are considered, God's Word has so much to say about that entity's destruction that the world's present focus on that area on the Euphrates engenders excitement—thoughts of Christ's soon coming again.

Iraq Today: The Bottom Line

Although Saddam Hussein began rebuilding a city on the site of ancient Babylon, it is many, many years away from even having a chance of again becoming a great world commercial or religious center. It is scarcely more than a tiny, token symbol of the magnificence that once occupied that area.

Some believed the war that removed Hussein would most likely disrupt that rebuilding effort. But some prophecy watchers suggest that with Saddam removed, the world community might now think to come together and make the present effort to rebuild Babylon into a true symbol of world unity and world peace. Some believe even the United Nations might be moved to a rebuilt Babylon as a gesture of world community and harmony.

We cannot know for sure whether defeating Saddam's evil regime will, in the near-term, bring about the prophesied end-time Babylon. However, those who look at Iraq as playing a significant role in prophetic fulfillment wonder if America's military involvement with the Islamic terrorists' constant death-dealing in the land of ancient Babylon might escalate to something of apocalyptic proportions.

No matter the skepticism among the world diplomats and journalists regarding Bible prophecy and the prediction of man's final military conflict in the region, they look warily at the possibility of a war that might produce just such an Armageddon scenario. And their fears are well-founded. Armageddon awaits.

The Tribulation Era

The Pressure for Peace

Already the world community is demanding peace between Israel and its Middle Eastern neighbors. The world's leaders see the Israeli-Palestinian conflict as holding the greatest potential for igniting all-out war. And the differences between Jews and Muslims are seen as explosive fuel that might be thrown on any war that might erupt in the region. Global leaders intend to do all within their power to force peace upon Israel and those who want to push the Jewish people into the Mediterranean.

Daniel the prophet foretold a peace that will destroy many people—both of Israel and of its enemies. The Antichrist will, according to Daniel 9:26-27, be the leader who guarantees that seven-year covenant of peace. When Antichrist brings together Israel and her foes for that peace treaty, the Tribulation era will begin.

The Tribulation is prophesied by the prophets Isaiah, Jeremiah, Daniel, and others, as well as by Jesus Himself to be a time of God's judgment upon rebellious people. This judgment will last seven years, concluding with Christ's return during the last battle of the Armageddon war taking place in the Middle East.

The Peace Agreement that Brings on Armageddon

Israel's agreement with the Antichrist to sign a peace covenant will begin the Tribulation, or apocalypse. This will also set in motion a series of conflicts that grows into the war called Armageddon.

So conflict in and surrounding Iraq won't in itself start Armageddon. But such conflict could, if reaching destructive enough levels, be the proverbial straw that breaks the camel's back. It could hasten the world community into forcing Israel and her enemies to finally agree to the so-called peace that has proved so elusive throughout the great diplomatic efforts since Israel's rebirth in 1948. In that sense, the awe-inspiring overthrow of the "Butcher of Baghdad," Saddam Hussein—and the occupation and accompanying violence involving Iraq—might fit significantly into the prophetic picture.

Diplomats look with increasing frustration toward the Middle East in general, and toward the place where ancient Babylon sat. This visceral discontent is destined to grow and evolve, according to Bible prophecy. It is not beyond the pale to think that the voracious thirst of the nations for the petroleum that pools beneath the region will ignite their lust and draw them to Armageddon.

Here is what Joel the prophet foretold about the ultimate actions by the world's nation-state forces, whose hunger for this, the most oil-rich region on earth, is growing by the day:

> Blow ye the trumpet in Zion, and sound an alarm in my holy mountain: let all the inhabitants of the land tremble: for the day of the LORD cometh, for it is nigh at hand; a day of darkness and of gloominess, a day of clouds and of thick darkness, as the morning spread upon the mountains: a great people and a strong; there hath not been ever the like, neither shall be any more after it, even to the years of many generations. A fire devoureth before them; and behind them a flame burneth: the land is as the garden of Eden before them, and behind them a desolate wilderness; yea, and nothing shall escape them (Joel 2:1-3).

America, Envy of the World

There is no other way to describe the vitriol that even America's internal political entities and foreign allies sometimes spew at the United States. It must certainly flow from envy, the internal political antagonists wanting political power, and foreign allies jealously wanting to be at the top of the governing chain of command, even though the United States has been primarily responsible for victory.

As stated previously, America seeks to build no empire; she helps her fallen foes to their feet after defeating them, often losing many soldier-citizens in the process. She provides financial assistance during the recovery process—assistance in greater amounts than that possessed by many national economies around the globe. America's largesse is legendary, with the consistently demonstrated desire, while watching out for our own national best interests (such as securing oil for the future), always to do all that is humanly possible to secure peace in the disturbed region involved in any action we take.

Does this mean America is always right in its foreign involvements—particularly in military conflict? No, absolutely not. Let me
be clear: I am not seeking to validate this nation in every foreign
intrigue, or for that matter, in her every action in internal matters.
I am simply pointing to the fact that America's enemies' criticism,
even hateful invective, stems more from envy and greed than from
genuine desire to serve the world in selfless sacrifice. America's record
of doing everything possible to secure the peace and safety of people
around the world is easy to document. Such human effort, however,
is doomed to fail because the Prince of Peace, Jesus the Christ, is left
out of man-made efforts to achieve earthly peace: "They [say]...Peace,
peace; when there is no peace" (Jeremiah 6:14).

Commentary from the Noncontent

There isn't much happiness out in the geopolitical world about
America having the reins of control right now in the Middle East. This
displeasure was expressed by a former Soviet KGB chief who himself
is doing all within his ability to garner absolute power.

Russia's outgoing president, soon-to-be prime minister Vladimir
Putin, said that rubble from the Berlin Wall was "hauled away as
souvenirs" to countries that praise openness and personal freedom,
but "now there are attempts to impose new dividing lines and rules,
maybe virtual, but still dividing our mutual continent."

The world, he said, is now unipolar: "One single center of power.
One single center of force. One single center of decision making. This
is the world of one master, one sovereign."[53]

Domestically, America also has its detractors concerning involvement in Iraq. Anthony H. Cordesman, Arleigh A. Burke Chair in
Strategy at the Center for Strategic and International Studies (CSIS)
think tank in Washington, D.C., pretty much framed the anti-Iraq
involvement sentiment: "You have seen this become a globally unpop-
ular war," Cordesman said. "Most of the world sees it as unjust and
sees the United States as having effectively lost because it went to war
for the wrong reasons."[54]

U.S. allies, even the closest of them in the Iraq action against Hussein, have joined in the criticism. Sir Menzies Campbell, the Liberal Democrat leader in Britain, took the political opportunity presented by an admission by Geoff Boone, defense secretary for Great Britain while developing Iraqi occupation plans with the American strategists. Boone said that the Americans had not listened to him when he advised against long-term Iraqi occupation.

Campbell said, following the admission:

> From the very beginning of the occupation, it became clear that London's advice was simply ignored in Washington… The Prime Minister's strategy of staying close in public so as to be influential in private simply didn't work. The problem for the British Government was that we became so enmeshed in American strategy that we had no option but to go along with it, even when it was palpably wrong.[55]

One world leader not so subtly reflected the smirking attitude many, both nationally and internationally, apparently hold. They think George W. Bush develops American Middle East policy based upon talking directly to the Almighty, who, I presume the critics believe, imparts to Mr. Bush what he should do, based upon Bible prophecy.

Former German chancellor Gerhard Schröder, referring to President Bush, with whom he dealt while in office during the invasion of Iraq, told *Der Spiegel* that "if a person adopts a policy based on what he gleans from his prayers, in other words, a personal talk with God, it can lead to difficulties in democracy."[56]

Open Invitation

Prophecy involving Babylon and the end times centers on the development of a ten-kingdom confederacy. We will learn more about that in due course. For now, let us consider whether the prophetic stage is being set. Are rearrangements underway that will allow a consortium of nations to supersede America's position as overseer in the region?

Such a plan has been under development for some time:

> Iraq's Deputy Prime Minister Barham Salih said that under the initiative, called the International Compact for Iraq, Baghdad would seek aid from governments and multilateral organizations while encouraging private sector investment into its strategic oil industry.
>
> "We hope the international community will step up in providing for any shortfall that there will be to get us to the point that we become a donor state as opposed to a recipient," Salih said.[57]

One geopolitical think tank assesses the future of the region, as far as international community interest is concerned, in this way:

> Major powers have been lobbying to establish a military presence in the Gulf, according to diplomatic sources.
>
> The sources said Britain, China and Russia were pressing GCC states to establish a permanent presence in the region. Their motivation is to advance political and defense industry interests.
>
> "The major powers have found that the best way to establish a relationship in the Gulf region is to be here on a permanent basis," a diplomat said.
>
> So far, the United States has been the only foreign power with a permanent military presence in the Gulf.[58]

Quest to Rebuild?

The open invitation to the world governments and business elite attests to the great desire to rebuild a modern-day city on the scale of Babylon in the grandest sense. The argument against such a city being re-established where ancient Babylon once stood is that nothing much is there now except a lot of sand.

Many prophecy watchers believe that based upon the inland geographical position and the primitive nature of the land in and around

Babylon in present-day Iraq, it would take decades to build a city like the prophesied end-times Babylon. With all other signals that the world is bumping up against the very end of the age just before Christ's second coming, these observers believe there simply wouldn't be time to build the city described in Revelation 18.

Prophecy scholar Dr. Mark Hitchcock weighed in on the matter:

> Amazingly, we have a very recent example of a new city in the Middle East rising from the sand dunes. It's called Dubai Internet City. This new city is referred to as an oasis in the desert. Dubai Internet City is being heralded as the most ambitious engineering, business, and political project in the Middle East. The new city, located in the United Arab Emirates, is just a few kilometers from the city of Dubai.
>
> In 2001, Dubai Internet City had ten buildings with 300 companies and 3,500 users. The site contains lakes, landscapes, trees, and oases and occupies over 400 acres. Currently, more than 350 additional applications from major enterprises for office space are being considered...
>
> Here is the astounding part. *Dubai Internet City was designed, built, and launched in only 12 months...*
>
> While no one is claiming supercity status for this phenomenon in the dunes, its rise as an economic and technological center in such a brief time shows how quickly a city can rise in the Middle East desert. With incredible oil wealth and the power of Antichrist, Babylon could be rebuilt in a relatively short time.
>
> It could be only a matter of months.[59]

Babel's New Tower?

Much progress has been made in Dubai since Dr. Hitchcock wrote those words in 2003. People from around the world have rushed to fill this Middle Eastern wonder metropolis in phenomenal numbers, both in bodies and in dirhams, the Dubai currency, according to the stories surrounding the soaring tower being constructed there.

> More than 300 people spent Friday night queuing up outside Emaar Properties' Burj Dubai sales centre, desperate to grab several new units in the developer's flagship project.
>
> In unprecedented scenes, some buyers are thought to have paid nearly 8 million dirhams ($2.18 million) for one bedroom apartments in the Burj itself, and over 2 million dirhams for one bedroom apartments in Downtown Burj Dubai...[60]

The report said of the people who came to get in on the first available living quarters: "Many were armed with cheque books and passports, keen to snap up anything they could."[61]

The massive building will indeed be a structure designed to reach into heaven:

> The Burj Dubai realized its "tallest high-rise building in the world" claim on July 21, according to developer Emaar Properties, when the concrete floors were poured and set on the skyscraper's 141st story. At 1,680 feet tall, the still-incomplete tower surpassed the previous height record of 1671 feet, established by Taiwan's Taipei 101, and surges toward an undisclosed height rumored to be 2,300 feet, some 160 stories, when the tower is finished in 2008...the Burj Dubai achieved its height record just 1,276 days after construction began. Its composite concrete and rebar floors are rising at an average rate of three days per level...
>
> The Burj's highest 50 floors will contain office space, while the remaining interior program is devoted to a luxury hotel, on floors one through 20, and penthouse apartments, on floors 20 through 110. Its floor plates will taper from 33,607 square feet, at the base, to 10,788 square feet at the top—half the size of floor plates in the 108-story Sears Tower, which contains nearly the same cubic volume as the Burj...

The $1.4 billion Burj tower is the focal point of Emaar's Downtown Burj Dubai, a 500-acre, $20 billion development where the operative word appears to be "big."[62]

Man's Elevated Self-Image Unchanged

The Dubai tower builders' accomplishments and goals are self-explanatory:

> The goal of Burj Dubai is not simply to be the world's highest building. It's to embody the world's highest aspirations. Burj Dubai looks different depending on where you're standing. For those living nearby, it is a shining accomplishment—tangible proof of Dubai's central role in a growing world. For those standing in other global capitals, it is a shining symbol—an icon of the new Middle East: prosperous, dynamic, and successful.
>
> In fact, Burj Dubai is both. It is a fact—an unprecedented example of international cooperation—and a symbol—a beacon of progress for the entire world.
>
> It is not by chance that it is being built in Dubai. In less than thirty years, this city has transformed itself from a regional center to a global one.
>
> This success was not based on oil reserves, but on reserves of human talent, ingenuity and initiative.[63]

Coming Home to Roost

World leaders, for the most part, agree on one thing: Most want a global unity that puts greater control over all aspects of life on earth. Some desire the control to be primarily in their hands, in particular. But in general, the idea is to unite so that peace will reign, and the worker bees will go about their lives doing the leaders' bidding, content to just get along with their neighbors.

The more nefarious idea, in effect, is to come back to Babel and the tower-building project man had to abandon when God saw that it was full of evil intentions. Babylon, at its earliest historical point, was instrumental in prophetically foretelling this latter-day return to a major one-world building effort.

Daniel the prophet learned that King Nebuchadnezzar of Babylon had had a dream-vision of a gigantic image of a man made of various metals. The whole story of Nebuchadnezzar's vision and its meanings is found in the second chapter of Daniel. The head of this image was of gold, the chest and arms of silver, the belly and thighs of brass, and the legs of iron. Its feet and ten toes were of iron mixed with clay.

Daniel and all of the counselors who were considered this all-powerful king's wise men—his soothsayers, who supposedly could look into the future—were told they would be put to death if they could not interpret the king's dream. Some of them told Nebuchadnezzar that it was unfair to ask them to interpret the dream when he didn't tell them the contents of it.

The king became furious, telling them that he was onto them. If they couldn't tell him what was in the dream, he certainly couldn't rely upon them for a true interpretation. They would all, he commanded, be put to death for their treachery and inability to do his bidding.

Daniel asked for and got an audience with Nebuchadnezzar, getting permission to first consult with God, then get back with the king to give him the answers he demanded. After meeting in prayer with God, Daniel told Nebuchadnezzar all about the image made of four metals. He then interpreted the dream:

> This is the dream; and we will tell the interpretation thereof before the king.
>
> Thou, O king, art a king of kings: for the God of heaven hath given thee a kingdom, power, and strength, and glory. And wheresoever the children of men dwell, the beasts of the field and the fowls of the heaven hath he given into thine hand, and hath made thee ruler over them all. Thou art this head of gold. And after thee shall arise another kingdom inferior to thee, and another third kingdom of brass, which shall

bear rule over all the earth. And the fourth kingdom shall be strong as iron: forasmuch as iron breaketh in pieces and subdueth all things: and as iron that breaketh all these, shall it break in pieces and bruise. And whereas thou sawest the feet and toes, part of potters' clay, and part of iron, the kingdom shall be divided; but there shall be in it of the strength of the iron, forasmuch as thou sawest the iron mixed with miry clay. And as the toes of the feet were part of iron, and part of clay, so the kingdom shall be partly strong, and partly broken.

And whereas thou sawest iron mixed with miry clay, they shall mingle themselves with the seed of men: but they shall not cleave one to another, even as iron is not mixed with clay. And in the days of these kings shall the God of heaven set up a kingdom, which shall never be destroyed: and the kingdom shall not be left to other people, but it shall break in pieces and consume all these kingdoms, and it shall stand for ever. Forasmuch as thou sawest that the stone was cut out of the mountain without hands, and that it brake in pieces the iron, the brass, the clay, the silver, and the gold; the great God hath made known to the king what shall come to pass hereafter: and the dream is certain, and the interpretation thereof sure (Daniel 2:36-45).

Most every student of Bible prophecy who views Scripture as literal rather than as literature to be spiritualized or allegorized understands Daniel's interpretation to be prophecy telling of five major kingdoms that will come to pass from this time onward in human history:

1. The Babylonian kingdom of Nebuchadnezzar

2. The Medio-Persian Empire

3. The Greek-Macedonian Empire

4. The Roman Empire

5. The final empire that will be Antichrist's regime

All the kingdoms have come to pass, history reveals, except for the final empire—the regime of the beast described in Revelation 13. This will be the last and most tyrannical empire, represented by the ten toes. It is also symbolized by the composite beasts—which are all the same beast—prophesied in Daniel 7:2-12, Revelation 13:1, and Revelation 17:3. This is the foretelling, also, of the final world kingdoms, the prophecy we read earlier in this volume: "The ten horns which thou sawest are ten kings, which have received no kingdom as yet; but receive power as kings one hour with the beast. These have one mind, and shall give their power and strength unto the beast" (Revelation 17:12-13).

Flying Back to Babel

The international community is determined to gather around the land of Shinar (Genesis chapter 11), the place America now occupies. It is a return to the land of Nebuchadnezzar's Babylon, the site of the tower that man was building with the intention of usurping God's authority over them.

I'm convinced that Zechariah foretold of this swift movement back to that strange land at the very end of days, just before the second coming of Christ. I believe Zechariah's vision foretells end-time Babylon's scheduled rebuilding:

> The angel that talked with me went forth, and said unto me, Lift up now thine eyes, and see what is this that goeth forth. And I said, What is it? And he said, This is an ephah that goeth forth. He said moreover, This is their resemblance through all the earth.
>
> And, behold, there was lifted up a talent of lead: and this is a woman that sitteth in the midst of the ephah. And he said, This is wickedness. And he cast it into the midst of the ephah; and he cast the weight of lead upon the mouth thereof. Then lifted I up mine eyes, and looked, and, behold, there came out two women, and the wind was in their wings; for they had

wings like the wings of a stork: and they lifted up the ephah between the earth and the heaven. Then said I to the angel that talked with me, Whither do these bear the ephah? And he said unto me, To build it an house in the land of Shinar: and it shall be established, and set there upon her own base (Zechariah 5:5-11).

America, firmly ensconced in Iraq, is at the very center of this movement back to Babylon. In effect, the United States seems to fit the description in Zechariah's prophecy of the base upon which this basket full of worldwide wickedness will sit.

11

GLOBALISTS SEEK ECONOMIC CONTROL

★ ★ ★ ★ ★

America's great influence for the past century has derived from the strength of the nation's ability to produce wealth. The dollar has stood as the world's most stable, most desired currency in countries around the globe. This remains the case for the most part, but powerful dynamics are now causing the U.S. dollar to quake, eroding its stability as the foundational monetary instrument for the world's economy.

We've looked before at how there is a sort of economic epilepsy associated with the intricate connections between the United States and other countries. Much of this is because the American dollar is tied to petroleum, which the movers and shakers of world finance view as an increasingly volatile commodity. Two factors are primarily responsible for this:

1. America's primary source of oil is the Middle East, where Israel, her chief ally in the region, sits surrounded by avowed enemies.

2. Oil is a finite resource, and is being used up at a tremendous rate that portends an ominous future not only for the fiscal but the physical well-being of global stability.

New Financial World Order

At the time of this writing the U.S. dollar has declined for some time in value, and the outlook isn't bright for recovery of lost prestige and buying power. The dollar's fall from its lofty perch doesn't concern the global elitists to any great extent. It is seen in their high enclaves as a positive thing. Many among them have long looked for a changed paradigm that would vault them into positions of power to determine the direction of planet Earth's future. Monetary manipulation is the key to gaining and maintaining such control. We will look into the thinking behind the global elitists' obtaining such manipulative power.

The following examination into the mind-set of those who would be earth's monetary puppet masters presents some interesting insights:

> The director of international economics at the Council on Foreign Relations has launched a scathing attack on sovereignty and national currencies.
>
> Benn Steil, writing in the current issue of CFR's influential *Foreign Affairs* magazine, says "the world needs to abandon unwanted currencies, replacing them with dollars, euros, and multinational currencies as yet unborn."
>
> In the article, "The End of National Currency," Steil clearly asserts the dollar and the euro are temporary currencies, perhaps necessary today. He argues "economic development outside the process of globalization is no longer possible."
>
> His inevitable conclusion is "countries should abandon monetary nationalism."[64]

The director of international economics seems to back away from appearing too radically against the continuation of the rights of nations to remain sovereign. He said,

> Governments should replace national currencies with the dollar or the euro or, in the case of Asia, collaborate to produce a new multinational currency over a comparably large

and economically diversified area...It is the market that made the dollar into [the global monetary standard] and what the market giveth, the market can taketh away. If the tailors balk and the dollar falls, the market may privatize money on its own.[65]

The article continues:

Steil's essay is antagonistic to the ideas of sovereignty and national currencies. He writes, "The right course is not to return to a mythical past of monetary sovereignty, with governments controlling local interest and exchange rates in blissful ignorance of the rest of the world. Governments must let go of the fatal notion that nationhood requires them to make and control the money used in their territory."[66]

The director makes no bones about the fact that he is certain the globalization of economics cannot be reversed. He implies national currencies are destined to disappear into the forgetfulness of history long past.

"In order to globalize safely," Steil says, "countries should abandon monetary nationalism and abolish unwanted currencies, the source of much of today's instability." Further, "the dollar's privileged status as today's global money is not heaven-bestowed. The dollar is ultimately just another money supported only by faith that others will willingly accept it in the future in return for the same sort of valuable things it bought in the past."[67]

Dollar in Dilemma

America's basic monetary unit, like the nation itself within the global milieu, is at the center of profoundly changing economic realities. The rearrangements are seen in the daily reports of the dollar and its position against other currencies.

In 2008, the Canadian dollar reached parity with the U.S. dollar for the first time since 1976. They are now equal in value. At the time of this writing the euro also soared to its highest-ever level against the dollar, trading above $1.40 for the first time since the currency was introduced in 1999.

The dollar is plunging in the world's money markets. Why is this happening? And more ominously, what does this mean for the rest of the world?

First, we must consider the difference between interest rates in the United States and other parts of the world. The United States has dropped its interest rates, but central banks around the globe have not followed suit.

Today the spread between the U.S. interest rate dictated by the Federal Reserve, residence of the dollar, and the interest rate governed by the Central European Bank, home of the euro, is less than usual. This means diminished value of the dollar against the euro.

Second, central banks in other countries are now diversifying, concentrating less on linking to the U.S. dollar, instead putting faith in other currencies such as the euro, the British pound, and others. More dollars are thus floating in world markets, causing a devaluation of the American basic monetary unit.

One authoritative source that analyzes such matters looks at the effects of the weakened dollar:

> Look at the record-high price of oil. Even if the same amount of oil is being pumped out of the ground, since it is traded in dollars and the dollar has weakened, the price of oil has increased to make up for the lost value of the dollar, creating a sort of vicious cycle.

> Oil-producing countries don't want to keep all the dollars they are getting for their oil, since it's worth less, so they are diversifying and converting their dollars into euros or other currencies. That pushes more dollars back out into currency markets, which in turn pushes down the dollar's value.[68]

Impact on the United States

Inflation raises its ugly head when the U.S. dollar becomes devalued.

We can remember the years of the Carter administration (1977–1981), when inflation exploded and prices in general skyrocketed. Each trip to the grocery store brought disgruntled frowns to consumers.

Inflation engenders higher prices for commodities imported from other nations, and the price of petroleum-based products escalates rapidly.

The bottom line is that whatever the American worker earns is worth less with every percentage point that rises because of inflationary pressures.

> If the dollar falls too much, foreign investors and banks won't be so interested in buying T-bills and bonds that keep the U.S. government and businesses humming. That's because the interest rate might not be enough to compensate for inflation. In other words, whatever is earned would be worth less money.[69]

The number of reports about the declining value of the dollar continues to grow, increasing pressures for rearrangements along the lines suggested by Benn Steil, the director of international economics at the Council on Foreign Relations. He concludes, "Economic development outside the process of globalization is no longer possible...countries should abandon monetary nationalism."[70] More about that after briefly looking into the mounting reminders of the dollar's problems.

Dollar's Fall Felt Around the Globe

According to a *Washington Post* article,

> The sharp decline of the U.S. dollar since 2000 is affecting a broad swath of the world's population, with its drop on global markets being blamed at least in part for misfortunes as diverse as labor strikes in the Middle East, lost jobs in Europe and the end of an era of globe-trotting rich Americans...
>
> It marks a shift for Americans in the global economy. In times of strength, a mightier dollar allowed Americans to

feed their insatiable appetite for foreign goods at cheap prices
while providing Yankees abroad with virtually unrivaled economic clout. But now, as the United States struggles to fend
off a recession, observers say the less lofty dollar is having
both a tangible and intangible diminishing effect.[71]

To be sure, there is optimism as well as pessimism within the
thinking that looks to the future of the dollar:

> A doomsday scenario has the U.S. economy spinning out of
> control: the dollar plunges, financial markets crash, and the
> Federal Reserve is powerless to halt the collapse since cut-
> ting interest rates would send the dollar down even further.
> Inflicting additional harm would be ever-rising oil and food
> prices.
>
> But two experts at the W.P. Carey School of Business
> believe that concerns of a dollar-triggered financial crisis are
> overblown.
>
> "I think it's a little bit dramatic and melodramatic," says
> Herbert Kaufman, professor of finance. While the potential
> for trouble exists, he says, the dollar's problems should not
> have widespread consequences. "I believe our economy can
> absorb it. The Federal Reserve can take appropriate action if
> necessary," he says.
>
> Economics Professor Kent Hill contends that the dollar's
> woes are really a "sideshow" to larger matters of the economy,
> such as the country's savings rate, Social Security and Medi-
> care liabilities, and government fiscal policy.
>
> "While I am concerned, these things are not going to play
> out overnight," says Hill. "I view the downside of all of this
> as a nibbling away at our future rather than a cataclysmic
> fall."[72]

Yet the majority of analysis on the dollar's future continues to be
of a negative variety, as seen in the following excerpts:

The ailing US economy seems to be driving the exchange rate of the dollar inexorably downward, with serious consequences for the global economy. Politicians and central bankers are looking on helplessly as the economic outlook worsens by the day and European companies rack up huge losses.

It costs about four cents to produce a one-dollar bill—a pittance, compared to the greenback's influence on the world's economy.

The exchange rate of the dollar can boost the fortunes of companies and entire economies—or plunge them into crisis. Its rate against the euro fluctuates by a few hundredths of a cent each day. But in the past five years that fluctuation has more often than not taken the US currency on a downward trajectory, causing consternation—and now despair—among people around the world.[73]

It's just straws in the wind so far. India's Ministry of Culture announces that foreign tourists can no longer pay in dollars when visiting the Taj Mahal and other heritage sites; they have to pay in good, hard rupees. Iran and Venezuela call for a joint OPEC statement on the weak US dollar…The Chinese imports that fill the big-box stores still cost the same, because the Chinese yuan is still pegged to the American dollar. But that may be about to change, along with many other things.[74]

The dollar's value has been sliding for about five years. But its weakness came into sharp focus this week after an official at China's central bank declared that the greenback is "losing its status as the world currency." His comments prompted a broad sell-off that drove the dollar to its latest lows.[75]

Time of Ten Kingdoms

That the nations of earth are in "distress…with perplexity" (Luke 21:25) comes into focus when looking at global rearrangements taking place today. Again, the U.S. dollar is at the heart of the problems, just as America is at the center of most all things of worldwide importance these days.

The forewarning Jesus gave included mention of events that would plague people to the point that they would be terror-stricken: "There shall be signs in the sun, and in the moon, and in the stars; and upon the earth distress of nations, with perplexity; the sea and the waves roaring; men's hearts failing them for fear, and for looking after those things which are coming on the earth: for the powers of heaven shall be shaken" (Luke 21:25-26).

Jesus' prophecy was not for this present dispensation (the age of grace, also called the church age). As discussed earlier, the era that follows this present dispensation of time, according to God's Word, will be the seven years that lead up to the second advent of Christ. This period is called the Tribulation, or Daniel's seventieth week. Jesus said this time will be worse than has ever been or will ever be again (Matthew 24:21).

Part of that terrible time will include a vastly changed, draconian economic system. As stated before, nation-states being in perplexity is merely setting the stage for the horrific era when the apocalyptic storm is full-blown. A ten-kingdom ruling force headed by a single leader will develop; its power will derive from economic controls unknown in all of human history.

A legitimate question to ask is this: Can we see any developments today that presage a paradigm change in the world economic power structure?

Forewarnings Setting the Stage

There are many signals in our present day that seem to be in-advance indicators of the storm that is the Tribulation. These are stage-setting issues and events that precede the full-fledged judgments that will burst upon the planet during the apocalypse as described by the apostle John throughout the book of Revelation. The following is a brief look at today's signals—signals that foreshadow major things prophesied for the Tribulation itself.

Israel in the Land

Israel is the most profound prophetic indicator given in biblical prophecy. As stated earlier, God said in Zechariah 12 that He Himself will see to it that Israel—Jerusalem, in particular—becomes a terrible burden to the world of nations because they come against His chosen people. What other city attracts more news coverage than this one? Modern Israel is the size of New Jersey, yet it gets the attention of more press than a country the size of Russia.

Russia in Place

Russia, in addition to Israel, is key to end-time prophecies. Russia is destined to present some of the most fearsome trials and tribulations for Israel. Gog, "chief prince of Rosh," is the leader of Russia described in Ezekiel 38 and 39. In ancient language, Gog means "leader." "Rosh" is the ancient name for the land of Russia. In the last days, Russia will lead the Gog-Magog coalition that will move against Israel only to be defeated by a supernatural act of God. These days, the Russian government is moving back toward a type of governance more like that of the Soviet system before it fell in 1989. Note especially the regathering of power under a single, authoritarian leadership, and the movement away from the parliamentary system meant to serve the people. It is more than a point of fascination to observe KGB-like secrecy and methodologies redeveloping in the country. The nation's increasing attempts to influence developments in the Middle East are of particular interest to those who watch for the Gog-Magog foreshadowing of things to come.

Iran a Chief Ingredient

Persia (Iran) comes right alongside Russia in prophetic parlance. According to Ezekiel 38:5, Iran will aid Russia in attacking Israel before or during the Tribulation. Even now, Iran acts as a destabilizing force in the world. All one must do to factor in Iran's part in the speed at which the world is heading toward Armageddon is to consider the threats by President Mahmoud Ahmadinejad of Iran. He has said at every opportunity that his desire is to see Israel and every Jew out of the Middle East. He wants these ancient enemies off the planet! Added to his vitriol is his desire to see Armageddon begin so the twelfth imam (an Islamic messianic character in the Koran) will come forth and rule the earth on behalf of Allah. Ancient Persia, or modern Iran, is in the news today and must be considered when thinking about how oil is destined to influence end-times events.

The Bible foretells the arrival of a false prophet. With Ahmadinejad proclaiming it is his job to bring about the coming of the twelfth imam to destroy all enemies and institute Islam as the only religion on earth, this prophecy, along with news from Iran, should be looked at closely in our time. Revelation 13:12 states the Antichrist will have a religious leader to aid him. The false prophet will direct the world to worship the Antichrist.

Iran, of course, represents the latest to desire to join the club of nuclear nations. The use of nuclear armament during the Tribulation will kill over a third of the human population, according to Revelation 9:18. Only in our time—with the availability of nuclear arsenals—does it seem possible this could happen. Jesus Himself said that if He didn't return by a certain time, every living being would be killed (Matthew 24:22).

Global turmoil that threatens peace at all times has never been at a more fevered pitch. The nuclear threats—particularly by nations that have achieved the bomb, along with terrorists who might have the bomb with which to threaten civilian populations—figures heavily in the end-of-days picture.

There has always been unrest in the world. However, the tremendous level of turbulence we see today is unique to our time. Terrorism was redefined in the twentieth century. Today, more wars take place concurrently than at any point in the past (see 2 Timothy 3:1 for the significance of all this peril).

Arms proliferation is an end-time signal that cannot be ignored in our day. Jesus said there would be "wars and rumours of wars" (Matthew 24:6). The armament trade is not going out of business anytime soon. In fact, it will soon supply the biggest conflict in human history, the war called Armageddon (see Matthew 24:6 and Revelation 16:16).

China, King of the East

"The sixth angel poured out his vial upon the great river Euphrates; and the water thereof was dried up, that the way of the kings of the east might be prepared" (Revelation 16:12). This prophecy, scheduled to coincide with Armageddon, when all the armies of the world will be gathered in the Valley of Jezreel, almost certainly will include the modern nation of China. I view that coming juggernaut as the king of the kings of the East—the leader of all countries of the Oriental world. This prophecy correlates to Revelation 9:16-18. China exerts hegemony today over its neighbors. It is a growing international player, harboring strength and potential that will soon vault it into superpower class alongside the United States and the European Union. China's leadership is still an oligarchy maintained and perpetuated by an ever-increasing military. This force is destined to eventuate in the 200-million-man army prophesied in Revelation 9:16.

European Union, a Revived Rome

Daniel 9:26-27 says,

> After threescore and two weeks shall Messiah be cut off, but not for himself: and the people of the prince that shall come shall destroy the city and the sanctuary; and the end thereof shall be with a flood, and unto the end of the war desolations are determined. And he shall confirm the covenant with many for one week: and in the midst of the week he

shall cause the sacrifice and the oblation to cease, and for the overspreading of abominations he shall make it desolate, even until the consummation, and that determined shall be poured upon the desolate.

Daniel was given this prophecy for the very end of human history as it is presently known. Daniel prophesies that the "prince that shall come," Antichrist, who will come out of the people who destroyed Jerusalem and the Jewish temple, the Roman Empire, will implement a peace covenant between Israel and its enemies. Great world turmoil will follow that action until the very end (at the second advent of Jesus Christ). Those who destroyed Jerusalem and the Jewish temple came from the region now inhabited by the nations of Europe and a few Mediterranean areas. Rome is the very heart of where the ancient Roman Empire resided. Antichrist will come out of an area near the center of that location. The European Union (EU) is comprised of 25 countries that now represent a growing world power. The EU, many prophecy students believe, forms the matrix out of which the Antichrist regime will grow to become the worst tyrannical government ever to exist.

The European Parliament meets on a regular basis now, in many instances usurping national autonomy and sovereignty of the European states that are members of the EU. Some believe the ten-kings economic power bloc prophesied to develop during or before the Tribulation will grow from the EU, which will be its nucleus: "The ten horns which thou sawest are ten kings, which have received no kingdom as yet; but receive power as kings one hour with the beast. These have one mind, and shall give their power and strength unto the beast" (Revelation 17:12-13). It is wise to observe developments such as the North American Union (NAU) and other such powerful economic trading blocs in considering this prophecy.

Globalists at Work

Back to the matter proposed earlier: Can we see any developments today presaging a paradigm change in the world economic power structure?

In my opinion, the just-examined geopolitical realities of our time, overlaid by God's prophetic Word, answers the question to some extent. Each of these nation-states or regions of the world are at stage-center. I believe they are aligned for fulfillment of things to come, as outlined in the scriptures above.

When these prophecies come fully into view and the Tribulation descends upon a world ripe for God's wrath, global economics will certainly be changed in ways that no amount of speculation can fathom. The signals are already here of the coming shift in the way the world does business. The globalist-elites are at the center of the stage being set for the mark of the beast economy.

Let us look at a few snippets to get a flavor of the globalists' setting up the world for the apocalypse—most likely unwittingly, as far as falling in line with Satan's evil plans is concerned.

The North American Union and the Larger Plan

[The Center for Strategic and International Studies (CSIS) is scheduled to release the] "final document on their 'North American Future 2025 Project.'" The Project has "an emphasis on regional integration," and the year 2025 AD was selected "on the basis of the data presently available on overall global projections."

Seven closed-door roundtable sessions have been looking at the methodology of global and North American projections, as well as labor mobility, energy, the environment, security, competitiveness, and border infrastructure and logistics.

Zbigniew Brzezinski has been a CSIS counselor, and at Mikhail Gorbachev's first State of the World Forum in 1995, Brzezinski revealed: "We cannot leap into world government through one quick step...The precondition for eventual and genuine globalization is progressive regionalization because by that we move toward larger, more stable, more cooperative units." This is why the CSIS Project has "an emphasis on regional integration." (Brzezinski also described the regions that would be formed, that Israel and the Palestinians would be part of a Middle Eastern region, how Communist China would be brought into an Asian region, and that Iran would be part of a Central Asian region which would have important oil and gas pipelines constructed.)[76]

Lou Dobbs Calls NAU "Orwellian"

Christine Romans [CNN correspondent (voice over): Waco, Texas, 2005]: Under [the leaderships of the U.S., Mexico, and Canada,] the Security and Prosperity Partnership was born. An effort, the governments say, to harmonize regulation and increase cooperation between three very different countries...

[With a new Canadian Prime Minister joining the effort] this North American partnership barrels ahead, with departments and ministries of all three governments working quickly to integrate North America by 2010...

[Worse than opening borders to the detriment of national sovereignties] critics say foreign policy elites are promoting a European-style union, erasing borders between the three countries and eventually moving to a single North American currency called the Amero...

Dobbs: The fact is—and everyone watching you and that report tonight—for any American to think that it is acceptable for the president of the United States and this executive department of his government, his administration, our government, to proceed without the approval of Congress or a dialogue and a debate and a...and a public voice from the people of this country is absolutely unconscionable.

Romans: The defense of those folks who are saying that they're involved with the SPP is that they're not doing anything that would require congressional approval or voter approval. They're just harmonizing the regulations between the three countries.

Dobbs: What they're doing is creating a brave new world, an Orwellian world, in which the will of the people is absolutely irrelevant. And I think we've had a sampling of what's going to happen to people who do that in the future. I can't imagine this standing. But then again, I couldn't imagine its beginning nor the fact that it's gotten this far.[77]

Orwell's *1984?*

Author George Orwell's 1947 novel, *1984,* had many prophecy observers a bit on the edge of their seats as that year approached. The advance of computer technology and increase of government's capability of keeping track of people as they went about daily life made the fiction seem in the realm of hideous possibility. In retrospect, we can look back and say the world hadn't seen anything yet.

Computer linkups between individuals, states, nations, and continents via satellites orbiting the earth have taken off in ways impossible to imagine in those pre-1984 years. Electronic funds transfer, with only a few manipulations on keyboards needed to move vast amounts of electronic money from and to anywhere in the world, has brought this generation into the time long wondered over by those who read the dreadful foretelling:

> He causeth all, both small and great, rich and poor, free and bond, to receive a mark in their right hand, or in their foreheads: and that no man might buy or sell, save he that had the mark, or the name of the beast, or the number of his name. Here is wisdom. Let him that hath understanding count the number of the beast: for it is the number of a man; and his number is Six hundred threescore and six (Revelation 13:16-18).

Such a system that would give "Big Brother" the ability to accomplish the mark and numbering system of everyone on the planet is no longer fodder for fiction. It exists, and only lacks the will of national leaderships to acquiesce to the globalists' blueprint to return to Babel with one world government.

The United States, by its very position as the most economically powerful nation on earth (despite what some might say to the contrary), has the keys to that shiny, new vehicle in which the global elitists want to drive all of us to Utopia. New world order is the vehicle's name.

Again, the apostle John was given the prophecy pertaining to developments in this regard that I believe we are witnessing today. The geopolitical architects are under directives of the same ancient engineer who convinced the Tower of Babel builders to produce a world government apart from God (read Genesis chapter 11). I reiterate the prophecy because I view it as perhaps the most important to the understanding of the economic rearrangements in today's world: "The ten horns which thou sawest are ten kings, which have received no kingdom as yet; but receive power as kings one hour with the beast. These have one mind, and shall give their power and strength unto the beast" (Revelation 17:12-13).

America, who holds the keys to one world order, must be circumvented or be caused to give in to the relentless assault on national sovereignty. To repeat: The United States is mentioned nowhere in Bible prophecy.

12

PEACE PUZZLE COMING TOGETHER

★ ★ ★ ★ ★

The jigsaw puzzle pieces are being fitted into place by the mighty hand of God in these strange and troubling though exciting days. Peace is the central segment of that puzzle. Mankind is looking diligently for an instrument, a document of peace that will put human history on a course away from nuclear Armageddon. And the most likely trigger to thermonuclear war resides in the Middle East.

Jerusalem will be at the center of world conflict just before Christ returns to earth (again, see Zechariah 12:1-3). Middle Eastern potentialities are scheduled to bring man to the brink of war; fears engendered by those possibilities will, at the same time, bring the world a peace of sorts.

And America, which is at the center of all crucial global matters today, is at the heart of this quest to find peace—particularly peace that will disarm the trigger to World War III.

Many students of Bible prophecy who watch the ongoings related to the peace process view the United States's involvement in putting pressure on its key ally in the region—Israel—as critically dangerous. For the Lord of heaven, the scattering of His chosen people down through the centuries and the dividing of the land He promised them are deadly serious matters. About this, God says through Joel the Old Testament prophet, "I will also gather all nations, and will bring them down into the valley of Jehoshaphat, and will plead with them there for my people and for my heritage Israel, whom they have scattered among the nations, and parted my land" (Joel 3:2).

Peace Process Underway

We have looked at the many geopolitical and other realities of our time, all of which appear to be circumstances and situations that are quite similar to prophecies scheduled for the Tribulation era.

The most profound signal that this generation is very near that time just before Christ's second coming has now joined the other signs. The American-spawned "Roadmap to Peace" is moving ominously within issues of war and peace involving Israel and its blood-vowed enemies.

Further division of Israel's land and of Jerusalem lies at the nucleus of the attempt at peace. God will not abide such a thing without severe ramifications upon the perpetrators.

The following gives an overview of the aforementioned peace process:

> In April 2003, the Quartet [the United States, European Union, United Nations, and Russia] published a road map aimed at bringing about a settlement of the conflict between Israel and the Palestinians. Israel and the Palestinian Authority accepted the road map and agreed to fulfill the commitments it placed on them.[78]

With the caveat that the perspective that follows is excerpted from the Jewish Virtual Library, a division of the American-Israeli Cooperative Enterprise, the principal obligations of each party and their progress or lack thereof toward fulfilling them are outlined below.

Palestinian Obligations

(A) PALESTINIAN OBLIGATION: Issue unequivocal statement affirming Israel's right to exist in peace and security.

- Palestinian Prime Minister Abbas has affirmed this principle while also calling Israel's creation a crime.

(B) PALESTINIAN OBLIGATION: Call for immediate and unconditional cease-fire.

- Abbas and Olmert agreed to a cease-fire at the end of November 2006.

- Abbas and Sharon agreed to declare an end to hostilities during a summit in Egypt.

- Palestinians continue to threaten violence if their demands aren't met.

- Even after Israel withdraws completely from Gaza, Palestinians continue to fire rockets into Israel on an almost daily basis.

(C) PALESTINIAN OBLIGATION: Take substantive and visible actions to stop terrorists and dismantle terrorist infrastructure.

- Abbas has explicitly said he would not disarm terrorist groups or dismantle their infrastructure.

- Abbas has said he will stop attacks on Israel.

- Abbas has also said he will not use force to confront terror.

(D) PALESTINIAN OBLIGATION: Confiscate illegal weapons.

- PA Interior Minister Abdel Razzak Yahya, who is formally in charge of the Fatah-controlled security forces in the West Bank, said that the PA was determined to disarm all armed groups as required by the road map plan for peace in the Middle East.

- Similar orders given in the past were never implemented.

- Militant factions vow resistance to surrendering weapons, and use the cease-fire period to enhance their weapons arsenal.

(E) PALESTINIAN OBLIGATION: Consolidate Palestinian security organizations.

• Abbas has acknowledged the need for such consolidation, and has said he will merge the security forces into three organizations. He has not yet done so.

• The Palestinian Authority has been unable to impose law and order and the areas under its control have grown increasingly chaotic. "It is a well-known fact that the vast majority of incidents that create the chaotic security situation in the territories originate with the security forces themselves...Abu Mazen has tried to compromise, mediate and outline agreements with the heads of the security services, but in practice, it turned out that he is incapable of controlling them and imposing security reforms" (*Haaretz,* November 29, 2005).

(F) PALESTINIAN OBLIGATION: Cut off public and private terror funding.

• Abbas has agreed to pay government subsidies to the families of terrorists. "On the very day of a suicide bombing in Netanya, it has been reported that the chairman of the Palestinian Authority gave budgetary approval to assistance for the families of suicide bombers. Each martyr's family will receive a monthly stipend of at least $250 from the PA."

(G) PALESTINIAN OBLIGATION: Official Palestinian institutions end incitement against Israel.

• Abbas has asserted his intention to reduce incitement, and initial actions are underway.

• Abbas called Israel the "Zionist enemy" during his election campaign.

• Incitement continues to be found in PA institutions, including the media.

(H) PALESTINIAN OBLIGATION: Appoint empowered
and independent interim prime minister and cabinet.

- Abbas appointed Salam Fayed as the new prime minister
to replace Hamas chief Ismail Haniyeh. "Salam Fayed is a
former World Bank economist, he ran as the head of a third
way group of independents in the elections that actually
brought Hamas to power, then the Hamas-led government
was boycotted by the international community, but when
Hamas and Fatah formed a unity government in March,
Salam Fayed was named the finance minister, and the US
and the EU resumed contact, at least through him."

Israel's Obligations

The Government of Israel—PRINCIPAL PHASE ONE
OBLIGATIONS

(A) ISRAELI OBLIGATION: Affirm commitment to two-
state vision.

- Implemented. "I extend my hand in peace to Mahmoud
Abbas, elected President of the Palestinian Authority. On
behalf of the State of Israel, we are willing to negotiate
with a Palestinian Authority" (Prime Minister Olmert
speech to U.S. Congress, May 24, 2006).

(B) ISRAELI OBLIGATION: Dismantle settlement outposts erected since March 2001.

- Israel has resumed dismantling illegal outposts. "Defense
forces were evacuating two unauthorized outposts in the
West Bank on Wednesday" (*Jerusalem Post,* January 16,
2008).

(C) ISRAELI OBLIGATION: Freeze settlement activity.

- Olmert reaffirmed the commitment not to build new

settlements. "Let's be straight, we committed ourselves in the road map not to build new settlements and we will not build any"—(*Jerusalem Post,* November 19, 2007).

(D) ISRAELI OBLIGATION: IDF [Israel Defense Forces] withdraws from parts of the Gaza Strip and West Bank.

- Agreed.

- Israel completely withdrew from the Gaza Strip and dismantled four settlements in the West Bank.

- Redeployments conditioned on a cessation of Palestinian terror. "Israel will continue to honor a cease-fire in the Gaza Strip even though rockets are being fired from there toward the Negev at the rate of about two a day, the security cabinet decided Sunday" (*Jerusalem Post,* December 4, 2006).

(E) ISRAELI OBLIGATION: End actions considered to incite Palestinians and undermine trust.

- Israel has agreed to undertake goodwill gestures (such as the release of Palestinian prisoners, which is not obligated by the road map), as well as to halt actions that are considered provocative, such as: deportations, destruction of Palestinian institutions and infrastructure, and other military measures.

(F) ISRAELI OBLIGATION: Work to improve the humanitarian situation in Gaza and West Bank.

- Agreed/Initial actions underway.

- Israel completely withdrew from the Gaza Strip, giving complete control within that area to the Palestinian Authority.

- Reconvened the Bilateral Committees established in the Oslo Accords to address the ongoing needs of the Palestinian Authority.

- Expanding economic cooperation. "The last IDF vehicle rolled out of the Gaza Strip through the Kissufim crossing at 6:40 a.m. Monday, marking an end to 38 years of military presence in the area" (*Jerusalem Post,* September 11, 2005).

- "Some 1,000 Palestinian workers from Gaza will be allowed to enter Israel and work. Several hundred businesspeople from Gaza and the West Bank will also be granted entry permits to Israel" (*Haaretz,* February 9, 2005).[79]

Daniel's Look into Our Day

The peace puzzle apparently coming together in our time makes it imperative to examine what the Bible prophesies, even at the risk of going over matters covered in previous chapters.

Daniel was given prophetic insights about the end of the age (the church age). The prophet obviously wasn't allowed to put the picture altogether in his own mind because the events prophesied were still far in the future. Answers to the mystery of all these end-time matters, however, are coming more and more into focus with every day that passes.

Nothing is more apparent, as evidenced by things concerning the Roadmap to Peace outlined above, than the fact that we are living in the middle of the prophesied end-time peace process. But it is a false peace process that will end up being a covenant or agreement made with death and hell, according to what the Bible says. God is graphic in His description of how He will ultimately deal with Israel's leaders and those who make peace with anyone other than with the Prince of Peace, His Son Jesus Christ:

> Wherefore hear the word of the LORD, ye scornful men, that rule this people which is in Jerusalem. Because ye have said, We have made a covenant with death, and with hell are we at agreement; when the overflowing scourge shall pass through, it shall not come unto us: for we have made lies our refuge, and under falsehood have we hid ourselves:

Therefore thus saith the Lord GOD, Behold, I lay in Zion for a foundation a stone, a tried stone, a precious corner stone, a sure foundation: he that believeth shall not make haste. Judgment also will I lay to the line, and righteousness to the plummet: and the hail shall sweep away the refuge of lies, and the waters shall overflow the hiding place. And your covenant with death shall be disannulled, and your agreement with hell shall not stand; when the overflowing scourge shall pass through, then ye shall be trodden down by it (Isaiah 28:14-18).

False Prince of Peace

Daniel prophesies that "a king of fierce countenance" (8:23) will come on the world scene at the end of the last of the four kingdoms predicted in Daniel chapters 2 and 7. By that time, people will have come to be very wicked indeed. The fierce king, Antichrist, will understand what he must say in order to get this evil generation to follow him. He will speak great words that will hypnotize the masses. He will be a thousand times more charismatic than was Germany's führer, Adolf Hitler. Scripture says his great abilities will not be human gifts, but will be given by Satan.

This satanically driven man will, the King James Version of the Bible says, "destroy wonderfully" (Daniel 8:24). This means that his destruction will be both deceptive and complete. In other words, the people of earth will believe he is a wonderful person interested only in their own good. He will promise plenty for everyone. He will especially promise the one thing they want most of all: peace.

The Bible says this dictator "shall cause craft to prosper" (Daniel 8:25). This is taken two different ways by various prophecy students. Either Antichrist will do this in the sense of deceit or craftiness, or he will do this in the sense of industry, meaning he will produce great prosperity.

I personally believe this could be a double reference, wherein both interpretations might be correct.

Antichrist will not be seen as "the beast" (Revelation 13) at this point. In the view of most of earth's inhabitants, he will be simply the greatest man who ever lived. Being a supreme egotist, he will agree totally with that assessment of himself: "He shall magnify himself in his heart" (Daniel 8:25). The action that will mark this satanically inspired man is his dealing with the peace process.

This leader will be the opposite of the true Prince of Peace, Jesus Christ. The Antichrist will be the false prince of false peace. Daniel 8:25 prophesies that he will, through peace, "destroy many." The Bible says further: "When they shall say, Peace and safety; then sudden destruction cometh upon them, as travail upon a woman with child; and they shall not escape" (1 Thessalonians 5:3).

A Cry for Peace?

A question we can ask ourselves to see where we stand on God's prophetic time line is this: Do we hear a cry for peace and safety today? And another: Do we see a peace process today involving God's chosen nation, Israel? These issues are crucial to understanding prophecy as it relates to Mideast war and peace.

I like the scenario my dear friend, the late Dr. Dave Breese, once wrote for one of my books. He called the piece "The Man with the Plan," describing this future false peacemaker as follows:

> One can easily envision such a leader presenting himself on international television as "the man with the plan." One could almost hear him say: "Dear friends of earth, brothers and sisters. Let me extend a great call to sanity. We are now presented with the possibility of nuclear holocaust, but such a thing does not have to come to pass. Why should millions die when it could be otherwise? Let us meet together under the great cause of world peace, and let us plan our tomorrows as civilized men. Yes, I have a plan whereby we can move beyond the threat of war into a millennium of peace, and yes, a new age of prosperity."
>
> With these and many other words, a beguiling voice could

easily attract the attention, the loyalty, and the cooperation of the nations of the world.[80]

The future world leader who will be Antichrist is called by other names in Bible prophecy. He is also called...

- the little horn (Daniel 7:8)
- the king of fierce countenance (Daniel 8:23)
- the king (Daniel 11:36)
- the man of sin (2 Thessalonians 2:3)
- the son of perdition (2 Thessalonians 2:3)
- the beast (Revelation 13:1-4,12,14-15,17; 19:19-20)
- six hundred threescore and six (Revelation 13:18)

The Antichrist's nomenclature as "the prince that shall come" (Daniel 9:26) will elevate him to the position that he will be able to "by peace...destroy many" (Daniel 8:25). He will be a masterful, mesmerizing global politician, and the people will lust after his every word. His promise to save the world from its greatest threat will do the trick. In actuality, it will be his setting up the world for Armageddon.

> After threescore and two weeks shall Messiah be cut off, but not for himself: and the people of the prince that shall come shall destroy the city and the sanctuary; and the end thereof shall be with a flood, and unto the end of the war desolations are determined. And he shall confirm the covenant with many for one week: and in the midst of the week he shall cause the sacrifice and the oblation to cease, and for the overspreading of abominations he shall make it desolate, even until the consummation, and that determined shall be poured upon the desolate (Daniel 9:26-27).

Nuclear Nightmares

Memories of the Cold War years, for those of us old enough to recall, bring up thoughts of when there were considerable apprehensions about nuclear war. We were taught to "duck and cover," as if this would somehow save us from hydrogen bombs going off in our hometowns.

There don't seem to be such apprehensions today—at least on a national or global scale. A time is predicted, however, when such nightmarish things will take place. Whether they will occur before the Tribulation is something we don't know. But, the bombs will go off at some point, if the scriptures describing those prophesied times are about nuclear detonations. Consider, for example:

> A fire devoureth before them; and behind them a flame burneth: the land is as the garden of Eden before them, and behind them a desolate wilderness; yea, and nothing shall escape them (Joel 2:3).

> I will shew wonders in the heavens and in the earth, blood, and fire, and pillars of smoke (Joel 2:30).

> This shall be the plague wherewith the LORD will smite all the people that have fought against Jerusalem; Their flesh shall consume away while they stand upon their feet, and their eyes shall consume away in their holes, and their tongue shall consume away in their mouth (Zechariah 14:12).

Births of the Bomb and Israel

Two developments in the mid-twentieth century took place almost at the same time. These occurrences cannot be mere coincidence, for God is in complete control of all that happens at all times.

Man's war-making ability was great until the middle of 1945. Millions had been killed in some 15,000 wars. But on the early morning when the night sky lit up brighter than any day that has ever been, man's ability to make war changed forever.

The first atomic explosion brought mankind to the brink of self-destruction. In fact, the scientists were not at all certain that when the bomb ignited on that early morning at Alamogordo, New Mexico, that the atmosphere itself would not continue to explode in a chain reaction that could not be stopped. True to man's fallen nature and his tendency to destroy everything he touches, the scientists were willing to take the risk.

Near the time of the first atomic test, the horrific facts about Hitler's murder of six million Jews were revealed before the eyes of the world. So great was the reaction that even the elite leaders who wanted to achieve a one-world government through the infant United Nations couldn't stop the sympathy for the Jews from producing the rebirth of Israel.

These two monumental events, the birth of the atomic bomb in 1945 and the rebirth of God's chosen nation three years later, set the stage for one of the most dramatic prophecies in the Bible regarding end-time matters.

Filling Up a Cup of Trembling

Again we come to Zechariah's forewarning about Jerusalem and the Middle East region. God Himself said He will make this area of the earth a cup of trembling for the whole world (Zechariah 12:3).

That cup of trembling is filled with an interesting mixture indeed. It is a mixture of ancient hatreds, nuclear weaponry, and Mideast oil. The Lord didn't fill up this cup of deadly ingredients. Fallen mankind filled it. God simply said He will use man's own sinful mixture to bring this corrupt world-system to a conclusion so that His Messiah, Jesus Christ, can restore order on this dying, decaying planet.

The cleansing scheduled to take place will see pillars of fire mixed with the blood of the rebels opposed to God. In a number of places, the Bible describes warfare that can only be nuclear. Even the remaking of the earth at the end of the Millennium seems to be thermonuclear in nature. But this is not surprising. Science has told us for many years about the nature of the atom.

The tiny atom is held together in some way no one really can explain. The electron, neutron, proton, and so on revolve and stick to each other in some mysterious way. Yet at the same time, the atom gives off great heat and energy.

Jesus, of course, is the one who ultimately holds all matter together. The Bible says "by him all things consist" (Colossians 1:17). It is Jesus, not the false peacemakers, who will take the burning fuse from the nuclear nightmare and bring real world peace.

Satan's Signature

Lucifer's handwriting can be seen across the world in this day when so many prophetic signals inundate the news. He has never ceased in his attempts to seduce mankind into trying to usurp the throne of God.

Satan's first effort to establish a world government was stopped; God personally came to earth and saw to that. As covered earlier, the Genesis 11 account of the tower builders of Babel on the plains of Shinar is the story of humanism. Humanism is mankind's philosophy about who should be in charge on planet Earth. That philosophy declares that man can take care of himself and the planet without any help from God. In fact, humanism asserts—according to humanist champions such as German philosopher Fredric Nietzsche—that God is dead.

Today there is a movement back to the attitude of the Tower of Babel builders. Satan's fingerprints are all over present-day attempts to kick the Creator off the planet. This attitude is evident in America's recent history.

As we saw earlier in this volume, prayer and Bible reading in public schools were stopped by U.S. Supreme Court decisions in 1963. In 1973, the Supreme Court's decision in the abortion case, *Roe v. Wade,* legalized the killing of more than 50 million babies in their mothers' wombs, according to the most recent estimates.

Since those decisions, the United States has endured a rise in deadly violence in public schools. Mass shootings in Jonesboro, Arkansas, and Littleton, Colorado, followed by the massacres on college campuses and in shopping malls starkly demonstrate the burgeoning insanity that equates real human beings to virtual targets on violent computer games. Life, in the view of many young people, seems to have been cheapened to the point that murder rather than scuffles are taking place with more regularity in school hallways and classrooms. Humanism seems to be ingrained in the thinking of our school children. The philosophy is "Do what is right in your own eyes," echoing the warning in Proverbs: "The way of a fool is right in his own eyes" (Proverbs 12:15).

The devoted humanist does what is right in his own eyes. He becomes a law unto himself. Satan's world dictator, Antichrist, will be the ultimate humanist.

No matter their intended altruism or lack thereof, the humanist power brokers, the movers and shakers in all human activities, are gathering to play God. They think they can force peace upon the rest of the world. These globalists, the international government leaders and politicians, intend to put an end to war so their new world order can bring heaven to earth.

The true Christ, of course, is always left out of their plans. And there is coming a day when the whole world will accept a false Christ who promises that elusive thing called peace. Satan will at last have achieved putting his Antichrist in place as absolute ruler of this fallen world. He will bring not peace, but man's worst war ever.

When the Lord lifts His mighty hand of restraint from the earth, all peace will disappear. In other words, God will give the humanists enough rope, and they will hang themselves.

The Dotted Line...

Daniel was given a staggering prophecy for the end of the age (Daniel 9:26-27). The prophecy indicates a peace process presided over by the devil himself. The Bible says Antichrist will force a peace that will destroy many. He will sign on the dotted line, confirming a seven-year peace agreement. Daniel prophesied that after the Messiah would lay down His life in sacrifice, the temple and Jerusalem would be destroyed.

The people of the prince who will come, that prophecy said, would be the destroying force. Who were these people? Of course, we've seen that they were the Romans. The prophecy tells us the prince will be from these people. This refers to the end-time world dictator, Antichrist. He will be from the revived Roman Empire. The prophecy says further that from the time the temple and Jerusalem would be destroyed until the end of human history (that is, the present age), there will be no true peace. Wars, the Bible says, will continue until the age reaches its consummation.

To reiterate, the prince to come will confirm a covenant with many. This means Antichrist will make and sign a covenant of security or peace for seven years. Three-and-one-half years into the treaty, this prince will break it. Then will begin what Jesus called Great Tribulation, and what Jeremiah 30:7 says will be a time of great trouble—a time unlike any experienced before and unlike any ever to come. This is also called the apocalypse.

The first part of these awesome prophecies was fulfilled when, in AD 70, General Titus attacked the rebels in Jerusalem and his Roman troops completely destroyed the Jewish temple on Mount Moriah. Jerusalem itself was almost completely leveled.

This fulfilled the prediction Jesus made to His disciples on the Mount of Olives just before His crucifixion: "Jesus went out, and departed from the temple: and his disciples came to him for to shew him the buildings of the temple. And Jesus said unto them, See ye not all these things? verily I say unto you, There shall not be left here one stone upon another, that shall not be thrown down" (Matthew 24:1-2).

Some of Daniel's prophecies have been fulfilled. Jesus' prophecy about the temple came true, but many other prophecies are yet to be fulfilled. The growing worldwide talk of global peace proves that tremendous pressure is building. Not only Mideast war and peace are at issue, but world peace is at stake.

One day Satan himself, working through the greatest world leader ever seen, will step forward to sign on the dotted line. The peace arrangement will supposedly promise peace between Israel and her enemies. But, as we saw earlier, the Bible says it will be a covenant made with death and hell.

Paving the Road

Earlier we looked briefly at the vehicle by which America and others are trying to drive antagonists in the Middle East to the table of resolving their ancient differences. The Roadmap to Peace has sputtered and popped without gaining the kind of traction that will one day be attained by the "prince that shall come"—Antichrist. The very fact that the majority of the globalist elite are trying to get Israel and her long-time enemies to talk peace, with Jerusalem itself apparently now at the heart of the process, is astounding. The process is creating the smooth roadbed that will soon be paved by more sophisticated efforts.

Let's look at a couple items of interest from recent reports on the progress of the roadmap.

America to Be Judge

The Quartet's Middle East envoy Tony Blair said Thursday that Palestinian security forces had significantly improved and were starting to carry out their part in the long-stalled "road map" peace plan.

The former British prime minister, now the envoy for the Quartet of Middle East peace mediators which include the European Union, the United States, Russia and the United Nations, urged Israel to respond by easing travel and trade restrictions imposed on the Palestinians in the West Bank.

The U.S. government will assess and judge whether Israel and the Palestinians are meeting their obligations under the 2003 road map as part of a push for a Palestinian statehood agreement.[81]

America Not to Be Judge

Three U.S. generals will monitor Israeli and Palestinian compliance with the road map for peace, but won't act as judges,

a senior U.S. official said Saturday. The same sources also said
that U.S. Secretary of State Condoleezza Rice plans frequent
Mideast trips as the sides attempt to fulfill their objective of
reaching a peace deal by the end of 2008.[82]

Confusion About Peace

So it seems that peace in the Middle East is still a quite confusing
reality. Headlines and news stories on these matters will change and
move forward, but the basic problems will still be in the mix. The
American government is right smack in the center of the confusion.

U.S. administrations will change, and prophecy tells us there will
be a continued perplexity over what it will take to bring peace to the
Middle East and to the whole world—at least until the only puzzle
piece that can complete the picture God has for world peace is finally
in place.

That key puzzle piece is the Prince of Peace, the Lord Jesus
Christ.

13

RELIGIOUS LEADERS PROPOSE WORLD UNITY

★ ★ ★ ★

America is undergoing tremendous change in every area of culture and society. Change in the arena of religion is no exception. Christianity in particular is undergoing alterations that portend developments that closely align with the apostasy foretold to occur near the time of Christ's second coming (2 Thessalonians 2:3).

False Worship System Foretold

A time is coming when all religions of earth will supernaturally gather under one faith umbrella. That faith will be directed by an individual God's Word calls "another beast." This second beast will call people to worship the one called "the beast" (Revelation 13:11-12).

This religious system will be the ultimate outgrowth of a gathering of all such systems, and that effort is already in view today. It will be, at first, a religious amalgamation for which God has some frightening things to say:

> There came one of the seven angels which had the seven vials, and talked with me, saying unto me, Come hither; I will shew unto thee the judgment of the great whore that sitteth upon many waters: with whom the kings of the earth have committed fornication, and the inhabitants of the earth have been made drunk with the wine of her fornication.

> So he carried me away in the spirit into the wilderness: and I saw a woman sit upon a scarlet coloured beast, full of names of blasphemy, having seven heads and ten horns. And the woman was arrayed in purple and scarlet colour, and decked with gold and precious stones and pearls, having a golden cup in her hand full of abominations and filthiness of her fornication: And upon her forehead was a name written, MYSTERY, BABYLON THE GREAT, THE MOTHER OF HARLOTS AND ABOMINATIONS OF THE EARTH. And I saw the woman drunken with the blood of the saints, and with the blood of the martyrs of Jesus: and when I saw her, I wondered with great admiration (Revelation 17:1-6).

The strange, terrible, agglomerate beast upon which the ghastly woman rides has been examined in previous chapters. It is the representation of the world governmental empires first seen in the vision of a huge man-image of various metals given to Babylon's King Nebuchadnezzar in Daniel chapter 2. Later, Daniel had a vision of this monster (in Daniel 7).

John saw this next in Revelation 13:1 as it arose out of the sea. Now, the woman described by John as appearing to be a prostitute sits astride the scarlet-colored monster, smiling, dressed gaudily though luxuriantly, her mouth streaming with the blood of the saints of Jesus Christ.

Woman on the Beast Revealed

Dr. J. Vernon McGee, an authority on Bible prophecy whom I respect greatly, had this to say about these verses:

> Here in chapter 17 it is mystery Babylon, the cosmic church. The Church of Thyatira, described in chapter 2, verses 18-29, which permitted Jezebel to teach, will become the apostate church of the Great Tribulation. It will attain the goal of the present-day apostates of all the great systems of the world: Romanism, Protestantism, pagan religions, cults and "isms." Even in our so-called independent Bible churches there will

be those who are not believers, and during the Tribulation they will join this great organization that may call itself a church but is not. The Bible calls it a harlot. There couldn't be a worse label than that! This is ecumenical ecclesiasticism of the one-world church. The location of this system could be in Rome. Rome, the city built on seven hills, is probably the city in mind here.[83]

America today is associated with Christianity as no other nation on earth. However, the fact that so many people in the United States claim to be Christians doesn't mean America is a Christian nation.

Not only does the United States have a large percentage of people who claim to be Christians, so too does it have many who subscribe to false teachings that divert from the doctrines of the Bible. Paul the apostle prophesied such diversion, which is defection of the apostate sort: "Now the Spirit speaketh expressly, that in the latter times some shall depart from the faith, giving heed to seducing spirits, and doctrines of devils; speaking lies in hypocrisy; having their conscience seared with a hot iron" (1 Timothy 4:1-2).

Diversion or defection from Bible doctrine doesn't have to be outright lies, such as claiming that Jesus wasn't virgin born, that He is not the Son of God, or that He didn't die and rise again to atone for the sin of man. Apostasy can be as simple as not preaching that man is in sin and needs redeeming. Or it can be as seemingly innocuous as teaching that God is love and would never condemn anyone.

Prominent Prophetic Signal

The ubiquitous signals that Christ is coming again, perhaps very soon, are clearly manifest. These signals, known as "sorrows"—that is, birth pang-like contractions—are punctuated by the development of an apostate Christianity that is leading people down the broad way to destruction. Bible prophecy expert Dave Hunt observes,

> There is no denying that these specific "sorrows" have been both prominent and accelerating since Israel, in 1948, became

a nation in possession of the land of her fathers again, in fulfillment of the specific promises God made to His ancient
people through His prophets more than 2000 years ago.
Since that remarkable rebirth of Israel, the intensity and fre-
quency of these signs has increased like the birth pangs of a
woman approaching her time of delivery, exactly as Christ
foretold. There has, however, been such emphasis upon these
oft-mentioned signs of the nearness of Christ's return that the
first words of Christ's response have been largely overlooked
and His solemn warning neglected:

> And Jesus answered and said...Take heed that no
> man deceive you. For many shall come in my name,
> saying, I am Christ, and shall deceive many.... (Mat-
> thew 24:4,5).

> And many false prophets shall rise, and shall deceive
> many...For there shall arise false Christs, and false
> prophets, and shall shew great signs and wonders;
> insomuch that, if it were possible, they shall deceive
> the very elect (verses 11,24).

It is essential to note that the very first sign (and thus the most
important one) Jesus gave in response to His disciples' query
was religious deception: "take heed that no man deceive
you." It is significant, too, that His revelation of this primary
sign was phrased as a warning: "take heed," or beware. He
repeated this sign two more times for emphasis and explained
the nature of the coming deception: it would involve false
Christs, false prophets, and false signs and wonders. More-
over, His repetition of the word "many" four times indicates
that this deception will not be hidden in a corner but will be
a worldwide delusion deceiving multitudes.

Paul uses similar language and issues a similar warning in
referring to the last days: "Let no man deceive you by any
means." A time of deception is coming, says Paul, so take care.
But in echoing Christ's warning about apostasy, Paul provides

an added insight. He reveals that the spiritual deception to which Christ referred, though it will of course involve rank unbelievers following false Christs and false prophets, will infect the professing church, it will involve a "falling away," or apostasy: "for that day [of the Lord] shall not come except there come a falling away first, and that man of sin [Antichrist] be revealed, the son of perdition" (2 Thessalonians 2:3).

While a true Christian cannot fall away, a false Christian can. Fall away from what? From the faith in Christ which he or she has outwardly professed but without inward reality. These apostates, however, will not leave the church and announce themselves as atheists. They will not convert to Buddhism or Hinduism.

While there are always some exceptions, it is important to understand that the apostasy doesn't represent a massive defection from Christianity but a turning away from the truth within the professing church.[84]

Falling Away in View

The turn of the century brought to the forefront of the dawning millennium a desire for a changed global paradigm—the call for a one-world religious union. No doubt the 1000 ecclesiastical leaders who gathered for the Millennium World Peace Summit of Religious and Spiritual Leaders in that crucial year, 2000, laid down their collective intentions:

> "This is very different than any interfaith meeting that has happened before," said Professor Lawrence Sullivan, director of the Harvard University Center for the Study of World Religions, who attended the Summit as an observer. "If you hold an ecumenical meeting in a church or synagogue or a mosque, that is not common ground. But the United Nations is a global common ground. It changes the nature of the conversation."

And the essence of the conversation was this: that it is time for the world's religious communities to stop fighting and arguing amongst themselves and, in an atmosphere of mutual respect and understanding, to begin working together—in cooperation with secular leaders at the United Nations and elsewhere—for peace, justice, the eradication of extreme poverty, the protection of the environment, and social harmony.

"Humanity stands at a critical juncture in history, one that calls for strong moral and spiritual leadership to help set a new direction for society," states the preamble of a declaration issued by the Summit. "We, as religious and spiritual leaders recognize our special responsibility for the well-being of the human family and peace on earth."[85]

Deluding Doctrines

The world of religiosity has made inroads into vaccinating evangelical Christianity with save-the-world serum that seems really nothing more than venom from the serpent. Below we read of an invitation for evangelical Christians to fall for this deluding venom:

Ban Ki-Moon, the secretary general of the United Nations and one of the world's most influential leaders, did the unimaginable a few weeks ago: He met with a diverse group of evangelicals near Washington, D.C., and asked for help from the church.

Speaking on behalf of 192 nations that committed themselves to cutting global poverty in half by 2015, Ban told evangelicals, "We cannot do it alone. We need good allies such as you. We need...the faith community to help be a voice to the voiceless people. Your engagement can push governments to push through on their commitments. Do not underestimate your power. With faith and the will, we can make a difference."[86]

Salvation Message

In recent decades, religious leaders have chosen to change the thrust of the message regarding what constitutes salvation. That is, *salvation* means "saving" the environment, redeeming planet Earth. Salvation of the soul and its redemption have been put on the back burner of priorities. Lucifer's plan seems on track as he infects Christianity with the apostate virus:

A number of scientists and religious leaders have joined in an effort to fight the perceived and much-ballyhooed global warming threat. These groups, often at the opposite ends of the spectrum in regard to questions about origins and the age of the planet, are on a quest to protect earth against ecological enemies such as pollution and other "reckless human activities." Their determination seems driven by fervent, religious-like zeal.

> "We believe that the protection of life on Earth is a profound moral imperative," according to the 'call to action' issued in Washington today by 28 scientists and evangelical Christian leaders..."

> It is significant that the National Association of Evangelicals (NAE) has endorsed the dialogue. The organization represents 45,000 churches, with membership totaling approximately 30 million churchgoers in America.

> In 2006, the NAE did not agree to endorse the "Evangelical Climate Initiative," a document signed by 86 religious leaders that proclaimed global warming a real and urgent moral problem.

> NAE officials said at the time that there was disagreement among their members about the importance of global warming and the dangers it presented to the planet.

> Now, those same officials say things are changing.

> "It's important to understand the profound changes occurring in the evangelical community in just the last year," said

Richard Cizik, Vice President of Governmental Affairs for the NAE...

Cizik says that the NAE board unanimously approved the new alliance between science and religion, and that he's also seeing more concern about climate and environmental issues coming from the local church level...

The statement declares that there is no excuse for further delay. It calls on leaders within science, business, religion, and politics to "work toward the fundamental change in values, lifestyles, and public policies required to address these worsening problems before it is too late."[87]

Change Sought

It is interesting that the word *change* is the incessant hue and cry in America today. "The people want change" is the mantra of politicians and media. The change agents can't seem to frame exactly the rearrangements we the people apparently are craving, but that seems of little importance while the unspecified "changes" go forward.

Clearly, much change is afoot in religion today, while a changed world order is preparing as religionists everywhere propose, even demand, unity. Unity, they say, is the change needed. This will help to save the planet, a thing that America and the world must make priority.

The doctrine of change must, they seem to be saying, be built around global warming and the dangers that in particular are presented by America, the superstate. We simply are burning too much fossil fuel. This: 1) pollutes the atmosphere, and 2) depletes the finite resource. Some add that this harshly affects third-world countries.

National and world leaders must come together to legislate the true teachings of Jesus and institute the changes He came to invoke. This must be made a religious cause in order to generate the fervor essential to accomplishing this noble quest.

Rick Warren, who has formulated his own peace plan for saving the earth, presents thoughts pertinent to this topic:

Warren says that he recently told a group of business leaders, "The future of the world is not secularism. It's religious pluralism...The world is becoming more religious, not less. Christianity is growing around the world at a rapid pace through conversion, and Islam is growing at a rapid [rate] due to births...We're going to have to minister in a context where we...learn how to get along."

The Saddleback pastor, we are supposed to infer, is trying to increase civility in a world out of kilter. He strives for a change in which those who call themselves Christians will participate in the world with the teachings of Jesus in the individual and collective mind.

"I think we need a second Reformation in the church about how we behave," he asserts. "The first Reformation was about creeds. I think the second Reformation needs to be about deeds...If Christians of all stripes...would just practice what we know Jesus taught, the world would be an incredibly different place."

He calls this second Reformation a "mobilization." Saddleback is developing a "peace plan" and worldwide mission to promote reconciliation through service...

Warren proposes a..."public, profit, and parish" approach to solving the planet's most difficult problems.

"The church is the most widely distributed organization in the world," he points out. "The church was global 200 years before anybody started talking about globalization."[88]

The pastor no doubt believes he, in unity with the religious, business, and political amalgamation proposing change, can contribute toward a new world of peace and plenty. To genuinely want to do all that can be done for the betterment of mankind is an honorable, even noble, aspiration. The problem is—and it is a 100 percent fatal flaw—such an undertaking is doomed to fail when God and His perfect plan—the gospel that Jesus Christ alone is the only way to salvation of the soul—is left out of the formula for genuine peace on earth. Jesus is the equation which all such construction must have at the nucleus. Any and every other formula for trying to make peace will lead to dismal failure.

Evangelicals who have signed on to help build the new world order think they can first build for the poor and downtrodden a better environment and living habitat, then come in the back door of the newly constructed quasi-utopia to share the gospel, and souls will be won. But the gospel of Jesus Christ must be at the forefront of everything and all things: "He is the head of the body, the church: who is the beginning, the firstborn from the dead; that in all things he might have the preeminence" (Colossians 1:18).

The Revelation Religionists

As I said earlier, American today is associated with Christianity as no other nation on earth. It is for this reason that I believe America is the home base for the false Christianity wing of the on-storming religionists' movement into ecumenism. The agglomerate organization will culminate in full-blown apostasy. These are the ecclesiastical clergy who willfully and ravenously drink from the golden chalice provided by geopolitical kingmakers. They think they do God a service, but by ignoring the true purpose of Christ's sacrifice on the cross at Calvary, thus putting their collective foot on the throats of true believers and prohibiting the declaration of the truth about salvation through Jesus alone, the religionist neo-Babel builders symbolically fill the figurative chalice with the blood of Christ and His true servants.

These are types of the false clergy who will do the bidding of the false prophet of Revelation 13. They ride the back of the scarlet beast that symbolizes the Babylonian humanist government that will be Antichrist's regime. Jesus had this to say about those who deny Him and His primary mission on earth:

> Beware of false prophets, which come to you in sheep's cloth-
> ing, but inwardly they are ravening wolves...Not every one

that saith unto me, Lord, Lord, shall enter into the kingdom
of heaven; but he that doeth the will of my Father which is
in heaven. Many will say to me in that day, Lord, Lord, have
we not prophesied in thy name and in thy name have cast out
devils? and in thy name done many wonderful works? And
then will I profess unto them, I never knew you: depart from
me, ye that work iniquity (Matthew 7:15,21-23).

Harlot's Fate Sealed

Bible prophecy doesn't hedge on the final disposition of this religious system, which is likened to a prostitute. She prostitutes herself
to the powers that be in order to garner influence and wealth during
the worst times in human history. The apostate church becomes Antichrist's mistress, the antithesis of Christ's bride, the church, who has
been taken safely to heaven at least seven years earlier. (Again, read
John 14:1-4; 1 Corinthians 15:51-55; 1 Thessalonians 4:13-18; and
Revelation 3:10.)

This whorish mistress's lover, the beast, will slaughter her once
she has served his purposes. He will abide no other worship system
other than that which idolizes himself. This is worship demanded
by Lucifer—Satan—who indwells Antichrist at this time: "The ten
horns which thou sawest upon the beast, these shall hate the whore,
and shall make her desolate and naked, and shall eat her flesh, and
burn her with fire" (Revelation 17:16).

Plainly, the evidence shows that America is at the heart of the
formative stages of the end-of-days false worship system. Which is
another reason to ask the question: Why, then, is the United States
not mentioned in Bible prophecy?

14

WORLD STUNNED AS MILLIONS VANISH!

★ ★ ★ ★ ★

A headline similar to this chapter title will one day leap from the front pages of the world's major newspapers. Newscasters will break into regularly scheduled programming on television and radio programs. The Internet will rage with the distressing revelation. Millions will have vanished, and it will be as if the planet had been turned upside down and inside out.

This is the one event that will grab and hold the attention of every individual on earth who has ability to understand what has happened. A panic will ensue that will make all other crises that have ever occurred seem as nothing.

What happened? What's going on? These will be the primary questions in the fear-filled thoughts of every person who learns of the disappearances. Many will have witnessed the sudden vanishings "up close and personal," as *ABC Sports* used to put it. The planet will be abuzz with terror.

America, a nation with among the largest numbers of Christians, will instantly lose its very heart. The greatest nation to ever exist, in terms of creative genius and industrial acumen and productivity, will be forever changed in a microsecond.

Doomsday Drivel?

Since 1947 the board of directors of *Bulletin of the Atomic Scientists* at the University of Chicago has maintained what is known as the Doomsday Clock. This clock, which is currently set to a few minutes before midnight, is meant to warn where this generation stands with regard to the potential for world-ending nuclear cataclysm. Those who have arbitrarily set this clock have been praised, not castigated, for sounding the alarm.

On the other hand, Christians who look for Christ's return are more and more being accused of wanting the prophecies about history's most terrible time and Armageddon to hurry up and arrive. Believers are called "doomsdayers" (and other less-than-flattering names), and are accused of wanting to influence American foreign policy in ways that will bring on war and bloodshed, particularly in the Middle East. At least that's the mantra of some media pundits.

This accusation is, of course, untrue. We who are Christians don't desire a Mideast (or any other) war, and God's time line is His own. No one and nothing can change it.

Those who have brought messages of impending doom have been literally or figuratively stoned throughout the centuries. Old Testament prophets were regularly ostracized or killed for bearing news of coming judgment and wrath from God. We who are Christians today certainly aren't prophets in the Old Testament sense of the word, but we are called to proclaim the whole Word of God, the Bible. Nearly a third of the Bible is about prophecy. Half of that is about prophecy that is future from our point in history. We are the messengers of that prophecy.

As many as two-thirds of the people alive at the time of the Tribulation will die. It will be a horrible time when 21 specific judgments will befall rebellious people. The Creator of all things will not let this happen before the world has been adequately warned. But it must be noted: People of the world have been in the process of being warned for many centuries. No other generation has had more warning than this one, due to the tremendous advancement in communications technologies in these times.

Much of God's warning tells of a coming time that will be the worst ever experienced. Killing the messengers, literally or figuratively, will not change things. Judgment and wrath are coming.

Despite the message of coming judgment, however, our viewpoint should be looked at as one of supreme optimism, not as one that says, "Bring on the apocalypse." The rapture is the way to escape the judgment and wrath God says are on the way. We look for Jesus Christ to come for Christians in that moment of rescue (see Titus 2:13). This view invites all people everywhere to join in this coming rescue by accepting Christ for salvation.

That our rescue through the rapture will happen doesn't mean Christians should just sit back and watch society disintegrate. That diatribe is yet another of the common accusations made against those who see the pre-Trib rapture in Bible prophecy. Our job is to tell people about their sinful condition. We should be striving to accomplish God's work until the day Jesus calls us home. That is what is involved in the assignment called the Great Commission, which Christ gave to His followers before He ascended into heaven:

> Jesus came and spake unto them, saying, All power is given unto me in heaven and in earth. Go ye therefore, and teach all nations, baptizing them in the name of the Father, and of the Son, and of the Holy Ghost: Teaching them to observe all things whatsoever I have commanded you: and, lo, I am with you alway, even unto the end of the world. Amen (Matthew 28:18-20).

When it comes to the following dire prophecy concerning the judgments involved about the end of this earth age, we believe carrying the message to everyone possible is validated: "For then shall be great tribulation, such as was not since the beginning of the world to this time, no, nor ever shall be. And except those days should be shortened, there should no flesh be saved: but for the elect's sake those days shall be shortened" (Matthew 24:21-22).

This chapter will examine why, with the world's downward spiral toward self-destruction, doomsday is not for planet Earth, which God will remake into pristine condition. This world will never end, God has promised. However, doomsday is coming for all that has gone wrong since man's fall in the Garden of Eden. He will make all things right again.

Meanwhile, however, those alive on earth will pay a heavy price for enmity with the God of heaven. God's judgment and righteous wrath must fall upon a wicked world that grows more so by the minute.

Reason for Reason

In His Word, God extends this invitation to mankind: "Come now, and let us reason together, saith the LORD: though your sins be as scarlet, they shall be as white as snow; though they be red like crimson, they shall be as wool" (Isaiah 1:18). The Lord, who created man in perfect harmony with Himself, now calls all to reconciliation from their fallen state. He pleads with us to accept the redemption He offers through the sacrifice His Son made on the cross. But His wrath and judgment are building. He is patient, but His patience is not without limits. At the same time, it is totally against His great character to want any to perish in the judgment that must befall all who are incorrigibly rebellious against Him: "The Lord is not slack concerning his promise, as some men count slackness; but is long-suffering to us-ward, not willing that any should perish, but that all should come to repentance" (2 Peter 3:9).

God has been reasoning with lost humanity in these modern times in ways as never before in history. Communication of every sort takes the message of the gospel instantly to every point on the globe. This is one of the reasons we can say with biblical authority that we are indeed in the end of days. The following prophecy has literally been fulfilled in the course of recent decades: Jesus said, "This gospel of the kingdom shall be preached in all the world for a witness unto all nations; and then shall the end come" (Matthew 24:14).

America the Witness

The United States, as we explored earlier, was brought into the world for two main reasons, at least in my observations. One was to be an unprecedentedly powerful nation-state protector for modern Israel. The other all-important reason was to develop the technologies that could reach into the world with the message that Jesus Christ is the way to redemption and reconciliation with God. Despite her plummet in every area of godly morality, America has been a true witness to the whole world. The nation has served its purpose. That is a chilling thought, isn't it? America *has*—the emphasis is on the past tense—served her purpose. That statement has an ominous ring to it; as repeated throughout these pages, America is mentioned no place in Bible prophecy.

Israel, on the other hand, is the most prominent nation in these last days, exactly as God said it would be. Nearly all nations—as proved consistently in the United Nations by votes made against the tiny Jewish state—are gathered against Israel, just as Zechariah the prophet predicted.

Israel in the Headlines

America has been instrumental in positioning Israel in today's headlines. Of that there can be no doubt. We have seen a number of times throughout these chapters that the world views the United States and Israel as joined at the proverbial hip. Those same nations have demonstrated a visceral dislike for both countries. The world community of nations lets Israel's Islamic-led Arab enemies get away with lies fabricated out of whole cloth in most instances.

Israel stands in the crosshairs of the anti-Semite vitriol, as captured in the following opinion piece about Israel's skirmish with Hezbollah terrorists when the latter attacked Israeli civilian populations with rockets.

> These are strange times.
>
> Perennially beleaguered Israel, for instance, was hit all summer long with rockets from Lebanon and Gaza, as the world watched and kept score in an absurd new game of

proportionality: Israel was to be blamed because its hundreds of air strikes against combatants were lethal, while Hezbollah was to be excused for shooting off thousands of rockets aimed at civilians because of its relative incompetence.[89]

The opinion piece said that a gathering hosted by Iran termed "international conference on Holocaust denial" included a collection of strange bedfellows, all with an anti-Semitic bent, under the guise of a forum that allowed a free exchange of ideas, unlike anything that could be found in Europe.

The article pointed out that during the same general time frame former president Jimmy Carter was remaining silent about Iran's call for holocaust against Israel and the Jewish people, while hawking his book that more or less compared Israel's way of dealing with Palestinians to an apartheid state, treating with cruelty the Palestinians and Christians of the region, bringing upon itself as an "occupier" retaliation such as suicide bombings.

The opinion went on to say,

> As with the writings and rantings of bin Laden and Dr. Zawahiri, these [international community] experts should perhaps listen to what is actually being said by the prominent Palestinians themselves—not what we keep thinking they should say...

The opinion writer implied it might be wise to, for example, pay heed to what Al-Jazeera editor-in-chief Ahmed Sheikh said to Pierre Heumann, the Middle East correspondent of the Swiss weekly Die Weltwoche. Heumann asked Sheikh (who the opinion writer said is not merely a propagandist for the Palestinian cause, but a keen observer of the mind-set of his people) if, in the end, the central thinking of the Palestinians is a matter of feelings of self-esteem.

Sheikh said, "Exactly. It's because we always lose to Israel. It gnaws at the people in the Middle East that such a small country as Israel, with only about 7 million inhabitants, can defeat the Arab nation with its 350 million. That hurts our collective ego. The Palestinian problem is in the genes of every Arab. The West's problem is that it does not understand this."[90]

Ego-Driven Doomsday

Ahmed Sheikh simply but succinctly told the world through the interview precisely why the Arabs hate Israel. In children's playground vernacular, the explanation is "just because."

It is really no more complicated than that, though astoundingly profound. It is wrapped up, he admits, in ego. Pride is the ingredient that foments millennia-long hatred. And, just as God's Word outlines in the saga of Israeli and her enemies, the greatest egotist of all—Satan, that old devil, the serpent—is at the center of the rage. Lucifer still plans to put his star above the throne of God.

This insanity in the Middle East has now infected all of humanity, and like a purulence-filled skin eruption, it will come to a head at Armageddon.

Israel-Initiated Inferno?

Hollywood punditry, of all things, put its finger on the problem regarding the world's fearful view of things to come in the Middle East:

> The aggressively photogenic John Edwards was cruising along, detailing his litany of liberal causes last week until, during question time, he invoked the "I" word—Israel. Perhaps the greatest short-term threat to world peace, Edwards remarked, was the possibility that Israel would bomb Iran's nuclear facilities.
>
> As a chill descended on the gathering, the Edwards event was brought to a polite close.
>
> Support for Israel in the U.S. has lately become bafflingly multi-cultural, representing an alliance between diaspora Jews, traditional Zionists and evangelicals.
>
> Support from Christian zealots, who now represent about

one-third of Israel's tourist business, is welcomed even
though, according to evangelical doctrine, Judgment Day
will bring the ultimate destruction of Israel and death to
most of its residents.[91]

This assessment is uncannily observant, even prescient, coming
from such a generally uncomprehending source as Hollywood. Israel
is indeed perceived as the entity posing the greatest threat to world
peace. That the Jewish state could well attack Iran's nuclear development facilities is what makes the diplomatic world tremble.

Even more amazing is that this writer had it right about Israel's
supporters—although he couldn't resist naming them in a way that
was laced with invective. "Diaspora Jews," "traditional Zionists,"
"evangelicals," and "Christian zealots"—each seem to be named with
a hissing scorn.

The writer's words are portentous.

Israel is in the crosshairs of its Arab neighbor-enemies; the nation
is in the world spotlight as the chief troublemaker; the Jewish state's
only true friends are about to be reduced by one-third or more from
its already small numbers.

Millions Vanish! A Scenario

At just such a time as today's world conditions present, millions
of people will disappear before the horrified eyes of those left to continue to walk the earth. The one-world drive is again being pursued
in a concerted effort by the powers elite. Yet in the past, when things
have reached a certain point of depravity, God has always intervened.
A prime example is when He destroyed Sodom and Gomorrah (read
Genesis 19 to learn about both mankind's depravity and the Lord's
intervention), which brings us to the point about end-of-days scenarios
I would like to explore.

Jesus Himself set the prophetic stage for a time when He will again
intervene—catastrophically—into depraved man's playhouse of las-
civiousness. He said: "Likewise also as it was in the days of Lot; they
did eat, they drank, they bought, they sold, they planted, they builded;

but the same day that Lot went out of Sodom it rained fire and brimstone from heaven, and destroyed them all" (Luke 17:28-29).

This is a description of a society, a culture, a generation going
forward with business as usual. Jesus prophesied that it would be
just like this when judgment from heaven would fall at the time of
His end-of-days intervention. It is not, however, a description of the
Tribulation era, when Jesus comes physically to earth, as foretold in
Revelation 19:11. At that time, as many as two-thirds of the earth's
population will have died in the apocalyptic judgments. It will not
be business as usual, like the Lord describes in Luke 17. The things
that transpire here, though not as disastrous as things will get later
in man's last grasp to rule himself, will still be calamitous. And the
possible scenarios are mesmerizing. Let us look at my postulations,
based upon the pre-Trib view of the rapture.

Jesus' description of Lot's being removed from that condemned
city is almost certainly a picture of the future removal of the only
good God sees on this earth—born-again Christians, the church Jesus
said He would build. Lot, Abraham's nephew, although not a perfect
example of living a godly life, was nonetheless considered a "just" man
in God's eyes. That is, the Lord saw Lot as righteous, one who accepted
God's authority over his life and His salvation plan. Lot and his family
lived in a society that was, well, much like ours. It was wicked to its
black core. Incidentally, in that society homosexuality had become
accepted as part of life in Sodom.

God removed Lot, and His wrath began to fall upon that wicked,
ungovernable people. Jesus indicated that this is exactly what will
happen near the time He comes again. It will happen at the rapture,
at least seven years before He comes back and touches down on the
Mount of Olives. The first part of God's wrath will be the removal
of His Holy Spirit from the consciences of earth-dwellers. The people
left behind will have rejected God's authority.

Now, raptured saints will perhaps from the balcony of heaven be
given a God's-eye view of whether the rebels' claim that they don't
need God to govern them is true.

Millions will vanish in a millisecond. The United States of America, which possesses at the same time more gospel light than any other nation of history and access to more filth and depravity than even ancient Rome at its decadent, orgiastic worst, will experience an implosion that staggers the imagination.

We have seen that Jesus forewarned that when He comes again to planet Earth it will be as it was in the days of Noah (Luke 17:26). That is, the characteristics of the end-time generation will be like those in the days presented in Genesis chapter 6. When we look at that chapter, we cannot help but conclude that it must have been a terrifying time. This must have been true especially for Noah and his seven family members just before the flood. Violence filled the whole earth, God's Word reports (Genesis 6:11,13). Though business was moving along at a good pace, terroristic activity filled the earth.

Does this sound familiar? What did President George W. Bush call the war declared upon an almost unidentifiable enemy following the 9/11 attacks? He called it the War on Terror. And now the whole international community is uptight about the possibility of ramifications of the terror—the violence—that threatens to ignite war in the Middle East.

Let us look at the potential calamitous things that will likely immediately follow the twinkling-of-an-eye intervention into this humanistic, last-days world.

In the United States, a young mother pregnant with her second and with a small daughter riding in the basket will be walking down an aisle in a supermarket. A truck driver will be steering a tractor-trailer rig onto a superhighway onramp, ready to merge into heavy traffic. A 757 pilot will push the throttles to full power and head down a runway at JFK in New York. A surgeon at a major hospital in Minnesota will make the initial scalpel cut to open a heart patient's chest for a bypass procedure. A funeral director will straighten the collar of a starched white shirt worn by a corpse, whose funeral is next on the services schedule.

In less than the time it takes for a neuroelectrical synapse to fire in the brain, the young mother's womb is empty. She sees her little girl vanish as she, herself, starts her fall to the floor from the shock of the changes taking place in her body. The 18-wheeler is careening into the traffic, driverless, out of control, crushing and demolishing vehicles and their passengers while raging ahead in its ungoverned course.

The 757 on the runway has reached full take-off speed, but the pilot and co-pilot are not at the controls, and the right wingtip dips toward the runway and catastrophe. The surgeon in Minnesota finds the scalpel cutting air rather than flesh because the patient is gone. The funeral director staggers backwards, astonished because the burial apparel he has been making just right for presentation has collapsed and the corpse is no longer in the casket.

Those snapshots of the paradigm-changing dynamics of the rapture will geometrically burgeon from the instant this stunning event takes place. It will be the most powerful event in human history since Christ's first advent intervened into the affairs of mankind.

Believers are translated, changed in a fraction of an element of time that cannot be divided. They now look into the holy, omniscient eyes of their Lord that are fathomless in the depths of His love. He leads them through the portals of glory to the city called heaven.

On earth, millions have vanished into nothingness before the stupefied eyes of billions of others. All earthly things that belonged to the departed ones remain behind, including clothing, jewelry, and prosthetics of every description.

I once heard a nationally known "reverend" (I don't like to use the word *reverend* in reference to anyone on this fallen planet, because there is only one Reverend, and He has just, in our scenario, whisked all who are His into heaven for their eternal rewards) say something like this: "A rapture—if it were to be something that really happens—would mean that there would be unbelievable carnage upon the earth. God won't let that happen."

Hello, reverend, but what about the judgments for the end of days as described in the Old and New Testaments? What about the book of Revelation? The seal, trumpet, and vial judgments don't exactly give us the warm, fuzzy feeling that the era of apocalypse will be a tiptoe through the tulips.

The "Kingdom Now" folk, with their replacement theology, however, see these things written in the areas of biblical judgments and God's wrath as allegory or symbolism. They spiritualize these prophecies or treat them as already fulfilled. They teach that the church (Christians) will make this earth a better and better place until Christ can safely return to occupy His earthly throne. My dear reader, they are simply not looking at the same headlines as yours truly. And the headlines I'm experiencing each and every day coincide precisely with what God's inerrant Word has to say about the end of days—again—as the secular media like to call the end time: "Evil men and seducers shall wax worse and worse, deceiving, and being deceived" (2 Timothy 3:13).

Jesus Himself made it clear how bad things will get: "Except that the Lord had shortened those days, no flesh should be saved: but for the elect's sake, whom he hath chosen, he hath shortened the days" (Mark 13:20).

This world is in for a very rough ride, and the reverend was wrong to pronounce that God would not allow carnage, and thus a rapture is not in the future of mankind. Nothing could be more ludicrous.

The thief-in-the-night prophecy is aimed particularly at the people who will be left behind after the rapture. That great event will certainly take most willfully ignorant Christians by total surprise, but it will not be like a thief-in-the-night experience to them. We can know this from Paul the apostle's words to the Thessalonians, and to all Christians of the church age:

> For yourselves know perfectly that the day of the Lord so cometh as a thief in the night. For when they shall say, Peace and safety; then sudden destruction cometh upon them, as travail upon a woman with child; and they shall not escape. But ye, brethren, are not in darkness, that that day should overtake you as a thief. Ye are all the children of light, and the children of the day: we are not of the night, nor of darkness (1 Thessalonians 5:2-5).

Note Paul's use of the pronouns "they" and "them" versus "you," "ye," and "we." He was differentiating between unbelievers and believers during this church age. The rapture, for all Christians who are alive at the time, will be an entirely different experience than the thief-in-the-night experience of those left behind. We see this in John 14:1-3 and in Paul's comforting prophecy: "Looking for that blessed hope, and the glorious appearing of the great God and our Saviour Jesus Christ…" (Titus 2:13).

America's very soul will be gone in that stupendous second of time. The United States will have changed in ways that will demand a profoundly different order of life.

15

UNITED STATES PURSUES PLACE WITHIN CHANGED INTERNATIONAL ORDER

★ ★ ★ ★

America will suffer loss as will no other country when the calamity of all calamities sweeps millions upon millions from the planet. The instantaneous disappearance of multitudes will leave the nation and the world terrified and searching for answers.

Shocking Scenes

So, getting back to the earthbound scenarios that we speculate will immediately follow the rapture, let us look at some dark probabilities.

The first thing that assaults the senses of those left behind are the clothing and other personal belongings things that fall to the ground. The only evidence that those who suddenly vanished were ever on earth are the clothing and other personal items they no longer need. The prosthetic devices of every sort, too, give the news pundits something to talk about on the programs that are dominated by one subject: the sudden and unexpected disappearance of millions.

Every single child who hasn't reached the age of accountability for his or her soul has vanished. Every womb of every left-behind woman who is pregnant is suddenly empty. God, in that astonishing moment, makes a monumental and unmistakable statement about His opinion of when life begins!

With the intimately personal cataclysms still raging, other just-as-staggering considerations flood the thoughts of the men and women who are left behind.

National Chaos

In America, martial law is immediately invoked. But before the much-denuded military and law enforcement personnel can regroup to enforce order, looters of every sort move freely throughout decimated society, pillaging, destroying, and raping whatever and whomever they find in their paths.

The consciences of people are no longer under the restraint of the Holy Spirit, as in the time just before the disappearances occurred. Homes, empty of their vanished occupants, are open game, and the looters don't stop to give a second thought to the horrendous future mankind now faces. They think, as I heard Dr. Charles Stanley once say, they have died and gone to their warped version of heaven.

We've only begun to explore what the left-behind world will be like and the likely dynamics that will rearrange planet Earth for Antichrist's appearance.

People have vanished all over the world in less time than it takes for light to enter the eye and strike the retina. The chaos is worldwide, but nowhere so profound as within the United States of America. Just a matter of time, however, will prove that the ramifications are geopolitically staggering—for one nation in particular, in addition to America.

The American government at every level soon determines that every child below—most likely—the teenage years is gone. Every pregnant woman who remains suffers the loss of the baby in her womb. But some other things are even more troubling to the officials: many leaders at every level of government are missing.

Government in Crisis

Government ongoings are totally disrupted, and the powers that be quickly recognize that not even martial law is going to help reestablish the revenue basis for carrying on government as usual. A huge part of the tax base—a fatally proportionate one—is no longer on hand to provide the funds to carry on government work. Much of the workforce that is the heart and soul of American industry and fidelity to the good work ethic has disappeared in that stupefying moment.

The carnage caused by the many accidents and other disappearance-engendered problems requires massive manpower and in many cases extraordinary skills to begin restoring order. Yet the people who would normally help restore order are gone in great numbers.

Europe, on the other hand—while dumbfounded, even extremely worried over the vanishings—seems to have suffered little infrastructure damage. The economy, well structured by the European Union parliament, experience only minimal glitches. Now it is bidden by the upper echelon of the American government that is left to advise and assist in helping with things—especially with reestablishing America's economic base on a sound footing.

Enemies on Alert

America's particularly bad circumstances do not go without notice by others within the nation-states of the world. Russia and China take special notice. They assess how America's military complex has been affected.

Islamics who want their religion to rule the world are delighted. The Great Satan (America) has gotten its deserved punishment from Allah. Although Islamic children, too, have disappeared, the adults who remain in great numbers are still available to make war—and love—in order to replenish the children. The Islamic terrorist organizations are delighted and immediately see opportunity for more aggressive jihad against their enemies—most particularly against the Jews of the world and Israel.

Israel Comes to Attention

Israel's governmental leaders come to two stunning realizations:

1. Their only ally, with the greatest thermonuclear deterrent in the world, is in chaos. The U.S. government officials who remain are doing all within their power just to make deals with the European Union in order—somehow—to regain their power. There is no time, or even facility, to see to Israel's protection.

2. The greatest supporters of Israel and the Jews—their best friends—are no longer on the planet! While America's top leaders are coming to realize a need for a complete re-arrangement of economy and monetary matters, Israel is getting reports of plans for attack by the Arabs, Persians, and other Islamics who view what has happened as an opportunity provided them by Allah to once-and-for-all eradicate the hated Jew and the impostor State of Israel.

The Jewish leadership is intact, and the Jews—even those of the Labor Party and the most liberal—know the tiny nation now stands alone. Even Mideast oil exigencies are for the moment off the table for the powers of the West, the industrial nations that must reorganize and are unable to send their troops on ventures into the sands of the Middle East.

What Israel determines to do, it must do quickly. Very quickly. The Israeli leadership realizes one thing beyond all others. They know their blood-vowed enemies will do everything within their power to wipe them—including the Labor Party and other liberal Jews—off the earth. But there is "the Samson Option," even the liberal Jews agree. The tiny state now in the crosshairs of practically every Arab state still has perhaps the third- or fourth-most lethal nuclear weapons force in the world. The Islamic fanatics—the entire world—must be shown that their vow "Never again!" is as strongly in the collective determination of the Jew as in the years immediately following the Holocaust.

Israel Friendless

Following the removal of all born-again believers, the leadership of Israel will look around to find its world support gone. All who truly believe Israel has a God-given right to the land will be missing. America will be in total turmoil, and desperately searching for ways to regain its national equilibrium. This can only be accomplished by reestablishing government that will provide structure for restoring order. The European Union, somewhat shaken, nonetheless will remain solid. All civilized parts of the Western world will rush to the European Union for help in trying to regain or preserve things lost in the greatest catastrophe in recorded human history.

The Islamic leaders of the Middle East, who have for centuries held the people under their despotic thumbs, will not be cowered by the disappearances—even of all of their young children. Rather, they will be emboldened to look toward Israel and see an Allah-sent opportunity to once and for all scour the Jew from the face of what they consider to be their land.

Author's note: There has been developed, in my view, a compelling recent dissection of Scripture that possibly involves modern Israel and her antagonist Arab neighbor nation-states. The prophecy is found in Psalms 83. Author Bill Salus, in his book *Isralestine: The Ancient Blueprints of the Future Middle East* has carefully examined this prophecy, which he believes is about a war that is separate from and precedes the Gog-Magog war of Ezekiel chapters 38 and 39. His look at this foretelling is so profoundly intriguing that I sense it warrants in-depth consideration for the reader who seeks to understand the full scope of these end times (see page 287).

This rumor of war will not escape Israel's leadership.

Israeli Preemption

While the Arab-Islamic forces gather in council of war, the military leadership of Israel will be given the top spot in doing whatever is necessary to ensure the nation's continued existence. The liberals and woolly minded who harbor delusional thoughts that peace is primary will be pushed to the margins. Israel must survive.

Gamal Abdel Nasser will be remembered in the councils of both

Israel and her enemies who spawned that Egyptian warlord. Nasser gathered the combined forces of Arab nations and attacked Israel in 1956. He was in the process of doing so again in 1967 when the Israel Defense Forces preempted the Egyptian dictator's plans and thoroughly defeated that collective foe. The people who declare they will never again sit still while forces gather to destroy the nation will now be in charge in Israel; the pacifists will be silenced. Dramatic action is called for; it will be taken.

Damascus Doomed

The leaders of the major Mideast terrorist organizations will gather at the one place they are all headquartered—the oldest inhabited city on earth, Damascus, Syria. Their drumbeat of hatred will make the inevitable obvious to the Israeli hawks—most all within Israeli leadership, who will decide to cut off the heads of the hydra-headed serpent in one mighty blow. That blow will be delivered by the nuclear sword: "The burden of Damascus. Behold, Damascus is taken away from being a city, and it shall be a ruinous heap" (Isaiah 17:1).

One Israeli jet with a 15-kiloton bomb will cut off the heads, bringing much of Islam into confusion and immense rage. Then there will be jihad of the most nightmarish sort. But preparation for such jihad will take time. Many of the diabolical terrorists most proficient at planning such a holy war will have gone to their 72 virgins in the nuclear blast.

War Jitters

Now, America will acquiesce to agree with European Union brainstorming. Something, all agree in the Western power sphere, must be done—immediately. World War III—which some have said has already begun with the War on Terror—will be about to get underway in full-blown fury. Israel will then sense the collective wrath not just of its Islamic neighbors but of the entire world, including its former staunchest ally—the United States of America.

Israel, through its preemptive destruction of Damascus with a nuclear weapon, will have enraged everyone, who now view the tiny Jewish state as the number one troublemaker on the planet. Zechariah 12:1-3 will come to prophetic fruition. The Jewish state will stare into the face of its worst nightmare at this time. Israel will be friendless. Most all Jews will know they are doomed. There will be no choice but to invoke the Samson Option. They will bring all who come against them down with their own deadly fall.

Prince with the Plan

But there will be one man within the hierarchy of the European Union who wants to try a diplomatic tact others haven't considered. Damascus lies in nuclear rubble, completely cut off from ever becoming a city again. The major jihadist terrorist heads were cut off in Israel's preemptive strike. But the collective wrath of the rest of the world's nations—led by the United Nations' Israel-haters—surround the tiny Jewish state, figuratively, at least.

The Islamic hordes of every stripe are in full rage. The battle cries scream from every media and diplomatic venue, as well as in the streets of Europe and other nations where Islam's populations have grown exponentially.

Israel's leadership—particularly the military leadership—know that it is fight or die as a nation and as a people.

But just as the Samson Option is about to be invoked (bringing down the house of Israel and all of its enemies with nuclear holocaust), a man from the European Union steps from among his fellows, speaking great things of the diplomatic sort: "Of the ten horns that were in his head, and of the other which came up, and before whom three fell; even of that horn that had eyes, and a mouth that spake very great things, whose look was more stout than his fellows" (Daniel 7:20).

Prince Befriends Israel

This European leader tells Israel that he is her friend. Almost the only friend she has among the voices of the United Nations and the newly developed superstate, thanks to the rapture of the church and America coming under the European umbrella, bringing with it the most powerful and sophisticated nuclear weapons arsenal on the planet.

He may be but one voice, but what a voice! No one would dare to make war with this man who commands such awesome might. In fact, this man will one day be worshipped as a god: "They worshipped the dragon which gave power unto the beast: and they worshipped the beast, saying, Who is like unto the beast? who is able to make war with him?" (Revelation 13:4).

This leader promises Israel that he, personally, will guarantee she is not attacked, and that she is accepted by other leaders of the nations now threatening an all-out assault on the Jewish state.

Peace at Last?

This leader will begin with his wondrous works of convincing the mesmerized world that he is the man of the hour. He is the ultimate negotiator—the great, longed-for peacemaker.

He even promises Israel it can build a temple on the most sacred spot to religious Jews—atop Mount Moriah, the Temple Mount. But in exchange, Israel must agree to put down all of its defense, especially its great nuclear arsenal. Israel must agree to rely totally on him to be its national protector, savior. Israel once rejected the true Messiah, but will readily accept this great leader's overtures of peace. Jesus prophesied about this: "I am come in my Father's name, and ye receive me not: if another shall come in his own name, him ye will receive" (John 5:43).

Although Israel and the world have been forewarned, this proud, arrogant, nefariously ambitious man will invoke his peace. It will—ultimately—produce catastrophic results.

However, he will appear at first to be a miracle worker of unprecedented magnitude: "Through his policy also he shall cause craft to prosper in his hand; and he shall magnify himself in his heart, and by peace shall destroy many" (Daniel 8:25).

He is called the man of sin, the son of perdition, Antichrist, the beast, the king of fierce countenance, the prince that shall come, and other names.

Prince Has Mideast Connections

Interestingly, among his other names, this man is called "the Assyrian" (I recommend that you get the book *The Assyrian Connection*, written by my friend Phillip Goodman, to read about the Bible's reference to this man). He and Antichrist seem to be one and the same in terms of considering the future tyrant that is referred to as the beast most prominently in Revelation chapter 13.

This man, the son of perdition who stands above all others of like mind to rule the world by hook or by crook, comes from the geographical area that comprised the old Roman Empire. While he hails from that region, his ethnic origin is from people (his fathers) of Middle Eastern extraction.

He honors the "God of forces" (Daniel 11:38). This is a most interesting proposition. And there are other fascinating factors and considerations in pursuing this line of conjecture. The prince—in our end-of-days scenario—has come forth from the people (the Romans) who destroyed the city (Jerusalem) and the sanctuary (the Jewish temple) just as foretold by Daniel (Daniel 9:27). He comes guaranteeing a peace that has already been negotiated, and through great, swelling words, aggrandizes himself in the eyes of many peoples throughout the world (Daniel 7:20).

Daniel 11:38 foretells: "In his estate shall he honour the God of forces: and a god whom his fathers knew not shall he honour with gold, and silver, and with precious stones, and pleasant things." The Assyrian beast magnifies himself above all. He has attained godhood and manifests the prideful arrogance of all of the great kings, princes, and tyrants of history in one egomaniacal, supernaturally empowered man.

The great leader, at the same time, according to Daniel 11:38, is in league with the "God of forces," and heaps riches upon a god his fathers would have no part of worshipping. These are a couple of fascinating foretellings about the prince who has come forth. He casts his lot, at least initially, with a couple of interesting "gods." The first god referenced invokes aggressive, militant, and deadly action to achieve its way. The prince uses this god and its forces to accomplish great things—for himself, of course.

The second god spoken of indicates a religious system whose love of the riches of life is at the center of all worship. The former "god" fits the profile of Allah, whose holy book, the Koran, demands that all who do not bow the knee to Islam be dispatched from this life. The latter "god" is further described in Revelation 17. The false religious system that seduces the kings of the earth is both Catholic and Protestant apostate religionists, all rolled cozily together with ecumenical entities from the various religions of the world. Antichrist will turn on both the god of forces and the god his fathers—Abraham and his predecessors—would not worship. He ultimately will abide no worship other than of himself.

While Islam grows more fanatic and proliferates through a birth rate that far outstrips any other militant ethnic people, the great leader from the European Union and other Western powers combine and turn against the "God of forces."

Leader Turns on Islam

Islam has gotten too threatening to the technological democracy the latest and greatest führer wants to institute. Islam will not adjust. These forces—whose god commands them to remain pure in Islam's draconian ways—recede and reconnoiter in regions native to their hordes. They join with powerful allies north of their comfort zone. The revived Russian military force is led by a leader who has special mention in end-of-days Bible prophecy.

Gog's Power Grab

Gog, which means "leader," looks with lust toward the south and all the oil-based riches of the Middle East. Economic and other factors make the Russian Gog think an evil thought. The Islamics, unwelcome in their interference with the Assyrian leader of the newly forming one-world plan, hitch their ambitions to the Russian leader's evil thought to rule the petroleum fields and to thereby destroy Israel. Destroying Israel is at the heart of Islamic thinking. The Jews must forever be eradicated from the land they proclaim belongs to them.

The great Western leader eyes the great Eastern leader. The supernaturally saturated prince of Bible prophecy—in our scenario—will know that Gog is about to get his comeuppance. The Western leader, directed by the same "god" as the Eastern leader, knows what is about to happen. He bides his time.

Israel Defenseless

Israel sits without means to defend herself. The Jewish nation's leaders have given their complete trust to the Western leader who has personally guaranteed their peace and safety. But this great Western leader, in spite of watching the situation develop, isn't quite confident in his assessment of what Bible prophecy has to say about this moment in human history. He's not certain developments are necessarily in his favor.

His own kingdom is still under construction. While he won't move until he fully consolidates his unstoppable power, he watches Gog and the Islamics gather for assault on the Middle East. His time will come. He will move, then, as no other leader in history has ever moved: in all-out aggression: "Tidings out of the east and out of the north shall trouble him: therefore he shall go forth with great fury to destroy, and utterly to make away many" (Daniel 11:44).

It will be another force that deals with Israel's great enemy at this particular moment. Israel, in our ongoing end-of-days scenario, has agreed to all stipulations the Western international community—under inspiration of a great world leader—has required of the Jewish state. Key to getting the leader to assure Israel's security—its peace—is the requirement that Israel give over her nuclear arsenal to the still-forming, growing superstate. God's prophetic Word has two things, basically, to say about this action by Israel:

1. The first involves not only Israel, but all who embrace this "peace" spawned by the Western superstar and the nations that back him. The world will get its much-desired, then ballyhooed "peace and safety," but it will come at a tremendous price. It will not, of course, be a true peace at all; it will be a horrific war.

2. The second thing God says about this attempt at peace is exclusively directed at God's chosen people and the nation Israel:

   > Because ye have said, We have made a covenant with death, and with hell are we at agreement; when the overflowing scourge shall pass through, it shall not come unto us: for we have made lies our refuge, and under falsehood have we hid ourselves...And your covenant with death shall be disannulled, and your agreement with hell shall not stand; when the overflowing scourge shall pass through, then ye shall be trodden down by it (Isaiah 28:15,18).

   > When they shall say, Peace and safety; then sudden destruction cometh upon them, as travail upon a woman with child; and they shall not escape (1 Thessalonians 5:3).

Again, Jesus, speaking to the nation Israel, prophesied that Israel would accept this Roman prince's overtures while rejecting Him, their true Messiah: "I am come in my Father's name, and ye receive me not: if another shall come in his own name, him ye will receive" (John 5:43).

Gog's Lust

Israel sits now—in our scenario—like an ungated community. It doesn't even have a local constabulary to protect it. It depends totally on the great Roman prince's promises of peace and safety. Just at this moment, the other leader of supernaturally infused power—the Eastern leader to the north of Israel—realizes all of the Middle East is ripe for the pickings, while the Western coalition is still consolidating power.

> Thus saith the Lord GOD; It shall also come to pass, that at the same time shall things come into thy mind, and thou shalt think an evil thought: and thou shalt say, I will go up to the land of unwalled villages; I will go to them that are at rest, that dwell safely, all of them dwelling without walls, and having neither bars nor gates, to take a spoil, and to take a prey; to turn thine hand upon the desolate places that are now inhabited, and upon the people that are gathered out of the nations, which have gotten cattle and goods, that dwell in the midst of the land (Ezekiel 38:10-12).

The only response of the prince and his cronies out of the West to the hordes they see coalescing in warlike configuration around Israel and the oil fields of the region seems wrapped up in the following prophecy:

> Sheba, and Dedan, and the merchants of Tarshish, with all the young lions thereof, shall say unto thee, Art thou come to take a spoil? hast thou gathered thy company to take a prey? to carry away silver and gold, to take away cattle and goods, to take a great spoil? (Ezekiel 38:13).

The "protectors" of Israel offer only a note of diplomatic protest. The Russian and Islamic heads of Russia's Arab and Persian allies seize upon the perceived weakness of the West's leadership.

The question to consider: Is the note of protest sent out of true weakness, or does the Roman prince realize what fate awaits the one called Gog and his Magog forces?

The demons, God's Word says, believe in God and tremble. The satanically driven prince that shall come will certainly know the Ezekiel prophecies. He will be the most brilliant military strategist ever to inhabit flesh on the planet. Can there be much doubt that he will think—in advance—to take advantage of every possibility?

Antichrist's Calculation

In our scenario, Antichrist takes a look at the gathering storm and sends his note of protest, all with a sly grin of belief in what Scripture says. He will let other forces take care of the insolent Russians and the deluded war lords of Israel's enemies. His own authority is not yet fully consolidated. He will, along with his great titans of wealth backers, watch the Russians destruct upon the mountains of Israel while he himself prepares to fill the most fortuitous vacuum that is about to be created in the Middle East.

Gog, the prophesied leader of the Israel-hating coalition north of Jerusalem, has hooks in his jaws—put there by none other than the Lord God of all creation. Our scenario has that hook lubricated generously with the black, liquid gold of the Middle East. The dictator who rules Russia has watched with Lucifer-inspired obsession the whole international rearrangements following the disappearance of millions. He receives an "evil thought" and thinks to take "great spoil"—the vast oil supplies of the regions surrounding Israel (Ezekiel 38:10,13).

It is the Tribulation era—Daniel's seventieth week—the last seven years of human history that will culminate in Christ's second advent. Man has always claimed in humanistic pride that he can make this world into paradise. This has been true since before the time of Nimrod and Babel (Genesis 11).

The leader of the newly formed superagglomeration of Western powers has brokered the peace that the prince promises will make things heaven on earth for the world. Israel has bitten into the apple from the great leader's garden of promises. God Almighty takes His hand off planet Earth to the extent He will now allow people to see if they can achieve their utopia. The Holy Spirit has withdrawn from acting as restrainer upon the consciences of human beings.

Gog Prepares

Gog knows the leadership of the Western nations is consolidating their power. Once that is done, the forces of the reviving Roman Empire will be formidable, perhaps impossible to defeat. They have the most awesome thermonuclear arsenal ever stockpiled. But Russia, China, and even some of Gog's other allies have such weapons, too— enough to destroy the world. The Western behemoth gathering strength is quite unlikely—in Gog's self-inflated estimation—to use military power to try to stop his invasion at this point.

Gog is inspired by one other profound realization. The West's true power has always been in its great technological capabilities—its fantastic, wealth-producing machinery that is far advanced of anything the humanity-oppressive regimes of the East have been able to match. The only true accomplishments of the Eastern world have been, for the most part, mere replication of things produced by the freedom-loving people of the West.

The Russian, in consort with his cohorts of the coalition he has gathered, knows that to take away the Western powers' ability to run their machinery—thus their technological production—is to cripple them. He will claim all the oil of the Middle East. The West, having long fallen prey to those who preached the politically correct ecological message that they were raping Mother Earth by drilling and refining petroleum, will be without resources to fuel their drive to dominate the world.

The leader who brokered the peace remains peaceful. He has sent his diplomatic protest. But he believes in Bible prophecy. His knowledge comes from the father of lies, who convinces him that all of prophecy is true except the part that says he—the prince that shall come—will ultimately lose to the returning King of all kings (Revelation 19:20).

Prince Surveys Situation

The Western leader watches the Gog-Magog forces gather. He is troubled, but bides his time.

While the beast of Revelation 13 watches, the beast of the East, Gog, doesn't keep his nemesis waiting long. The assault is quick, all out, and, seen from satellite reconnaissance, looks like a massive storm moving southward toward Jerusalem. Israel sits vulnerable, without defense. The leader squints from Brussels at the many monitors while waiting to see if the things his special minion-mentors are telling him will play out on schedule.

Gog Destroyed

He is not disappointed. Here is how Ezekiel, under God's direction, reported this battle thousands of years before it takes place:

> Thou son of man, prophesy against Gog, and say, Thus saith the Lord GOD; Behold, I am against thee, O Gog, the chief prince of Meshech and Tubal: and I will turn thee back, and leave but the sixth part of thee, and will cause thee to come up from the north parts, and will bring thee upon the mountains of Israel: and I will smite thy bow out of thy left hand, and will cause thine arrows to fall out of thy right hand. Thou shalt fall upon the mountains of Israel, thou, and all thy bands, and the people that is with thee: I will give thee unto the ravenous birds of every sort, and to the beasts of the field to be devoured. Thou shalt fall upon the open field: for I have spoken it, saith the Lord GOD (Ezekiel 39:1-5).

Many, particularly the Jews within Israel, will believe that God has won the victory. And indeed, there is no evidence to the contrary. God did it all.

Even the great pseudopeacemaker from his proud perch in Europe has to say to himself that God has done this marvelous thing. But, so far as he is concerned, it only means advantage to his ambition. All resistance has been crushed for him, paving his way to fill the power vacuum. All of the oil riches are his. Now he will truly be able to build his one-world kingdom. To him belongs the great spoil Gog foolishly thought would be his.

Conquering Hero

Antichrist rides into the region a conqueror. He has—in his more and more demonically possessed mind—correctly understood the "dark sentences" given him by his minion-mentors from the father of lies. Jerusalem, the very capital of Jehovah on earth—is his for the taking. He himself will be the god of this planet:

> Let no man deceive you by any means: for that day shall not come, except there come a falling away first, and that man of sin be revealed, the son of perdition; who opposeth and exalteth himself above all that is called God, or that is worshipped; so that he as God sitteth in the temple of God, shewing himself that he is God (2 Thessalonians 2:3-4).

Antichrist has revealed himself. He demands worship. The greatest holocaust of history will begin. It is the time of Jacob's trouble: "Alas! for that day is great, so that none is like it: it is even the time of Jacob's trouble; but he shall be saved out of it" (Jeremiah 30:7).

Jesus said of this time: "For then shall be great tribulation, such as was not since the beginning of the world to this time, no, nor ever shall be" (Matthew 24:21).

Here is the scenario that Bill Salus, author of *Isralestine: The Ancient Blueprints of the Future Middle East* (Crane, MO: High Way Publishing, 2008) proposes:

Humanity must immediately prepare to experience four powerfully prophetic episodes. The parting of the Red Sea at the time of the Hebrew exodus out of Egypt, will undoubtedly pale in comparison to the magnitude of these epic events. Coming soon, and likely ordered as follows are:

1. The rapture of the church, fulfilling the prophecy of 1 Thessalonians 5:9.

2. The Israeli conquest over the Psalm 83 Arab confederacy, putting an end to the ancient Arab hatred described in Ezekiel 35:5, and fulfilling the sworn oath of God in Ezekiel 36:7.

3. The divine decimation of the nuclear equipped Russian-Iranian led coalition targeted against Israel, commonly referred to as the Gog and Magog invasion. This fulfills

Ezekiel 39:7, whereby God upholds His holy name before the international community.

4. The rise of the Antichrist on all lying signs and wonders as per 2 Thessalonians 2:8-12, whereby this crazed individual leads the world into "Tribulation," provoking God's wrath upon the entirety of unsaved humanity.

Like a domino effect, each event stated above sequentially sets the stage for the next event to follow. The church "age of grace" is about to conclude, causing the marquis lights to flash brightly over the Middle East theater once again. Immediately after, if not before the rapture, the deafening shout "Allah Akbar" will echo throughout the Holy Land as the Psalm 83 jihad begins to unfold.

In victory, the Israeli Defense Forces of today will become the "exceedingly great army" of Ezekiel 37:10. They may be a "twinkling of an eye" away from showing their superior strength.

ARE YOU PREPARED?

★★★★

We come, in our scenario, to the time of Antichrist's apex of power. America has been emulsified and absorbed within the satanic mixture—Antichrist's regime. No longer is the United States recognizable by name within the end-times scene. She is now a non-descript part of the ten-nation kingdom of Revelation 17:12-13.

A Concluding Perspective

America, the most glorious nation in history so far as her material contribution to modernity is concerned, seems nowhere in view. On the other hand, a strong case can be made that the United States is still present with her influence. It is the vast body of technology—the majority of which America has invented, produced, and disseminated—that has "given power and authority unto the beast" as prophesied in the ten-kingdom reference in Revelation 17:12-13.

No doubt, as stated before, it is America's nuclear arsenal and the unmatched ability to deliver the horrific warheads to anywhere at any time that puts the exclamation point upon the Antichrist's capability to cause all the world to worship him or be killed (Revelation 13:16).

Perhaps those who say Babylon is a reference to America in end-times prophecy are right to some degree. Again, Jeremiah 51:7 says, "Babylon hath been a golden cup in the LORD's hand, that made all the earth drunken: the nations have drunken of her wine; therefore the nations are mad."

It is a tragedy of the worst sort to consider: The blessings bestowed upon our nation turned to cursing in the sense of her God-inspired technological wonders being put at the disposal of the final führer.

Antichrist, in his satanic madness, using every technological device known to control the peoples of earth, will inflict holocaust upon the Jews and all others who refuse to worship him. His cruelty will be many times more horrific than Adolf Hitler's.

Of course, the story is far from over. The beautiful part of this scenario—and it is God's scenario, which is absolute truth—is found in these last few words of the old prophet Jeremiah's declaration about Jacob's trouble: "He shall be saved out of it" (Jeremiah 30:7). All of Israel—the believing remnant—will be saved out of the Tribulation holocaust (read Revelation 12).

So, too, will all Tribulation saints who survive the seven years of horror be rescued when Christ returns (Revelation 19:11). It is wise, however, to receive God's redemptive offer of reconciliation today, before that terrible time of His judgment and wrath.

The American Apocalypse Approaches!

My prayer is that if you don't yet know Him, you will accept Jesus Christ as Savior now, before these prophesied end-of-days events overtake this judgment-bound nation and the world.

"If thou shalt confess with thy mouth the Lord Jesus, and shalt believe in thine heart that God hath raised him from the dead, thou shalt be saved" (Romans 10:9).

Notes

★★★

1. Based upon information compiled by The New York Times Co.

2. David Barton, "Revisionism: How to Identify It in Your Children's Textbooks," Wallbuilders .com, http://www.wallbuilders.com/LIBissuesArticles.asp?id=112.

3. Chuck Missler, "Decline and Fall of the American Family," in William T. James, gen. ed., *Earth's Final Days* (Green Forest, AR: New Leaf Press, 1996), 260-62.

4. Ibid., 262-63.

5. Barton, "Revisionism."

6. R.K. DeArment, "Gambling and Recreation in the Old West," *Wild West*, April 2005.

7. Ibid.

8. Ibid.

9. "Gilded Age," http://en.wikipedia.org/wiki/Gilded_Age.

10. "Flapper," http://en.wikipedia.org/wiki/Flapper.

11. Mark Gribben, "Bootleggers Paradise," http://www.crimelibrary.com/gangsters/purple/purple main.htm.

12. "Dust Bowl," http://snr.unl.edu/metr351-03/jnothwehr/introduction.html.

13. William T. James, "Israel, the Clear Signal," in William T. James, gen. ed., *Storming Toward Armageddon: Essays in Apocalypse* (Green Forest, AR: New Leaf Press, 1992), 162-70.

14. Quotes and facts from Michael T. Benson, *Harry S Truman and the Founding of Israel* (Westport, CT: Greenwood, 1997), 54.

15. Robert H. Bork, *Slouching Towards Gomorrah* (New York: ReganBooks, 1997), 2.

16. "*Roe v. Wade,*" http://en.wikipedia.org/wiki/Roe_v._Wade.

17. "The Death of Character: Moral Education in an Age Without Good or Evil," *Legislating Morality,* Spring 2001.

18. National Center for Health Statistics, http://www.cdc.gov/nchs.

19. Calculated using the *2006 National Survey on Drug Use and Health.* J. Gfroerer of the Substance Abuse and Mental Health Services Administration, David H. Jernigan, September 17, 2007.

20. National Research Council and Institute of Medicine, *Reducing Underage Drinking: A Collective Responsibility,* eds. R.J. Bonnie and M.E. O'Connell (Washington, D.C.: National Academies Press, 2004), 35.

21. Calculated using the *2003 National Survey on Drug Use and Health.* J. Gfroerer of the Substance Abuse and Mental Health Services Administration, David H. Jernigan, September 14, 2004.

22. Johnston, L.D., O'Malley, P.M., Bachman, J.G., Schulenberg, J.E. "Overall, illicit drug use by American teens continues gradual decline in 2007," University of Michigan News Service, December 11, 2007, www.monitoringthefuture.org, accessed 12/11/07.

23. T.S. Naimi, et al., "Binge Drinking Among US Adults," *The Journal of the American Medical Association,* 289, no. 1 (January 1, 2003): 70-75.

24. Pacific Institute for Research and Evaluation, *Drinking in America: Myths, Realities, and Prevention Policy,* prepared in support of the Office of Juvenile Justice Delinquency Prevention Enforcing the Underage Drinking Laws Program, U.S. Department of Justice (Calverton, MD: Pacific Institute for Research and Evaluation, 2005).

25. Substance Abuse and Mental Health Services Administration (2007); results from the *2006 National Survey on Drug Use and Health*. According to SAMHSA, binge alcohol use is defined as "five or more drinks on the same occasion (i.e., at the same time or within a couple of hours of each other) at least once in the past 30 days (includes heavy use)." Heavy alcohol use is defined as "five or more drinks on the same occasion on at least 5 different days in the past 30 days." Substance Abuse and Mental Health Services Administration (2007); results from the *2006 National Survey on Drug Use and Health: National Findings* (Rockville, MD: Office of Applied Studies, NSDUH Series H-32, DHHS Publication No. SMA 07-4293).

26. Pacific Institute for Research and Evaluation, *Drinking in America*.

27. H. Wechsler, J.E. Lee, T.F. Nelson, M. Kuo, "Underage College Students' Drinking Behavior, Access to Alcohol, and the Influence of Deterrence Policies: Findings from the Harvard School of Public Health College Alcohol Study," *Journal of American College Health* 50, no. 5 (March 2002): 223-36.

28. Pacific Institute for Research and Evaluation, *Drinking in America: Myths, Realities, and Prevention Policy*, prepared in support of the Office of Juvenile Justice Delinquency Prevention Enforcing the Underage Drinking Laws Program, U.S. Department of Justice (Calverton, MD: Pacific Institute for Research and Evaluation, 2005); S.E. Foster, R.D. Vaughan, W.H. Foster, J.A. Califano, "Alcohol Consumption and Expenditures for Underage Drinking and Adult Excessive Drinking," *Journal of the American Medical Association* 289, no. 8 (February 26, 2003): 989-95.

29. Gary Hedrick, "Distress of Nations with Perplexity," in William T. James, gen. ed., *Foreshadows of Wrath and Redemption* (Eugene, OR: Harvest House, 1999), 118.

30. Zola Levitt with Lawrence Ford, "Israel at Ground Zero," in William T. James, gen. ed., *Prophecy at Ground Zero* (Lancaster, PA: Starburst, 2002), 27-28.

31. Ibid., 28.

32. Michal Zippori, CNN, http://www.cnn.com/2005/WORLD/meast/12/14/iran.israel/.

33. *The State of Industry: Assessing the Impact of September 11,* report by Ernst & Young, at www.ey.com/global.

34. *Global Competitiveness Report* by *Center for International Trade* (Harvard University: UNDP Report on Trade and Development), 2002.

35. "Overview of EU action in response to the events of the 11 September and assessment of their likely economic impact," European Commission Report, Brussels, October 17, 2001, at www.europa.int.eu.

36. *Financial Times,* ibid.

37. Ms. Farzana Noshab, *Global Economic Implications of 9/11 Attacks* (Islamabad: Institute of Strategic Studies), Autumn 2002, www.issi.org.

38. Chuck Missler, *Strategic Trends Update,* 2007.

39. Wilfred Hahn, *Eternal Value Review,* August 2, 2007.

40. John MacArthur on church growth outreach, *Christianity Today,* October 1, 1991.

41. Dale Hurd, "Europe Forsakes Christianity for Islam?" CBN News, September 12, 2006.

42. "Lutherans consider boycotting Israel," episcopallife.com, January, 2008.

43. David B. Rivkin Jr., "Commentary: The Weekend Interview, Henry Kissinger, Diplomacy in the Post-9/11 Era," *The Wall Street Journal,* November 18, 2007.

44. John Walvoord, "Antichrist, Armageddon, and the Second Coming of Christ" in William T. James, gen. ed., *Forewarning: Approaching the Final Battle Between Heaven and Hell* (Eugene, OR: Harvest House, 1998), 345.

45. Pew Global Attitudes Project, *America's Image in the Word: Findings from the Pew Global Attitudes Project,* released March 13, 2007, http://pewglobal.org.

46. Testimony of Andrew Kohut, United States House of Representatives, International Relations Committee, Subcommittee on Oversight and Investigations, November 10, 2005.

47. Guy Faulconbridge, "Russia's Gorbachev Says US is Sowing World Disorder," Reuters, July 27, 2007.

48. Rivkin, "Commentary."

49. Clifford Krauss, "Economy and Geopolitics Decide Where Oil Goes Next," *International Herald Tribune,* January 4, 2008.

50. *Petroleum News,* vol. 13, no. 2, January 13, 2008.

51. Kristen Robertson, "Students talk about their political views," *The Graphic* (Pepperdine University), July 4, 2006, http://graphic.pepperdine.edu/news/2006/2007-07-04-politicaltrends.htm.

52. See http://www.raptureready.com/rr-iraq.html. Sources: 1. *The Seattle Times,* "On the Brink: Understanding the U.S.-Iraq Conflict," January 26, 2003. 2. "President Bush Discusses Iraq in National Press Conference," March 6, 2003; www.whitehouse.gov. 3. "Iraq: U.S. Says It Has Captured Baghdad Airport, Closing in on Other Side," by Kathleen Knox, April 4, 2003; www.globalsecurity.org. 4. *Middle East Forum,* "Iraq Has Voted," by Michael Rubin, January 31, 2005; www.meforum.org.

53. Thom Shanker and Mark Landler, with C.J. Chivers contributing reporting from Moscow, "Putin Says U.S. Is Undermining Global Stability," *The New York Times,* February 10, 2007.

54. William J. Kole, "U.S.-led Iraq coalition withering fast," October 9, 2007; accessed at http://abcnews.go.com/International/wireStory?id-3708007.

55. Toby Helm, "Blair Was Overruled by Bush on Post-War Strategy, says Hoon," Telegraph.co.uk, December 9, 2006.

56. Judy Dempsey, "Schroder Targets Role of Religion in America," *International Herald Tribune,* October 25, 2006.

57. Daliah Merzaban, "International Organisations, U.N. and Donors Prepare Road Map for Rebuilding Iraq," Reuters, Abu Dhabi, September 10, 2006.

58. Accessed at www.geostrategy-direct.com, January 20, 2008.

59. Mark Hitchcock, *Second Coming of Babylon* (Sisters, OR: Multnomah Publishers, 2003), 152-53.

60. Anil Bhoyrul, "Hundreds Queue All Night for Burj Dubai Units," *Arabian Business,* February 10, 2008, www.arabianbusiness.com.

61. Ibid.

62. David Sadighian, "Burj Dubai Breaks Record...and Keeps Going," *Architectural Record,* July 24, 2007.

63. Burj Dubai official Website, www.burjdubai.com

64. Jerome R. Corsi, "Goodbye U.S. Dollar, Hello Global Currency," *The New World Disorder,* May 9, 2007, WorldNetDaily.com.

65. Ibid.

66. Ibid.

67. Ibid.

68. Charles Herman, "Why Is the Dollar Losing Value? A Closer Look at the Dollar and the Euro and What the Dollar's Drop Means for You," ABC News Business Unit, September 20, 2007.

69. Ibid.

70. Corsi, "Goodbye U.S. Dollar."

71. Anthony Faiola, *Washington Post,* December 24, 2007.

72. "The Dollar: Down But Not Out," accessed November 21, 2007 at http://knowledge.wpcarey .asu.edu/article.cfm?articleid-1508.

73. Spiegel Online, November 30, 2007, http://www.spiegel.de/international/business/0,1518 ,520700,00.html.

74. Gwynne Dyer, "The Middle East's Leading English Language Daily," *Arab News,* November 27 2007.

75. *The News & Observer* (Raleigh, NC) via Thomson Dialog NewsEdge, November 10, 2007.

76. Dennis L. Cuddy, "The North American Union and the Larger Plan," *The August Review,* August, 2007.

77. *Lou Dobbs Tonight* from the CNN transcript, aired November 29, 2006, http://transcripts.cnn .com.

78. "Keeping Track of the Road Map," February 21, 2008, from the Jewish Virtual Library, a division of the American-Israeli Cooperative Enterprise. Used with permission.

79. Ibid.

80. David Breese, "Europe and the Prince that Shall Come," in William T. James, gen. ed., *Storming Toward Armageddon* (Green Forest, AR: New Leaf Press, 1994), 190-91.

81. "Mideast Envoy Blair Says PA Beginning to Abide by 'Road Map,' " Reuters, www.haaretz.com/ hasen/spages/952278.html.

82. Mazal Mualem and Barak Ravid, "U.S. Official: American Roadmap Monitors Will Report, not Judge," Haaretz Service, December 1, 2008.

83. Dr. J. Vernon McGee, *Thru the Bible Edited Messages,* vol. 5, 1029-31.

84. Dave Hunt, "Flashes of Falling Away," in William T. James, gen. ed., *Forewarning: Approaching the Final Battle Between Heaven and Hell* (Eugene, OR: Harvest House, 1998), 27-29.

85. "Religious Leaders Gather for Their Own UN Summit, Also Pledging to Work for Peace and Tolerance," *One Country: The Online Newsletter of the Baha'i International Community,* vol. 12, issue 2, July-September 2000.

86. "How We Fight Poverty, U.N. Millennium Development Goals Are Good—As Far as They Go," *Christianity Today,* December, 2007, www.christianitytoday.com/ct/2007/december/17.20 .html.

87. Clayton Sandell and Bill Blakemore, "Science + Religion = New Alliance to Save the Planet, 'Saving the Creation' Makes Strange Bedfellows of Scientists and Religious Leaders," *ABC News,* Washington, January 17, 2007.

88. The source for these quotes and others within this narrative is Cathedral Centennial Website home page, Sunday, January 27, 2008. "A New Century: A New Reformation, with Rick Warren, founding pastor of California's Saddleback Church and author of the international bestseller *A Purpose-Driven Life.*"

89. Victor Davis Hanson, "Israel Did It! When in Doubt, Shout about Israel," National Review Online, December 15, 2006.

90. Ibid.

91. Peter Bart, "The Real Hollywood Politics," Variety.com, January 19, 2007.

Other Great Harvest House Reading

NORTHERN STORM RISING
Ron Rhodes

The Bible describes a massive end-times invasion into Israel by a coalition of nations. Who are these attackers? Why will they invade Israel? What will be the outcome? A fascinating overview of what's happening today in the Middle East, and what the future holds.

THE POPULAR ENCYCLOPEDIA OF BIBLE PROPHECY
Tim LaHaye and Ed Hindson, General Editors

A comprehensive wealth of Bible prophecy knowledge at your fingertips! This A-to-Z encyclopedia, put together by an outstanding team of more than 40 prophecy and theology experts, includes more than 400 pages of fascinating facts, information, and charts about the last days.

THE POPULAR BIBLE PROPHECY COMMENTARY
Tim LaHaye and Ed Hindson, General Editors

It's all here—clear and concise explanations for key prophetic passages from Genesis to Revelation. Among the notable features are more than 500 pages of commentary, useful charts and diagrams, helpful word definitions, and simple format for easy referencing.

UNDERSTANDING BIBLE PROPHECY FOR YOURSELF
Tim LaHaye

If you've ever wanted to have a clear understanding of Bible prophecy and current events but were unsure where to begin, this book was written especially for you. Includes examples of how to interpret prophetic Bible passages and exercises that help you maximize your understanding of key prophecies.

HARVEST HOUSE
PUBLISHERS